DIRECT FOREIGN INVESTMENT

ALSO FROM PRAEGER

FOREIGN CAPITAL AND TECHNOLOGY IN CHINA
Richard D. Robinson

THE INTERNATIONALIZATION OF CAPITAL: Imperialism and Capitalist Development on a World Scale
Berch Berberoglu

ON EDGE: International Banking and Country Risk
Ellen S. Goldberg and Dan Haendel

OVERSEAS ACQUISITIONS AND MERGERS: Combining for Profits Abroad
Duane R. Hall

MANAGING EXPORT ENTRY AND EXPANSION: Concepts and Practice
Philip J. Rosson and *Stanley D. Reid,* editors

JAPANESE MULTINATIONALS IN THE UNITED STATES: Case Studies
Duane Kujawa

ECONOMIC INTEGRATION AMONG DEVELOPING NATIONS: Law and Policy
Beverly May Carl

JAPANESE DIRECT MANUFACTURING INVESTMENT IN THE UNITED STATES
Mamoru Yoshida

DIRECT FOREIGN INVESTMENT

Costs and Benefits

Edited by
RICHARD D. ROBINSON

PRAEGER

New York
Westport, Connecticut
London

Library of Congress Cataloging-in-Publication Data

Direct foreign investment: costs and benefits/[edited by] Richard
  D. Robinson.
    p. cm.
   Includes index.
   ISBN 0-275-92717-2 (alk. paper)
    1. Investments, Foreign—Government policy—Congresses.
I. Robinson, Richard D., 1921–
HG4538.D557   1987
332.6732—dc 19   87-17750
                                                CIP

Library of Congress Catalog Card Number: 87-17750
ISBN: 0-275-92717-2

First published in 1987

Praeger Publishers, One Madison Avenue, New York, NY 10010
A division of Greenwood Press, Inc.

Printed in the United States of America

The paper used in this book complies with the Permanent Paper Standard
issued by the National Information Standards Organization (Z39.48-1984).

10 9 8 7 6 5 4 3 2 1

Contents

Acknowledgments

These chapters were prepared for a conference in Hangzhou, China, March 1985, made possible by generous grants from

The Asia Foundation
Computer Peripherals Incorporated
General Electric Corporation
General Motors Corporation
Motorola Corporation
Unilever Ltd.

The chapters in this book were originally created to brief the participants of a March 1985 conference in China on various national policies relative to foreign business, the costs and benefits of such intervention, and corporate response to it. These chapters complement the companion volume dealing more specifically with the Chinese situation, *Foreign Capital and Technology in China*.

What is missing is discussion of corporate strategic decision making. The following few pages attempt to fill that gap, thereby putting in context the various forms of government intervention, and the presumed costs and benefits of such.

Although not always made explicit, it would appear that corporate strategic decision makers have a model in their heads, a mental map representing a systematic approach. In the more internationally experienced firms, one suspects, this model, or process, tends to be more explicit. Essentially, it consists of five continuous and interactive steps:

1. Identifying the separable links in the firm's value-added chain.
2. In the context of those links, determining the location of the firm's competitive advantages, considering both economies of scale and scope.
3. Ascertaining the level of transaction costs between links in the value-added chain, both internal and external, and selecting the lowest cost mode, which implies conscious steps to minimize those transaction costs.
4. Determining the comparative advantages of countries (including the firm's home country) relative to the production of each link in the value-added chain and to the relevant transaction costs.
5. Developing adequate flexibility in corporate decision making and organizational design so as to permit the firm to respond to changes in both its competitive advantages and the comparative advantages of countries, both being highly dynamic.

Each of these steps requires some further definition and expansion.

A firm's product, whether it be "hard" (a good) or "soft" (a service), consists of a bundle of activities—a value-added chain—some or all of whose links may be performed by the firm itself (i.e., internalized). Others may be purchased from unrelated parties, or contracted out (i.e., externalized). It is often rewarding to look at what theoretically could be performed by a

Exhibit 1.   The Value-Added Chain

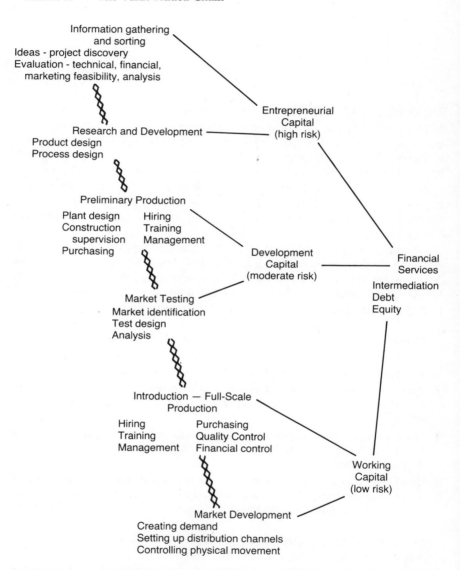

Information gathering
and sorting
Ideas - project discovery
Evaluation - technical, financial,
marketing feasibility, analysis

Entrepreneurial
Capital
(high risk)

Research and Development
Product design
Process design

Preliminary Production

Plant design   Hiring
Construction   Training
supervision   Management
Purchasing

Development
Capital
(moderate risk)

Financial
Services

Intermediation
Debt
Equity

Market Testing
Market identification
Test design
Analysis

Introduction — Full-Scale
Production

Hiring   Purchasing
Training   Quality Control
Management   Financial control

Working
Capital
(low risk)

Market Development
Creating demand
Setting up distribution channels
Controlling physical movement

firm that is legally and geographically separate from the first. The purpose of such examination is to determine wherein the real competitive edge of the firm lies—that is, which links are the real source of its profit? The more successful firms in the long run, one suspects, are not interested in maintaining

Exhibit 2.   Changes in the Value-Added Chain According to Comparative National Advantages

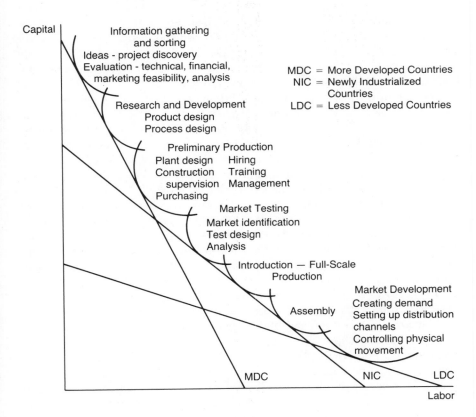

Capital

Information gathering and sorting
Ideas - project discovery
Evaluation - technical, financial, marketing feasibility, analysis

Research and Development
Product design
Process design

Preliminary Production
Plant design   Hiring
Construction   Training
    supervision   Management
Purchasing

Market Testing
Market identification
Test design
Analysis

Introduction — Full-Scale Production

Assembly

Market Development
Creating demand
Setting up distribution channels
Controlling physical movement

MDC = More Developed Countries
NIC = Newly Industrialized Countries
LDC = Less Developed Countries

MDC   NIC   LDC

Labor

control over a given function or set of functions simply for the sake of control (i.e., power), but only if by so doing it is more profitable.

The value-added chain may be portrayed as in Exhibit 1, which is a grossly oversimplified representation in that each link consists of many possibly separable inputs, only some of which are listed. Certain skills, or competitive advantages, may not be related to a specific link in the chain, such as the financial function. The management function may be another, although the management of certain links may vary substantially. For example, the managerial skills required to make the research and development (R&D) function most effective may be very different from the managerial skills required to manage the production or marketing links effectively.

It should be noted that there is a tendency for the links to become relatively more labor-intensive as one moves down the value-added chains (see Exhibit 2), which may have some explanatory power relative to the flows of direct investment and of subcontracted services internationally, given the different relative costs of capital and labor of various categories among countries. In Exhibit 2, the three lines represent the relative costs of capital and labor in the more developed countries, in the newly industrialized countries, and in the less developed countries. From this representation one may get a very rough notion of where various links in a value-added chain might be undertaken at least cost.

The point is, of course, that each link may or may not be performed by the firm itself, and each link may be performed in a different location—domestically or internationally. What is the least-cost mix, or at least perceived to be such by the firm's decision makers, both in respect to the activity embedded in each link and the transaction cost involved?

Two concepts are useful in making that analysis: economies of scale and economies of scope. The first is familiar to most. It has to do with the employment of functionally specific or product specific factors so as to achieve minimum unit production cost (that is, optimum intensity of use). It is useful to think of these factors as representing fixed costs over a broad range and included within the production function in that they are identified with a particular function or product and, hence, may be allocated to that function or product.

Economy of scope, on the other hand, relates to the utlization of factors *not* identified with a specific function or product, in such manner as to achieve the lowest overhead burden per unit of production and, thereby, gain an optimum spread (or scope) of use. We refer here to those factors representing relative fixed costs over a broad range, but which are not identifiable or attributable to specific function or product and, hence, are not part of the production function. Though at the border, whether a particular economy results from scale or scope may be somewhat fuzzy, Exhibit 3 may be useful in separating the two concepts. It should be borne in mind that reduction in cost resulting from "organizational learning" (i.e., moving down a learning or experience curve) can impact on both scale and scope, although *special practices developed by a firm to accelereate learning is an economy of scope IF* such practices can be applied effectively to various functions and/or products. A firm's ability to transfer learning internationally with least cost may be an economy of scope of signal importance, likewise the capacity to operate effectively within a specific country—which is a learned capacity. Both skills are perhaps generally applicable. That is, they are not limited to function and/or product, and, hence, represent a potential economy of scope.

A classic example of an economy of scope lies in the area of negotiating with a foreign government that, given the importance of government intervention relative to the entrance of foreign business, is of utmost importance in international business. Negotiating success may be a function of

Exhibit 3   Economies of Scale versus Economies of Scope

These economies arise because of a sunk cost or binding commitment to either:

Specific factors, which lead to economies of scale OR	*Non-specific factors*, which lead to economies of scope
Such as:	*Such as:*
1 Special purpose machines, buldgs., other capital assets (e.g., transport)	1 General purpose machines, bldg., other capital assets
2 Specific technical skills (the results of in-house training and/or experience)	2 Generally applicable technical skills, but with experience in working together
3 Specific product and/or process-related development capability	3 General research and development capability
4 Specialized financial skill (i.e., function or product-related)	4 General financial services and skills
5 Accepted brand names identified with specific services or products	5 Established corporate name (or accepted image) which facilitates market entry and/or access to lower cost capital and other factors (e.g., labor resources)
6 Specialized marketing skills and services	6 General marketing skills and services
7 Direct labor (that which embodies specific experience and can be terminated only at considerable expense)	7 Direct labor (which embodies non-specific experience and can be terminated only at considerable cost.
8 Specific information network	8 Multi-purpose information network
	9 Scanning functions and skills
	10 Project evaluation skills of a nonspecific sort
	11 Legal capability
	12 Managerial skills
	13 Public affairs skills (i.e., developing and maintaining political leverage, negotiating skills)

---

knowledge and experience, communication skills, personal attributes (i.e., employing the right people), training, and political leverage. Political leverage, in turn, may be a function of the corporate image, personal relations with key government personnel, and the development of trust and confidence—all of which take time and practice to acquire. Such negotiating skill may not be specific to a particular function or product, perhaps not even to the firm's own activities. Hence, the firm may be able to contract with other firms for the use of its negotiating skill and thereby enhance the *scope* of its investment in developing such skill.

Having thus determined wherein the competitive advantage of the firm lies, the corporate strategic decision maker, whether consciously or not, moves to ascertain the transaction costs between separable links in the firm's value-added chain. That is, is it less costly for the firm to perform a given activity itself (internal) or to have it performed by another firm (external)? Continued production of a given activity by the firm itself may be justified if the transaction cost in dealing with an unrelated party more than soaks up any potential advantage that externalization of that activity might otherwise offer. The point is that, all other things being equal (which they are often not), internal transaction costs tend to be lower than external transaction costs. That is, it is cheaper to deal within the firm than without. Why? Several reasons suggest themselves: (1) People at both ends of the transaction speak the same language in an organizational and technological sense. (The stronger the corporate culture, perhaps the greater the advantage in dealing internally). (2) Negotiating time and associated legal costs are reduced, though not necessarily. (3) There is little risk of nonpayment for commercial reasons (that is, lack of integrity or bankruptcy on the part of the supplier of an activity). (4) No performance bonds or guarantees are involved. (5) Claims based on failure of the technology or know-how to generate the expected results are unlikely.

It is also possible to introduce measures so as to reduce the cost of internal transactions still further. First, the firm may undertake activities to accelerate its learning by maintaining a low employment turnover rate (and thereby capturing its own experience), by creating an internal environment such as to facilitate learning and the dissemination of that experience rapidly throughout the organization (perhaps by creating a strong sense of trust and confidence, a low level of threat, a sense among employees of the fundamental equity in the way in which the benefits of business success and costs of reverses are distributed, and by maintaining open communication throughout the organization and a sense of participation), by developing a strong organizational culture, by restraining direct interpersonal competition, and by locating in a culture supporting the values underlying such practices (we return to this last point later on).

Even so, there may be advantages in external transactions in that by externalizing certain activities the firm may gain greater flexibility in sourcing, thereby reducing its risk and enabling it to take advantage more easily (that is, to do so at lower cost) of a national competitive edge in countries with which it is not familiar. Also, there are at least two important ways in which the cost of external transactions might be reduced. The first of these is for the firm to maintain a long-standing relationship with the other party, be it a supplier, service dispenser, processor, marketer, distributor, financer, or user. A second way, which commonly arises out of the first, is the rotation of individuals between the firm and its external associate. In effect, through these measures, the firm may move toward a relationship that incorporates most of the advantages of an internal transaction, as well as of an external transaction. In this day of volatile exchange rates, the instability inherent in mounting foreign debt, political volatility in many areas, and uncertainty of tomorrow's laws and regulations which may impact on a firm's costs and/or earning in virtually all countries, perhaps it is best to minimize the firm's commitment of its own resources in the bricks and mortar and machines of plants overseas that it itself owns. Perhaps it may be better to induce someone else to make the investment at risk and to limit the firm's own involvement to the supply of technology and know-how under contract (which may well include quality control), a relationship from which the firm may withdraw over a relatively short time with relatively little loss—that is, relative to withdrawal from its own plant. The firm thereby maintains a position of maximum flexibility that, given the dynamic nature of the world environment it faces, may be of critical importance in minimizing risk.

This discussion leads one into the fourth step in the strategic decision-making process, that of determining the comparative advantage of countries relative to each link in a firm's value-added chain and to transaction costs. In so doing, one is necessarily alert to *trading costs* of countries perceived important to the firm (that is, transportation and communication costs, tariffs and nontariff barriers in both directions, risk and uncertainty of political intervention, and of exchange rate volatility), *factor costs* (the relative costs of capital and labor of various categories actually faced by the firm), and *social/political costs*. Differences in trading costs are fairly clear and straightforward, though often difficult to tie down, given their dynamic quality. The notion of factor costs is likewise fairly clear. The relevance of national differences in factor costs in siting various links in a firm's value-added chain is graphically demonstrated in Exhibit 2. The notion of differing social/political costs, however, is even more complex and, yet, relatively little discussed in this context.

By social/political costs, we refer to costs imposed to a greater degree by some countries than others by reason of the fact that they provide structurally incompatible—that is, high cost—environments for modern enterprise by reason of a number of factors:

1. There may be valued modes of personal behavior that render it difficult for a firm to minimize its internal transaction costs—such factors as exaggerated individualism, aggressiveness, intense interpersonal competition.

2. The manner of resolving conflicts may require expensive and time-consuming litigation rather than less costly and more rapid modes of conflict resolution.

3. The time-horizon of decision making, both personal and otherwise, may be so limited as to render it virtually impossible for the firm to consider other than very short-term costs and benefits.

4. The level of security of person and property may be such as to require armies of security guards, heavy investment in sophisticated security equipment, and expensive insurance.

5. The ability to shift resources may be structurally inhibited, thereby making it costly for a firm to adjust its resources appropriately as markets become increasingly international, as the firm's competitive advantage moves along its value-added chain, and as national comparative advantages shift.

6. The degree to which a nation holds individual enterprises responsible for unintended injury to consumers (product liability), to employees (health hazards), and/or to the general public (toxic waste liability, liability for disturbing ecological balances and/or environmental aesthetics) may be relatively high and thereby result in heightened cost to the firm, either in actual expenditures or contingent liability, which may or may not be insurable.

7. The level one country feels compelled to an active role in the affairs of other nations may be substantially higher than for another. Such involvement can lead to politically motivated control of trade, finance, and/or movement of persons, also to relatively high military investment.

8. The degree to which governments feel compelled to intervene to control the involvement of foreign business in its society varies from country to country, so likewise the frequency of such change and its apparent arbitrariness (i.e., unpredictability).

The point is, of course, that such social/political regimes can impact on national enterprises, whether locally or foreign-owned, in a number of ways such as to induce relatively high cost. Some of these costs include: repeated entry training and socialization costs, work slowdowns or stoppages, blocked internal communications, slowed introduction of new technology on factory floor or office, heightened litigation and associated legal expenses, major investment in maintaining security, high insurance premiums (or increased risk inherent in self-insurance in the absence of insurance), blocked trade opportunities, high taxes (whether direct or via high interest rates and/or heightened inflation and/or shifts in major foreign exchange rates), and the imposition of a wide variety of government controls. One could go on. The measurement of such social/political costs are made doubly difficult by their constantly changing nature.

This last brings us to the fifth step in the process of corporate strategic decision making, which is perhaps the most difficult of all. This step has to do with designing and developing adequate flexibility, *on an ongoing basis*, in decision-making processes and organizational design so as to permit the firm to respond to changes in both its competitive advantages and in the comparative advantages of countries. Books have been written on this subject, and many more are sure to appear. It goes beyond the scope of this chapter to plumb the subject—suffice to mention it, and its inherent difficulty.

One might, however, introduce a word of advice to host governments. In developing national policies designed both to attract and to control foreign business, government policy makers and negotiators are well advised to note the wide variance between firms in terms of flexibility. Careful study of how a firm has entered and operated in other national markets relative to such factors as ownership, control, technology and know-how transfer, and the willingness to externalize (or internalize) various links in its value-added chain, may be rewarding.

Part One

GOVERNMENT INTERVENTIONS

Chapter One

Government Policy Options vis-à-vis Foreign Business Activity: An Academic View

Richard D. Robinson

In general terms, a government has only four administrative levers with which to encourage or discourage an enterprise, whether foreign or domestic, to do something it would not otherwise do: regulation, tax incentive, subsidy, and reduction or increase of uncertainty.

A government is inclined to intervene positively (that is, provide incentives) when it perceives, rightly or wrongly, that the *external benefits* expected from an enterprise's activities will not be reflected in its internal financial results, within the time relevant to a firm's decisions. Or, the government objective may be to prevent an enterprise from doing something that it would otherwise do, but which the government deems socially undesirable in the sense that the associated *external costs* are not reflected in the firm's internal financial results within the time frame of decisions. The assumption in either case is that an enterprise can be expected to respond only to the expected financial consequences of an activity, not to external costs and benefits. In such case, the government may impose disincentives. It is useful to consider the characteristics of these four administrative levers.

DEFINITIONS

Regulation, as a device to induce an enterprise to do something it would not otherwise undertake on its own volition (or the reverse), will work only if the enterprise perceives that, even though the act required may be less profitable than the prohibited alternatives, it is nonetheless sufficiently attractive in terms of anticipated financial results to warrant undertaking. If the enterprise has much to lose in the form of "sunk" cost (that is, expenditures already made that cannot be recovered), or is threatened with the loss of a significant market possessing the promise of future profit, then this approach may be effective—*but* at the possible cost of discouraging subsequent investors (new entrants). The discouragement will be particularly intense if the regulation is viewed as arbitary and changeable (that is,

3

unpredictable) without compelling rationale. Uncertainty is thereby increased. Compliance, of course, is mandatory for the enterprise choosing to proceed.

Tax incentives imply a tax reduction (or increase) from that normally imposed on inputs, outputs, and/or financial results (profits), provided the enterprise satisfies certain conditions (or fails to do so). Compliance with these conditions is voluntary. That is, the enterprise need not comply if it is willing to accept the tax consequence. (In a sense, regulation is equivalent to an infinitely high tax.)

A *subsidy* is the provision, by a government to an enterprise, of specific services or other inputs at below-market prices. The notion really should be viewed as a continuum from what amounts to a concessionary ("subsidized") price, an outright gift ("grant"), to an actual payment. That is, included under the general heading of "subsidy" are inputs provided at specially discounted prices (market price less some percentage), at zero price, or at a negative price. The latter, of course, results in a payment to the enterprise, such as a transfer of funds for doing research and development locally, or for maintaining employment at a given level, or payment for its output at a price above the market price (for example, government procurement at a premium price). This subsidy continuum may be represented as in Figure 1.1.

Figure 1.1   The Subsidy Continuum

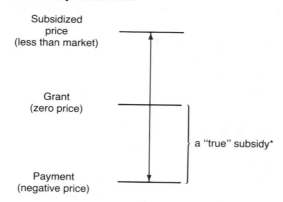

---

* A "true" subsidy is often identified as a payment, either to pay the firm for doing something that it would not otherwise undertake, such as research and development, or to reimburse the firm for certain expenditures.

As in the case of a tax incentive, the firm has the option of complying with the qualifying conditions or not. If not, it simply forgoes the subsidy.

The *reduction of uncertainty* as perceived by a management has the result that a firm's anticipated financial return need not be discounted to the same degree as might otherwise be the case. Uncertainty may be reduced by guarantee, but only if perceived by management to be enforceable. Examples of uncertainty reduction are (1) a commitment by a government to purchase part or all of the product of a project at a known price, (2) to assure a measureable market by prohibiting further entry, (3) to render local agreements enforceable under international law by permitting binding external arbitration, (4) to enter into international agreements in respect to the payment of compensation in event of expropriation of assets or breach of contract, and (5) to participate in international conventions for the protection of proprietary rights (trade marks, patents, copyrights, and trade secrets).

The purposes of all four devices are similar. Generally, they are designed to encourage any combination of the following responses:

1. the investment of foreign savings
2. development of a production facility on a particular site
3. investment from specific sources (country or corporation)
4. investment in a given sector of industry or activity
5. the processing of local materials prior to export (that is, the increase of local value added)
6. the use of locally manufactured components so as to induce the development of ancillary industry
7. the use of local labor
8. the transfer of foreign technology of a certain type
9. the development of certain functions locally (such as data processing, research and development)
10. the transfer of foreign skills (technical or managerial)
11. the development of exports
12. the transfer of ownership and control to local nationals
13. the public sale of equity in an enterprise
14. lower prices on outputs
15. production to certain standards (such as employee health and safety, product quality)

In all four cases, application of a specific incentive or lever may be limited in respect to nationality (e.g., domestic or foreign), to undertakings only above a certain minimum size, or to a certain time in the development of an undertaking.

In regard to the last—the *timing* at which a regulation is imposed, or tax incentive or subsidy given, or an uncertainty-reducing guarantee provided—it is useful to consider the life cycle of a project, which may be diagrammed as in Figure 1.2. Bear in mind that some activities may be conducted simultaneously and others added; it all depends on the nature of the project.

Obviously, the further removed an activity is from a predictable result (the point at which aggregate investment is recaptured, plus a reasonable profit, say at point Z in Figure 1.2), the greater the uncertainty perceived by the enterprise. Early on, it can have no real measure of the potential market, for it may not know precisely what it is going to market, at what price, under what competitive conditions. It can only assume the best and worst scenarios, as informed as these may be. *Risk* for the enterprise is greatest at the point of maximum investment, that is, at the point of maximum exposure prior to certainty of outcome (say, at point Y). By this time, the enterprise should be able to estimate the probability of various financial

Figure 1.2   The Project Life Cycle

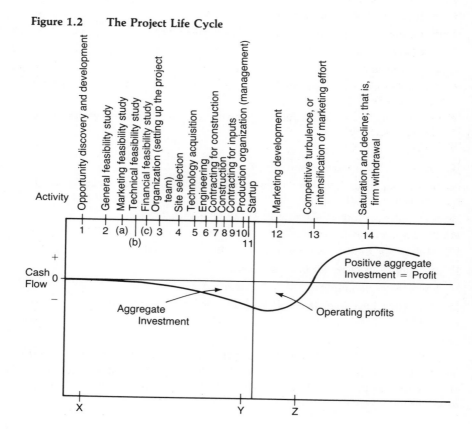

results. Costs, prices, competition, and consumer response can now be fairly accurately estimated. Both uncertainty and risk, in the sense we are using the terms here, evaporate to zero at some point in the curve at which investment and responsible profit have been captured (say, at point Z).

Therefore, for regulation, tax incentive, subsidy, or uncertainty reduction to be truly effective in achieving those objectives implicit in any given activity (such as stimulating investor interest, which is implicit in activities 1, 2, and 3, Figure 1.2), it must be applied at or before that point. The most effective intervention will probably be that occurring at or between the point of maximum uncertainty for an enterprise (point X on the project life-cycle diagram) and of maximum risk (point Y).

DISTINCTIONS

This brings us to a major difference between the four policy levers, namely, the timing of application during the project life cycle. Other differences relate to specificity of application, tax consequences, measurement of cost, visibility, risk of nonperformance, and possibility of unexpected impact.

Timing

Regulation cannot work unless an enterprise has already made a commitment of some sort based on purely market considerations, certainly not before activity 4 (site selection), if then. That is, regulating site selection will be effective only if the enterprise perceives the site to be acceptable on its own terms based on financial feasibility, even though it is a "second best" choice. The same could be said of activities 5, 6, 7, and 8. In each case, the regulation must be perceived by management as tolerable in terms of internal financial results within the planning time horizon. It will, of course, add on uncertainty cost to its calculations; regulations can change, thereby adding unanticipated costs. A management cannot know, *unless* it is convinced that the guarantees offered by the host government will be enforced. It should be noted that regulation—unlike tax incentive and subsidy—cannot create lower costs, a better market, or higher results. Hence, it is not positive, except possibly in one case: a regulation prohibiting additional entry, thereby creating the possibility of monopoly profit for the enterprise. It is more appropriate, perhaps, to think of such prohibition as an infinitely high tax on potential competitors. In any event, my own research in U.S. corporations[1] indicates that few managements are willing to make substantial investment on the assumption that regulation will be enforced effectively or will continue indefinitely. There are too many cases to the contrary on both counts.

An uncertainty-reducing guarantee cannot be realized until after the start-up of production and possibly only after revenues have begun to flow. We have found that an *up-front government commitment to purchase* a certain percentage of an enterprise's output at a specified price for a given time can be singularly effective, although management must perceive the existence of an attractive share of an ongoing competitive market. Managements, we have learned, are somewhat more skeptical—and, hence, less influenced—by government promises to prohibit new entry. Historically, too many have reneged, as eventually they must (or install some sort of price control so as to prevent extraction of monopoly profit). In any event, the real implementation of such a promise comes well after start-up. However, commitments to render breach of contract and expropriation of assets actionable under international law are important to a management right from the start of significant investment or anticipation of involvement in a project, say between activities 3 and 6 in Figure 1.2 (organization, site selection, technology acquisition, and engineering). We were told over and over during the course of our research[2] that a firm could live with *any* regulatory system so long as the flow of returns from contracts and investments made under that regulatory system were more or less assured for a reasonable period of time. Ten years was often mentioned.

As already indicated, a tax incentive can be applied only after some commercial activity has been commenced. If sales or value-added taxes are important, their reduction can impact as soon as activities 7 or 8 contracting for inputs and construction begin. The same is true of a tax reduction on imported capital equipment and materials, that is, lowered customs duties. The reduction of taxes on capital equipment is of special importance in that it comes at the time of maximum risk and means a one-time reduction in costs that cannot be taken away subsequently. Also, the enterprise management can see immediately whether the tax reduction is, in fact, implemented. If not, it could still withdraw with minimal loss in many cases.

Tax incentives promised in anticipation of a flow of profits (that is, a reduction of profits' taxes) are rarely effective in stimulating the development of new projects. Many international executives told us[3] that such incentives were seldom factored into investment decisions. They cited several reasons: (1) uncertainty and risk of the venture's ultimate profitability; (2) uncertainty as to whether the host government would live up to its commitment; and (3) the inability of certain foreign-based corporations (most notably, the United States) to realize advantages from a reduction in profit of wealth taxes (a subject to which we will return).

In contrast, a subsidy may be applied effectively for any activity from activity 1 (opportunity development) to activity 14 (saturation and decline, that is, firm withdrawal).[4] No purchase of inputs or commercial activity need to have taken place. This means that subsidies can be given during those activities identified with period of highest uncertainty (that is, opportunity development, feasibility studies, and organization), for which neither regulation, tax incentive, nor uncertainty-reducing guarantees are really applicable.

Specificity

Unlike a regulation or tax incentive, a subsidy or guarantee may be given quite easily to specific, named enterprises. The point is that under many bilateral friendship, commerce, and navigation treaties, trade treaties, and tax treaties, the signatory nations pledge themselves to desist from imposing discriminatory taxes, laws, and regulations. Subsidies and guarantees are normally not mentioned, other than export subsidies and market protection, which are, for example, restricted by the General Agreement on Tariffs and Trade. A country may determine, however, that it wishes to attract investment by, or the technological-managerial input from, specific corporations or countries. It may do so either because it "knows" certain companies and has confidence in their sense of responsibility and technical proficiency, or it wishes to diversify national sources of investment and technology, or it desires (or is obligated) to give preference to certain countries with which it has special relationships. In such cases, a host government can offer appropriate subsidies and/or guarantees without running afoul of its international treaty obligations, which it might do if it were to apply discriminatory tax or regulation.

Tax Consequence

Another distinguishing feature among the three approaches is the tax consequence. A regulation or guarantee generally has no direct tax consequence, but tax incentives and subsidies are another story.

For purposes of calculating the parent country tax liability in respect to income from foreign investment (or from a transfer of technology, or from technical or managerial skills), reduced taxes on local inputs (such as sales, value-added, or transactions taxes) and subsidies increase taxable income when earnings are remitted to the parent corporation abroad. That is, if the parent country were taxing foreign-source income when remitted, as though it were domestic income (as does the United States and a number of other countries), something like half of the added profit (depending upon the income tax level in the parent country, currently 46 percent in the United States) would end up as tax revenue for the foreign—that is, parent—government. Such taxes give rise to no tax credits that may be applied to the firm's parent country tax bill. They are "expensed," that is, they are deducted from taxable income as other business expenses.

A tax imposed on profit by a host government may, of course, be credited, dollar-for-dollar, against the parent government's tax bill, provided the latter taxes worldwide income. So, if that tax were reduced or waived, no benefit would accrue to the investing firm unless it were to reinvest its profit abroad—or unless the parent government recognizes the tax-sparing principle (which the United States does not), or unless the parent government does not tax foreign source income (or taxes it at a substantially reduced rate). In the worst case, the investing firm benefits from a reduced or waived profit tax abroad only to the extent of the interest on the amount it otherwise would have had to pay in tax to its parent government for the period that the relevant earnings are held abroad. The Appendix to this chapter gives numerical examples of the tax consequences of a subsidy, complete and partial reduction of taxes on inputs, and reduction of the profit tax. It should be noted that under U.S. law, a corporation has the option of either expensing or crediting foreign profit taxes.

Measurement of Cost

There is no way in which a host government can measure the cost (or benefit) of a regulation or of a guarantee (with the possible exception of government procurement). One has to make assumptions as to what would have happened if there had been no regulation or guarantee. What investment or activity has been forgone? How much does acquiescense to the regulation cost the firm in out-of-pocket expenses (for filling in forms, delay, expert assistance) and in forgone opportunities? To what extent will the costs imposed by regulation be passed on to the consuming public via higher prices or back to the government in the form of lower taxes (by reason of reduced profit and/or purchase of inputs)? And what benefit will a guarantee ultimately bring to the firm, unless in the form of government purchase?

The cost and benefit of income or profit tax incentives are likewise difficult to calculate. In the absence of such incentives, what would have happened? The cost of such incentives to the host government includes the forgone tax revenue. But was the tax critical to the relevant enterprise decision? According to my research among U.S. corporations,[5] very few overseas projects are either abandoned or implemented because tax incentives are absent or present. Managers tend to view tax incentives as "frosting on the cake," which could very easily melt away if the host government were to change its mind.

The situation is quite different for subsidies for two reasons. First, the direct cost of a subsidy is known. Second, its effectiveness can be tested. A host government need not offer a subsidy at the start of discussion of a project, but only when it is perceived that a subsidy might be critical—and justified because of externalities. In that subsidies are for specified amounts, or their cash value can be determined fairly accurately, and are paid early on ("up front") at the time of high uncertainty and high risk for the firm—that is, prior to commercial production—they are cited by many international executives as being peculiarly effective. Such subsidies are almost always plugged into their financial feasibility studies, we found, in that the amount is known and receipt is relatively certain. As indicated, management response to tax incentives tends to be very different.

Perhaps equally effective is the promise of reduced taxes on the import or the local purchase of capital equipment and on the purchase of land and buildings. Again, the timing is such that they correspond to a firm's period of high exposure. They not only reduce the amount of that exposure, but their up-front one-time nature reduces the perceived uncertainty of actually receiving such tax incentives. Also, their impact on production costs can be calculated quite easily. That is, inasmuch as such benefits bestowed by a government on an enterprise are not dependent upon long-delayed financial results, the cost of the benefits to the government can be more precisely calculated than can the cost of a reduced tax on profits. They cannot be measured with the same precision as outright subsidies, but almost so if the engineering has been completed. Of course, the earlier in the development of a project such incentives are promised, the less exactly can the host government measure their cost, whereas a "truly subsidy" (that is, grants or specific payments for performance) is almost always subject to precise measurement, although the need for the subsidy may remain somewhat problematical. Was it really necessary to induce the enterprise to do whatever was intended?

Visibility

Although subsidies thus possess several advantages over regulation, tax incentives, and guarantees, they have two important weaknesses: greater visibility and greater risk of nonperformance.

Just as subsidies may be awarded more easily on a discriminatory basis (to specific firms, projects, or nationalities) and are subject to more precise measurement, so likewise are they more visible. A subsidy of a million dollars given to Corporation X—either in grants of land or buildings or in outright payments to secure certain performance—is highly visible. In contrast, a tax incentive in the form of reduced tax on profits or on purchase of inputs is much less visible in that the amount is not specified, only a percentage reduction after some commercial activity has taken place. In any event, the local attitude toward the payment (or nonpayment) of taxes may be very different than that toward the give away of visible public resources. The reward, in the former case, comes after the firm has shouldered major risk; a subsidy may not. Subsidies thus tend to become politically vulnerable, particularly if the recipient is a large, foreign-owned corporation, and the donor government has, what some perceive to be, unfulfilled obligations to its own citizens. Guarantees are obviously triggered only by a specific contingency.

Risk of Nonperformance

For the very reason that preproduction (up-front) subsidies are apparently so effective in terms of attracting management attention, they may be high risk from the point of view of the host government. In that such subsidies are given before the event in order to induce an enterprise to develop a project, undertake feasibility studies, set up a project team, select a site, do the relevant engineering, and so on, there is little to prevent a corporation from taking a subsidy and not following through, except its sense of integrity and fair play. The firm may, at that point, have assumed little risk in terms of exposure. Hence, where an up-front subsidy is given, it may make sense to require the posting of some sort of performance bond by the firm, although this is not the general practice and would largely vitiate the appeal of a subsidy.

Of course, the promise of a subsidy, payment of which is *contingent* upon the firm's doing something (for instance, employing a given number of local personnel, undertaking local research and development, etc.), is somewhat less risky for the host government. However, by the same token, it is less effective, because there is always doubt in management's mind that the government will, in fact, live up to its commitment. An uncertainty-reducing guarantee involves little or no risk to the government because it is triggered only upon some specified event within control of the government; but again, management may doubt compliance, *unless* underwritten by an internationally enforceable commitment.

Possibility of Unexpected Impacts

It is probably true that a subsidy is more likely to achieve a desired impact without counterproductive secondary effect. For example, a payroll tax to finance the training of skilled labor used by the firm adds to the firm's labor cost, thereby inducing it to substitute capital for labor. Likewise, the elimination of import duties on capital equipment, out of a desire to promote employment by increased investment in productive capacity, may in fact increase the capital intensity of a project by rewarding the use of capital (that is, reduce its cost to the firm), but not of labor.

It might be more effective to pay an outright grant for each man-year of employment offered by a project.

Concessionary prices—another form of subsidy—may also produce unintended effects. An example would be a concessionary interest rate that encourages local borrowing, but only for fixed assets in that such rates are almost never available for working capital needs. Consequently, the more capital-intensive project is rewarded, even where the concessionary rates were offered to stimulate employment by encouraging expansion of productive capacity. The extreme case is where land and/or buildings are provided on a grant basis, or on a long-term concessionary lease-back basis where the buildings have been constructed specifically by the government for the investing firm. The cost of capital for the firm is, thereby, reduced, and a more capital-intensive project than might otherwise have been the case is encouraged.

A subsidy that has the effect of reducing the price of an input—be it electric power, water, certain raw materials, land, capital—has the result of stimulating greater use of the subsidized factor, but, by doing so, may cause a different technology to be employed. In the longer run, as subsidies are removed or reduced and the relevant inputs are priced closer to the market price, the technology (and associated skills) may prove to be uneconomic. The opportunity cost of the subsidies should be examined very carefully from the point of view of the costs they may induce by leading an enterprise to employ other than the least-cost mode of production.

Payment of a premium price for locally manufactured or processed products is another form of subsidy to the producing firm, but one so far removed from the original commitment to explore and develop a project that its cost-effectiveness may be limited. Moreover, to the extent that it is effective, such a subsidy has all the problems and costs associated with outright protection unless the subsidy is limited strictly in time so as to be associated only with the period of market development. Of a somewhat different nature is the guarantee of government purchase of a specified minimum amount of the product at a reasonable price (reasonable in relation to a truly competitive price for a period of time). Such procurement gets a firm past the difficult start-up period. So likewise does permission for a firm to import goods, and retain the ensuring sales revenues, for a period prior to—or during the early phases of—a project in order to test the market. We have found that this is a little used, but very effective, device to stimulate interest in foreign firms to become involved in local production.

NOTES

1. Reference is to Richard D. Robinson et al., *Performance Requirements for Foreign Business: U.S. Management Response* (New York: Praeger, 1983).

2. Ibid.

3. Ibid.

4. Although I have no knowledge of any such subsidy in practice, theoretically a government might pay a firm to retire a product or entire venture so as to make it worth its while to do so (for example, a drug found to be injurious after the market had been developed). A government might do so in order to reduce investor perceptions of costs arising out of uncertainty in respect to government intervention, and thereby encourage subsequent investors.

5. Robinson et al.

Financial Consequences of Tax Incentives and Subsidies When the Parent Government Taxes Worldwide Income

	With no Incentive or Subsidy, Profit Tax Credited	With no Incentive or Subsidy, All Taxes Expensed	With Taxes on Inputs Reduced 50% Profit Tax Expensed	With All Taxes on Inputs Waived	With Profit Tax Waived	With a Subsidy Equal to ⅓ of Costs
	A	B	C	D	E	F
1. Revenue	$100	$100	$100	$100	$100	$100
2. Deductible expenses						
(a) Taxes	(20)	(20)	(20)	(20)	(20)	(20)
(b) Other	(60)	(60)	(60)	(60)	(60)	(60)
3. Taxes waived	0	0	10	20	0	0
4. Subsidy	0	0	0	0	0	20
5. Actual costs	80	80	70	60	80	60
6. Profit before profit tax	20	20	30	40	20	40
7. Local profit tax (30 percent)	6	6	9	12	0	12
8. Remittance	14	14	21	28	20	28
9. Tentative foreign profit tax	9.2[a]	6.44[b]	13.8[c]	18.4[d]	9.2[a]	18.4[d]
10. Foreign tax credit	6.0	0.00	9.0	12.0	0.0	12.0
11. Foreign tax liability	3.2	6.44	4.8	6.4	9.2	6.4
12. Host government revenue[e]	26.0	26.00	19.0	12.0	20.0	12.0
13. Foreign government revenue[f]	3.2	6.44	4.8	6.4	9.2	6.4
14. Total tax burden for firm less subsidy[g]	29.2	32.44	23.8	18.4	29.2	8.4

[a] .46 × 20   [e] 2a + 7 − (3 + 4)
[b] .46 × 14   [f] 11
[c] .46 × 30   [g] (12 + 13 + 4) − 4
[d] .46 × 40

Assumptions: Local (host) government profit tax is 30 percent; foreign (parent) government profit tax is 46 percent.

Notes: The six columns indicate the results in financial terms of six different policies in respect to tax incentives and subsidies. Of course, the actual results in each case will depend on: (1) the level of taxes imposed on inputs (that is, sales, transactions, and import taxes), (2) the extent to which they are waived by the host government, (3) the level of profit tax imposed by the host government, (4) the level of profit tax imposed by the parent government (assumed to be .46 in this example), (5) whether the host government profit tax is expensed or credited (assuming that the firm has the option), and (6) the level of subsidy provided by the host government.

As can be seen, in our example the most favorable case for the enterprise is the subsidy (column F). Although its total tax burden is $28.4, this is reduced to $8.4 by the $20 subsidy. For the host government, the most favorable tax outcome is with no tax reduction; next, is with the profit tax waived.

Part Two

REGIONAL EXPERIENCE

Chapter Two

Evaluating Foreign Investment: With Special Reference to Southeast Asia

Louis T. Wells, Jr.

When a potential host country examines its policies toward foreign investment, perhaps the most fundamental issue that it must face is whether foreign investment is helpful or harmful in the development process. For two decades or more this has remained a burning issue in the development literature. The multinational enterprise has been attacked by some as a hindrance to development, and it has been praised by others as one of the important motors to pull poor countries out of their poverty. Every country makes an implicit assumption about the effect of foreign investment when it establishes policies toward would-be investors. Unfortunately, the assumptions have to be based on a great deal of faith; the empirical evidence for determining the impact of foreign investment on the development process remains rather weak.

There have been many fine studies that have examined the impact of foreign investment on certain aspects of development. Researchers have gathered information on the choices of technology made by foreign investors, on the wages that they pay, on their propensity to use imported inputs, on their willingness to export, on their alliances with local elites, and so on.[1] However, relatively little work has been undertaken to determine the overall impact of foreign investment on economic development.

To be sure, a few studies have attempted to draw conclusions about the economic impact of foreign investment based on macro data. Although some analysts have enterpreted those studies to support foreign investment, the studies most favorable to foreign investment show only that countries that have high incomes have been hosts to a larger amount of foreign investment that those that have been less wealthy. As tempting as it is to conclude that foreign investment is a cause of the better performance, it is equally convincing to argue that those countries that perform well simply attract more foreign investment because of their better economic performance.[2] The case either for or against foreign investment based on studies of macro data is very unconvincing.

A number of authors have taken a quite different approach to assess the impact of foreign investment on development. They have used piecemeal studies, anecdotal evidence, some plausible arguments, and several major leaps of faith to argue the case against foreign investment based on the overall impact of that investment on the host country. Perhaps the best known of the writings in English of this genre is *Global Reach*, a book that attracted considerable attention when it appeared in 1974.[3] The argument relies particularly heavily on anecdotes and allegations without strong empirical support. The best-argued of this category of work is that of the so-called dependencia school, in which Latin American representation is particularly strong.[4] But the empirical base of this literature is rarely sufficiently powerful to convince those who are not already converts to the cause.

Not surprisingly, there is a parellel set of literature on the other side of the argument with, at best, a weak empirical base. Some of this literature has been put out by business organizations and evidences little understanding of the macroeconomic issues that must be faced when the impact of such investment is evaluated.[5]

There is, to be sure, a body of literature that rather carefully weighs the arguments of both sides and the available empirical evidence on the impact of foreign investment. Whatever the conclusions the authors draw about the net effect of foreign investment, those conclusions are subject to many qualifications.[6] Many of the studies of this character have been of a high quality, but based on piecemeal data collected in a single country. These studies have attempted to weigh data on the propensity of foreign firms to export, to use imported inputs, to hire local workers, and so on, in order to reach a judgment about the net impact of foreign investment on the development of the country.[7] Whatever the overall evaluations made by such authors, the conclusions are not easily accepted by the avid supporters of foreign investment or by the opponents of such investment. The evidence that has been available to support the conclusions has simply not been able to give overwhelming support to either side of the debate.

Some Empirical Results from Micro Studies

One of the principal problems with the studies just mentioned has been that they have relied on bits and pieces of data that could be combined only with considerable faith into a net judgment. They have not attempted to capture in a single measure the economic impact of foreign-owned projects. This weakness had been partially overcome in two particularly helpful studies that attempted to use economic techniques to measure the overall effect of foreign investment on economic development. A third study, using a similar approach, has recently been completed based on data from an Asian developing country. One of these previous studies was done by Lall and

Streeten in the early 1970s for the United Nations Conference on Trade and Development;[8] another was done by Grant Reuber in the same time period under the auspices of the Organization for Economic Cooperation and Development.[9] The third study was done by this author and Dennis Encarnation in a developing country in 1983.[10] Although the tones of the conclusions of the two earlier studies differ from each other and there are differences in the methodologies of all three studies, the results are surprisingly consistent. When the three studies are viewed together, the results are quite helpful in addressing the issue of the impact of foreign investment on the development process.

The Recent Study

The results of the 1983 study have not been published, so a brief summary of the methodology and findings follows.

Data. The data were collected from application forms submitted during a recent five-year period by foreign firms to the authority responsible for screening investment proposals in one large Asian developing country, one that had been following a "mild" import substitution policy that gave protection against import competition to a wide range of industries. These applications generally contained ten-year forecasts of income statements and balance sheets for the proposed projects. Further, they contained estimates of the costs of imports that would be equivalent to the projects to be produced by the proposed plant.

Since the data were submitted by private investors but the projects were not yet in existence, we had no way of directly verifying the accuracy of the data. One might suspect that the bias of the would-be investor might lead the firm to submit figures that would make the project look better from an economic point of view than it would look if the data were accurate. The manager might, for example, understate the capital required for the project or overstate the value of imports that would be saved by local manufacture. The investors were quite aware that their proposals were being evaluated, and the form of the questions they were asked suggested that the evaluation would be of a common social cost/benefit approach.

There is, however, one reason to suppose that the firm might adjust numbers in ways that make the project look worse. Since the investment authority granted exemptions from import duty on capital equipment according to a list of equipment needs submitted by the investor, the investor might feel safer by overstating the capital required. If the total list were not approved, then the accepted sum might be enough for the actual requirements of the plant. Alternatively, if the entire sum were approved, items might be imported duty free and sold in the local economy. In fact, we were able to perform a weak control to check for the influence of this bias.

Overstating the capital requirements would lower the projected return for the private investor. Consequently, by separating the sample into firms for which projected income statements indicated a reasonable rate of return for the investor and those where the projected private return was low, we would test to see whether there was a difference in economic evaluation in the two groups. There was no indication in this test of a bias in reporting.

The sample was drawn from the pool of all foreign investment proposals completed and submitted to the investment authority of the country. We selected 50 applications for manufacturing (we included projects for fishing and fish processing). The sample covered a wide range of industries and the firms that proposed the investments were of a number of nationalities. (The Appendix to this chapter provides some details of the sample.)

Analysis. To determine the impact of foreign investment, we evaluated the *contribution to national product* made by each firm in the sample of 50 projects proposed by foreign investors. We did not attempt to estimate any impact the projects would have on local culture, defense capability, income distribution, or other areas not captured in national income. To determine the impact on national product, we extended the ten-year forecasts provided in most investment proposals to a twenty-year basis by using common fiancial techniques. The proposals were then evaluated using cost/benefit analysis. (The details of the methodology are available in the Appendix.) The approach used is closest to that described by Roemer and Stern.[11] There are differences between this and other methods, such as the so-called Little and Mirrlees approach.[12] The variations do not yield different cutoffs for selecting projects, although the different approaches can yield different rankings for projects. Further, the differences in techniques for analyzing the projects are less important than the errors in the data that are available for such analyses.

In the analysis, the benefits from the proposed projects are considered to be the contribution of the project to national income in the form of goods and services produced by the project and consumed or invested in the country, or the earnings from those goods and services if they are exported. In the calculations of the value of the goods and services to the economy, world market prices were substituted for the sales prices assumed by management. This reevaluation of the benefits was based on the assumption that the products and services could be imported if they were not locally manufactured. The figures for the cost of equivalent imports were supplied by the investor in the application.

The costs to the economy of proposed investments consist of the resources used in the project. These are labor, local capital, locally purchased goods and services, and the foreign exchange costs associated with the project. The foreign exchange costs include imported raw materials and components as well as dividends, royalties, interest, debt repayment, and similar costs. Where there were reasons to suspect that market prices underestimated or overestimated the value to the economy of a resource used by the project, we substituted shadow prices for the prices reported by the would-be investor. The shadow prices were intended to reflect the opportunity cost of the resources to the economy. Thus, if energy could be exported for more than the project paid for it, the shadow price would be above the market price. If labor would be unemployed in the absence of the project, its shadow price would be lower than the market price. In various calculations, we used shadow prices for oil, foreign exchange, labor, and domestic capital.

Results. No matter what calculation is examined (see the Appendix for the various assumptions), the results are quite similar and consistent with earlier research. They indicate that the majority of the projects increase the national product; at the same time, they clearly show that many investments proposed by foreigners would decrease the national product if they were accepted. That is, they would use resources in a way that yields less goods and services for the host country than those resources cost the country. They are unattractive to the host country even though the projects are profitable to the private investor. Moreover, there is a striking pattern that explains why investors propose so many projects that seem to be harmful to the host country.

The overall results are quite clear. In the measure most favorable to the foreign proposals, nearly three-quarters of the projects yielded a ten percent or better return to domestic resources; but the remaining one-fourth failed to yield a ten percent return to the host country. Nearly all (eleven out of the thirteen) unattractive projects showed a negative rate of return to the host country. In the measure least favorable to the foreign proposals, more than two-fifths of the projects failed the test of a 10 percent return. Regardless of the assumptions, the majority of the projects proposed by the investors are good for the economy, but a large percentage are harmful. At least one-quarter of the proposed projects do not pass the test of yielding a ten percent rate of return on the country's resources. The actual percentage of projects failing this test could be more than forty percent. The most probable figure is around one third.

At the risk of confusing the less technically oriented reader, a detour into some of the details of the assumptions underlying the alternative calculations is necessary.

First is the measure most favorable to foreign investors: The key assumption in this measure was that figures for imports as reported by the investor bore a 20 percent duty. Although there was no way of determining what duties the investors assumed in answering the questionnaire provided by the investment authority, it is likely that some part of the investors assumed lower or no duties when they reported the import requirements. This is especially the case since exemption from duties had regularly been granted to previous investors. Under the extreme assumption that investors included a tariff, about three-quarters of the projects passed the ten percent return test.

Consider the opposite assumption. If one assumes that the investors included no duties in their import figures, slightly more than two-thirds of the fifty projects yield at least a ten percent return; about one-third fail the test. Again, most of these failing projects show negative returns. Thus, we feel safe in concluding that the lack of certainty about investors' assumptions on import duties for materials does not have a major impact on the outcome of the evaluation of the proposals; only three projects were shifted from the positive to the harmful category when the assumption was changed dramatically.

In other versions of the calculations, we carefully examined the prices of domestic inputs that were used by the projects. The two inputs for which market and shadow prices were likely to differ were oil and labor. For a number of the proposals, we could determine the value of oil used, at market prices. Since oil prices in the host country were subsidized, we substituted the international price of oil for those reported by the investor. When this was done, almost 45 percent of the projects yielded less than a ten percent return for the country. In some calculations, we assumed that the shadow price of labor was as low as 70 percent of its market price. Such changes in the shadow price of labor had very little impact on the percentage of projects that were harmful to the economy.

In sum, regardless of the assumptions, a significant fraction of the projects that are proposed seem to be unattractive to the host country, although the majority remain attractive. Moreover, there are striking differences in the impact on the host economy of different kinds of projects. Some types were consistently beneficial; others were very likely to be harmful.

The Reasons for Bad Projects

It is important to understand why a large fraction of the proposed projects are harmful for the host country. A breakdown of the proposals by industry is instructive. First, consider the import-substituting projects. In total, 30 percent of these projects were harmful to the local economy even under the most favorable assumptions. In industries with high rates of protection, a particularly large percentage of proposed projects were harmful to the host economy; where protection was low, most projects were beneficial. The extreme case was made up, of course, by the export projects. In these cases, the firms had to compete without any protection on the world market. All eight such projects were beneficial. Table 2.1 shows the relationship between protection and the attractiveness of proposals to the host country:

Table 2.1

Industry[a]	Percent of Proposed Projects that Fail Test	Nominal Tariff Protection in Industry (percent)	Effective Tariff Protection in Industry (percent)[b]
Export	0	0	0 or less
A	30	about 10	26
B	33	20–25	150
C	50	50–100	191
D	70	about 100	717

[a]Includes all export projects and all import substituting projects for industries with three or more import substituting projects.
[b]From a World Bank report on effective protection in the country.

High rates of protection are quite clearly the principal cause of unattractive investment proposals. Investors in protected industries can build plants that do not contribute to the local economy, but the investors can nevertheless profit because of the protection.

Interpreting the Results of Three Studies

Remember that the analysis evaluates foreign investment against only one criterion: its direct impact on national product. Although this particular criterion is inevitably an important one, it does not address all the concerns of a would-be host country. First, we did not capture at all any economic effects of the project external to the project itself. Those effects might be positive or negative: the project might generate costs in the form of pollution or by creating competition so severe that domestic entrepreneurs decide to invest outside the country; or it might generate external benefits for the economy by training workers who leave the firm and apply their skills elsewhere. Second, the project might have important social impacts. The presence of the firm and its foreign managers may generate tastes for goods and behavior that are destructive of local values. Or it might increase income disparity among regions of the country. On the other hand, the activities of foreign managers may set good examples for local managers. The project might reduce the dependency of the country on overseas sources of defense goods. These and other effects that are not captured in the measurements used for this study might well make some seemingly attractive projects unattractive. Some projects that do not contribute directly to national product might be attractive if other criteria were taken into account.

While recognizing the potential importance of other criteria, I suspect that the direct positive impact on the national product is the contribution most sought by countries when they accept foreign investment. Equally important, of the projects that were unattractive when measured by their contribution to national product, the vast majority actually yielded negative returns to the economy on the resources they used. In addition, the majority of beneficial projects showed very high positive returns. Relatively few were close to the margin. The large portion of projects that showed either very positive or very negative impacts on the economy suggests that introduction of other criteria would probably not result in dramatic shifts in evaluations of the projects. Whatever the adjustments made, the evaluation would probably continue to show that the majority would be beneficial, but also that an important minority would be harmful to the host country.

The results of this study are, as was mentioned, quite consistent with the findings of two other studies that examined a number of investments at the micro level.

Lall and Streeten examined 133 foreign controlled projects in six countries.[13] For 88 of the firms they were able to calculate income effects, using a cost/benefit framework. For two-thirds of those firms, the effect was positive; for one-third, negative. The findings are thus similar to ours.

The Lall and Streeten study also reinforces the conclusion of our study as to the cause of bad projects. The Lall and Streeten work included not only foreign owned projects, but also some locally owned manufacturing plants that had been established to substitute for imports. It is important to note that Lall and Streeten found no statistically significant difference between the effects of the locally owned projects on the economy and those of the foreign owned projects. Although the lack of significant difference between foreign and domestic projects might at first seem surprising, it is easily understood when one considers the principal reason that explained the private profitability of socially unattractive projects in our sample of only foreign owned projects. High rates of protection from import competition allow private profits for socially unattractive projects regardless of whether the investor is local or foreign. Further evidence for the importance of protection in determining whether projects are likely to be attractive or not lies in Lall and Streeten's observation that competitiveness of sales had the greatest impact on the final results of their calculations.[14]

The Reuber study provides similar results. That study evaluated the costs of production for 45 foreign owned projects from a sample drawn from 30 host countries.[15] The analysis did not use a conventional cost/benefit approach, but rather compared the production costs of the subsidiaries to production costs in the parents' home countries (among other calculations). The results are a crude approximation of cost/benefit calculations. They come close to the results of social benefits analysis if in those social calculations all resources used are charged at market prices, but adjustments are made in the value of output to reflect world market prices. Using this simpler measure, the Reuber study finds that a little more than one-quarter of the subsidiaries had costs that were equal to or lower than those of the parent operations; about three-quarters had higher costs.

Reuber also broke down the projects according to whether they were export-oriented or not. Of the 14 export projects, 70 percent had costs that were equal to or lower than home costs. Reuber calculated that for the nonexport projects the country could have imported the equivalent products at a 30 percent savings over local production. Thus, the Reuber study found export projects more attractive than the average projects that were import substituting.

The results of the Reuber study are surprisingly similar to those of Lall and Streeten and to our own work. While the percentages differed a bit, all the studies concluded that the majority of projects appear to be beneficial and an important minority seem to be harmful.

Whatever one concludes about the exact percentages of good and bad projects proposed by investors, one must accept the fact that the typical package of proposals is a mixed bag. That protection is the principal cause of the difference between the private and social evaluations.

The policy implications of such findings are significant. The rewards of eliminating the bad projects appear to be quite significant. The desired results could be achieved in either of two ways. The price signals given to the investor can be made to match the social prices involved; alternatively, the host country can administratively screen out or reshape through negotiation the projects that are likely to be harmful to the economy.

In the country that we studied, a lowering of the effective rates of protection would lead to the desired results. If investors, local or foreign, had to compete based on international prices for their output, virtually all of the socially unattractive projects would have been unattractive to foreign (or domestic) private investors. Private profits and social profits would have been closely aligned. In a country where internal prices of resources depart more from social values than in the country that we studied, less protection from imports might not be sufficient to match private and social values. Major subsidies would probably have to be eliminated, for example. Most Western economists would consider the reduction in effective protection, improvements in the pricing of domestic resources, and effective domestic competition as the first-best solutions to the problem of eliminating unattractive investments. Nevertheless, few countries with high rates of protection are likely to eliminate tariffs and quotas quickly. Further, most countries find it politically difficult to effect quick dramatic reductions in subsidies. Consequently, one is left with second-best alternatives: administrative screening of investment proposals to eliminate those that are likely to be harmful to the economy.

SCREENING AND NEGOTIATING FOREIGN INVESTMENT

Establishing an effective organization for screening and negotiating foreign investment has proved frustratingly difficult. The task poses at least two dilemmas for host countries.

First, countries must decide how centralized to make the negotiating process. On one extreme, they might have potential investors negotiate with all the agencies of government that are considered to have a concern with the impact of the proposed investment. On the other extreme, they might vest authority in a single organization that has full power to negotiate with and to screen foreign firms. The choice between a centralized and a decentralized process is a frustrating one. Each type of approach has its advantages and disadvantages. Further, efforts to avoid the choice by establishing compromise organizations also generate advantages and disadvantages and, in fact, often fail to accomplish their objectives.

A second dilemma is posed by the nature of the tasks to be accomplished in dealing with foreign investors. Some organizations that might be particularly effective in negotiating with investors for the most favorable terms and in screening unattractive proposals are likely to discourage would-be investors. Few countries have established a single organization that is effective both in screening out bad proposals and in promoting foreign investment.

In a study of the organizations used to negotiate with potential investors and to evaluate their proposed projects, Dennis Encarnation and I found that countries differ considerably from each other in their choices of approach.[16] Moreover, the same country is likely to use different approaches for different industries at one time and its approach for the same industry might well be different at different times.

In spite of the number of choices that we observed, we do believe that we could discern a rational pattern in the selections that are made. The choices appear to reflect a country's attitude toward foreign investment in general, the salience of a particular industry in the development plans of the country, and the degree of competition that the country faces in attracting particular kinds of investors.

The Choices

In our study we observed four basic ways of handling the tasks of screening foreign investment proposals and negotiating the terms under which projects would be accepted.

The first approach, an unusual one for developing countries, was a "policy approach." Countries following this approach did not, in fact, conduct individual negotiations with investors over important issues. Rather, they had determined in advance overall policies that specified, at least for the majority of investors, the industries in which they would be accepted or excluded and the terms under which they could operate. Such policies might be lenient toward foreign investment, excluding few potential projects, or they might be very restrictive, virtually closing the country to foreign investment. Hong Kong and the U.S. federal government illustrate the first type; Burma is an example of the second.

Three remaining types cover the approach to screening and negotiation in most developing countries. The various approaches can be viewed as falling on a continuum that has a decentralized approach at one extreme and a centralized approach at the other. The countries that have decentralized negotiations include in the screening and negotiation most government ministries and agencies whose interests would be affected by the investment. Under this approach, a would-be investor must negotiate with each agency separately to emerge with the necessary permits and with a set of terms to govern entry. In Sukarno's Indonesia, for example, this approach governed discussions with many potential investors. On the other extreme, authority to negotiate with an investor is concentrated in one organization that has the full authority to accept or reject an applicant and to conclude the terms that will govern the investor's sojourn in the country. In recent years most investors seeking to invest in Singapore dealt with the Singapore Development Authority, which represents this type of approach.

Advantages and Disadvantages

The extremes of the continuum offer quite different advantages and disadvantages to the host country.

A decentralized approach is attractive for several reasons. First, the technical skills of specialized agencies and departments can be brought to bear directly in negotiations. Tax expertise is likely to be in the finance ministry; knowledge of labor and laws and issues, in the labor ministry; technical skills for the relevant industry, in the ministry of industries, health, or whatever; and so on. Second, these units of government are likely to be the agencies that will eventually have to administer the terms of any agreements that might be reached. Having them conduct the relevant part of the negotiations is likely to make for terms that can be effectively administered with available resources. Further, if the administrators are the negotiators, there is a reasonable chance for learning from past mistakes.

Decentralized negotiations cause serious problems, however. First, there is no way to evaluate the overall benefits offered by a foreign investor's proposal and to weigh the package of incentives and performance requirements that are negotiated. Each ministry acts on its own. If a particular ministry concludes that the project has a favorable impact on the issues that are of concern to that ministry, it is likely to approve and offer incentives. As a result, if all ministries like the project, the total package of incentives might well exceed what is required to attract the investor. On the other hand, if one ministry finds that the project has a negative impact on matters of concern to that agency, it is likely to disapprove or to impose burdensome performance requirements on the potential investor. In fact, it is quite possible that one ministry will block a project that is attractive to the country when the net impact on the country as a whole is considered.

A second problem is that individual ministries are likely to give little attention to overall policy issues and to the precedents that their negotiations set for other proposals. The implicit decisions may or may not be good for the overall interests of the host country. The results of such dispersed negotiations are not likely to provide a consistent pattern of decisions.

The third problem, and the most important for many countries in Asia, is that the costs of decentralized negotiations are particularly high for the foreign investor. Since outcomes are difficult to predict in advance and since the process is likely to be slow and to cost a great deal of management time, would-be investors are discouraged from even initiating negotiations. Consequently, the pool of investors applying to a country with a decentralized process might well be less than for a similar country with a process that is quicker and that yields more predictable outcomes for the investor. It is this problem that has led many countries to abandon the decentralized process for a more centralized approach.

A centralized process, of course, is in most ways the opposite of a decentralized one. In fact, centralized processes come in two quite different forms. The disadvantages and advantages of the two forms are somewhat different.

In a few countries, such as Singapore, negotiations with the vast majority of foreign investors are centralized in one autonomous body. Such an organization is able to negotiate quickly and to establish a predictable pattern of outcomes. This process addresses directly the problem of greatest concern to most countries that abandon a decentralized approach. But a centralized approach can offer other advantages. An autonomous body that covers a wide range of negotiations can consider the overall impact of a project on the country and it can weigh the total package of incentives and performance requirements to determine what is required to attract a desired investor. Moreover, it is very likely to consider carefully issues of precedent in its negotiations and decisions.

On the other hand, the use of autonomous negotiating units leads to a separation of negotiations from implementation. Implementation usually remains the problem of the relevant technical ministry. The distance between negotiator and administrator can lead to terms that may well be difficult to administer. Moreover, broad autonomous units pose one additional problem. The breadth of the task assigned to such agencies almost assures that it will not have in-depth expertise in technical and industry-specific issues.

An alternative approach to obtain some of the advantages of centralization is to place responsibility for negotiations in a specialized unit that covers only one industry or one type of investment. Oil agreements might be negotiated by a state enterprise. Or agreements with potential exporters might be the sole responsibility of an export processing zone authority. In contrast to the autonomous unit with authority for a wide range of industries, this more specialized agency is particularly likely to develop industry expertise. Moreover, this kind of organization is likely to conduct quick and reasonably predictable negotiations. But such organizations rarely take into account the impacts of their agreements on other investment negotiations outside their area of authority. State oil companies, for example, are unlikely to worry about the impact that the terms of their petroleum agreements have on discussions with mining or manufacturing firms.

Both types of centralized organizations have one advantage that usually explains their creation: they reduce the problem of high costs for potential foreign investors inherent in decentralized negotiations. They can be quick and predictable. But both types of centralized organizations do also impose a very important cost on the host country. Their creation entails high political costs. Establishing such organizations requires the government to "disenfranchise" ministries and agencies that consider that they have a legitimate interest in the outcome of negotiations and thus a right to participation. Centralization means, for example, that tax matters are decided outside the Ministry of Finance, foreign exchange issues outside the central bank, and so on. It is this reason that makes broad-based autonomous agencies for foreign investment so unusual. Governments are not willing to incur the political costs of centralization without strong reason.

Unwilling to incur the political costs involved in the choice of centralized structures and displeased with the disadvantages of decentralized approaches, many countries have tried to combine some of the advantages of each by efforts to coordinate the activities of various agencies of government that might be interested in the negotiation process and have been, at one time, participants in a decentralized system. They do this without going to the extremes of centralization.

The intermediate step of coordinating negotiations also takes at least two forms. Most common is the investment coordinating board, which is run jointly in some manner by a number of ministries whose interests are typically affected by foreign investment. Indonesia, for example, negotiates with many investors through one wing of the BKPM, the Foreign Capital Investment Board, a coordinating board that has representation from the Ministry of Finance, the Ministry of Industries, the Ministry of Agriculture, and other ministries that might be affected by foreign owned activities.

Coordinating boards have their advantages and disadvantages as well. They do provide a mechanism for examining the overall benefits and costs of proposed projects and for weighing the total package of incentives and performance requirements. Moreover, coordinating boards consider the precedents that are generated by individual negotiations. Particularly important, they do, when they work well, reduce the costs of negotiation for the investor.

Rarely, however, do coordinating boards work as well as intended. First, coordinating boards typically develop little expertise in particular industries. Perhaps even more important, very often powerful ministries often refuse to cooperate in the coordination efforts. Thus they may not honor the agreements reached by the coordinating board, or they may slow down the negotiating process by sending low-level personnel, or no one at all, to meetings. The result is usually a board that does not function as intended. Wise investors then learn to negotiate with the separate ministries regardless of the public descriptions of the alleged power of the boards. Those investors who do depend on the board find their agreements not honored; their experience damages the reputation of the investment climate of the host country.

In an effort to overcome these latter weaknesses of coordinating boards, governments sometimes take another approach to coordination. They form special ad hoc coordinating committees to deal with particular investments. These are quite similar to the centralized approach that covers one industry. The hope in creating such ad hoc committees is that ministries will not sabotage negotiations that are viewed as extremely important and that such a committee can assemble a special team with in-depth knowledge of the industry involved. Like their centralized counterparts, however, such committees generally pay little attention to matters of precedent and overall policy.

In fact, most countries establish a portfolio of approaches that reflects the various types of investment under consideration. Thus, in the 1970s Indonesia negotiated with most investors through the BKPM, its coordinating board. At the same time, however, a state enterprise, Pertamina, had almost full authority, in practice, to negotiate oil and gas agreements. Negotiations for a large petrochemical project were simultaneously being handled by an ad hoc committee with representation from several government agencies. Moreover, some consideration was being given to the creation of export processing zones where the authority for negotiation might, like other countries in the region, be centralized in an organization responsible for the operation of the zone.

Factors Affecting the Choices

The choices that countries make when they establish negotiating structures seem to follow quite regular patterns. Three variables seem to play critical roles in the decisions: The choices appear to be determined largely by the overall policies of the country toward foreign investment, the salience of particular industries, and the degree of competition faced by the country for particular types of foreign investors.

We found that a country's *overall attitude* toward foreign investment determined the approach that would govern negotiations with most would-be investors. Countries that are not eager to attract foreign investment tend to choose the more decentralized approaches. On the other hand, countries that desired more foreign investment tend to establish more centralized organizations. For most countries that eagerly sought foreign investment, the choice was some kind of coordinating agency. The driving force behind the choice of approach for the wide range of general investors appeared to be a trade-off. The country must weigh the political cost involved in centralizing the negotiation process against the high costs that decentralized processes imposed on would-be investors. Only countries that evidenced a strong desire for more investment were willing to pay the costs of diluting the authority of ministries by taking away their rights to conduct negotiations on matters of great concern to their interests.

The impacts of a country's changes in attitude toward foreign investment are frequently well-documented in its changes in the entry process. As has been pointed out, Indonesia required investors to negotiate with a large number of government agencies in the Sukarno days, when it was particularly suspicious of the supposed benefits from foreign investment. Under the Suharto regime, attitudes changed. Eager to attract foreign investment, the government moved toward coordinating the negotiating process. Complaints about the effectiveness of coordinating efforts led to an increase in the role of the coordinating board in the mid-1970s. Similarly, more favorable attitudes toward foreign investment in India have led to some reduction in the dispersion of the negotiating process in recent years.

Whatever the choices countries make for negotiating with the majority of investors, they tend to make special arrangements when the industry is particularly important, or "salient." When faced with proposals in such industries, few countries have been willing to live with the possibility that a decentralized approach would result in a poor agreement, or none at all. And they have not been willing to live with the lack of industry expertise that typically characterizes a broad coordinating board or investment authority. The most suitable approach for countries facing a particularly salient project, it seems, has been to vest negotiating power in a specialized state enterprise, if such existed, or to create a special ad hoc coordinating committee if no relevant state firm existed. Both approaches have offered the possibility of speedy negotiations, the potential of an overall view of the net benefits of reaching agreement, the possibility of weighing the incentives and performance requirements as a package, and most important, the potential for bringing to bear considerable industry expertise in the negotitions.

There were other cases when the countries that we examined decided not to use the negotiating approach that they used for most investors. Special arrangements were generally established when the *competition among countries* for particular kinds of investors was particularly intense. The most common examples involved export-oriented projects. A country with a large domestic market could attract foreign investors for the local market by offering the most effective incentive: protection from import competition. This incentive was not applicable, however, for firms that wanted to set up facilities for export. Competition was quite intense for such firms, since they could locate their plants in any of a number of countries that offered cheap production resources. In most cases, they required only inexpensive labor, sufficient infrastructure, and good transportation and communication facilities with the rest of the world. Fearful of losing the battle for such investors, many countries have centralized negotiations for such firms in one unit. The goal of centralization is to create an organization that can act quickly and decisively, thereby increasing the attractiveness of the country to investors in the face of intense competition from other potential sites. Many countries, such as the Philippines and India, have offered export processing zones for potential investors in export plants. Not only do these zones offer infrastructure, but they generally are run by an organization that is fully vested with authority to reach agreements quickly and according to well-understood, predictable guidelines.

Operation of Screening and Negotiating Bodies

The task of the organizations that deal with foreign investors could be divided into at least four categories: (1) attracting potential investors, (2) screening applicants, (3) negotiating the terms of entry for the acceptable investors, and (4) administering the agreements that have been negotiated. Some observers would add an additional task: determining when the terms under which investors operate should be renegotiated.

None of the countries in which we did research seemed to have resolved adequately the apparent dilemma posed by the tasks of attracting potential investors and evaluating proposals to screen out those that were not attractive. Most organizations placed almost all of their emphasis on one or the other of these two functions. The Economic Development Board (EDB) in Singapore, for example, puts most of its effort into promotion. The tendency is reinforced by the unit's management system. Target amounts of investment are assigned to sector heads. Further, the fact that many employees of the EDB remain for only a short time and eventually work in industry probably encourages this orientation. In contrast, the BKPM in Indonesia devotes little of its resources to effective promotion, but requires long application forms and lengthy negotiations of would-be investors. Screening appears, at least on the surface, to be its principal function.

Even where screening appears to be the major function, the effectiveness of screening is often questionable. Not one organization that we studied regularly performed economic analysis. One board, with long negotiations and little promotion activity, explained the unwillingness of the organization to perform relevant economic analysis as follows: Rejections would have a negative impact on the number of potential investors that would apply to the board. The dilemma posed by promotion and screening had, in this particular case, especially unfortunate consequences. The board did little to attract investment. At the same time, it did not screen out bad proposals. We were, in fact, not able to find any relationship between the economic cost/benefits of proposed projects submitted to this board and whether or not they were accepted.

We had no firm basis to evaluate the performance of organizations in the actual negotiation process. We did, however, have some indications of difficulty on the implementation side. We encountered frequent discrepancies between the seeming intent of an agreement negotiated by one organization and the implementation of that agreement when that implementation was done by another body. For example, ministries of finance would occassionally not honor tariff exemptions granted by investment authorities. In other cases, tax authorities would later negotiate tax terms more favorable (or less favorable) to the investor than those that had been negotiated with the investment authority. These differences usually arose during the implementation stage, when practical problems of administering the original terms began to appear, when ministries needed to collect more revenue, or, we occasionally suspected, when unofficial payments were passed to particular officials.

IMPLICATIONS

What do the experiences of the countries that we studied suggest for other countries concerned with foreign investment? The results clearly show that most developing countries cannot have confidence that projects that are attractive to investors are attractive to the country. There is some assurance of a match between private and national interests only under certain conditions: (1) prices that face the investor must be good guides to the opportunity costs of resources that the project will use, and (2) the prices for the output of the project must be close to those that indicate the social value of the product. In the projects that we studied, the absence of this second factor was usually the cause of investment proposals that were privately but not socially attractive. In the absence of policies that establish accurate price guidelines for managers, the government must seriously consider careful screening of proposals on their economic merits.

The existing research, all on market economies, says a great deal about where the emphasis should be placed in the screening process. Since price distortions on the output side were the principal causes of unattractive investment proposals, careful evaluation is most necessary when the proposals are for projects that would service a domestic market that is protected from import competition. On the other hand, bad projects are less likely to be proposed, and thus evaluation is less essential, when projects are to manufacture for export markets. Further, these are the projects for which international competition demands quick and predictable decisions.

An important caveat. One cannot be so sanguine about the effects of export projects in an economy where many domestic prices are administered, rather than determined by market competition. I know of no research that evaluates a sample of proposals or projects in countries with a large number of administered prices for domestic resources, but some anecdotal evidence suggests that in such environments even export projects can easily be wasteful of national resources. One case is of an onion drying plant, which would import onions to a free trade zone, dry them with fuel oil that was priced below export value, and export the dried onions, at world market prices. A study of the proposed project indicated that the country would be better off exporting the oil (or importing less oil) and rejecting the drying plant. A similar study of a metal smelter in a non-OPEC oil-producing country concluded that the country would have earned more foreign exchange by exporting the fuel oil and the ore concentrate than it did by processing the ore in the country in an inefficient (by world standards) plant. The examples suggest that screening may be necessary even for export projects in countries with administered prices that depart considerably from opportunity costs.

Although the potential benefits of screening foreign investment are clear for a country with import protection and with price distortions in the internal market, the experience of other countries suggests that those benefits are in fact quite difficult to achieve.

First, the screening process is not an easy one. Of all the organizations that we studied, none actually performed careful economic cost/benefit calculations. The reasons were numerous. Scarcity of skilled personnel was certainly one factor. Another was the difficulty in assembling adequate data. Moreover, the failure was, on occasion, blamed on the supposed incompatibility of screening and investment promotion.

The problems in undertaking economic analysis suggest that efforts should be made to concentrate analytical skills on those areas of investment where economic and private profits are most likely to differ. One approach, suboptimal from a theoretical point of view but perhaps necessary as a practical matter, is to make crude classifications of types of investment proposals. This enables the screening bodies to devote resources to the most likely trouble areas. Such a classification system might, for example, separate out export projects for a very simple, quick test. In the country we studied, a simple test of the ratio of energy used (underpriced to the investor) to labor employed (overpriced to the private firm) could be used. A ratio above a certain figure would separate out proposals for special attention. Since the vast majority of projects with lower ratios would be beneficial, they could be approved virtually automatically. Proposals for serving the local market might be divided into industries categorized according to priority and according to effective protection. Scarce analytical resources might be devoted first to high-priority sectors and special attention paid to industries with high rates of effective protection. Model terms might be prepared to improve predictability for would-be investors. Some poor projects might slip through such a screening process, but the increased speed of analysis is likely to generate more proposals for consideration. Proposals for low-priority sectors might have to wait for evaluation and negotiation until time is available. Some potential projects might, of course, be lost due to slow processing, but the losses are likely to be unimportant if the sectors are low-priority.

The second set of lessons derives from the difficulties posed by the organizational issues. If negotiations were decentralized, they were particularly likely to be ineffective and to discourage potential investment. On the other hand, centralization came at a high political cost. Only when the stakes seemed particularly high were governments willing to disenfranchise ministries in order to centralize the negotiating function. Coordination was, because of lack of political commitment at the top, often ineffective and, in some cases, deteriorated into decentralized negotiations soon after the initial attempts at coordination. Coordination can work only if government is actually willing to remove authority from departments with legitimate interests in the outcome of negotiations with potential investors.

The experiences of various countries indicate where the problems lie. Understanding the likely sources of problems in different structures is an important step in designing effective organizations.

NOTES

1. A few examples include the impact of multinationals on technology [e.g., Robert Stobaugh and Louis T. Wells, Jr., eds., *Technology Crossing Borders* (Boston: Harvard Business School, 1984); for a summary of some of this literature, see Sanjaya Lall, "Transnationals, Domestic Enterprises, and Industrial Structure in Host LDCs: A Survey," *Oxford Economic Papers* 30 (July 1978), 271–248], transfer pricing [e.g., Constantine Vaitsos, *Intercountry Income Distribution and Transnational Enterprises* (Oxford: Clarendon, 1974)], and exports [e.g., G. K. Helleiner, "Manufactured Exports from Less Developed Countries and Multinational Firms," *The Economic Journal* 83 (March 1973), 21–47].

2. For a critical review of studies based on macro data, see C. Stoneman, "Foreign

Capital and Economic Growth," *World Development* (January 1975), 11–26. See also S. J. Kobrin, *Foreign Direct Investment, Industrialization, and Social Change* (Greenwich, Conn.: JAI, 1977); and V. Bornschier, "Multinational Corporations and Economic Growth: A Cross-National Test of the Decapitalization Theory," *Journal of Development Economics* 7 (June 1980), 191–210.

3. R. J. Barnet and R. Mueller, *Global Reach: The Power of the Multinational Corporations* (New York: Simon and Schuster, 1974). See also *A Critical Comment on Global Reach* (Washington, D.C.: The Center for Multinational Studies, 1975).

4. For one of the best of the many dependencia works, see Peter Evans, *Dependent Development: The Alliance of Multinational, State, and Local Capitals in Brazil* (Princeton, N.J.: Princeton University Press, 1979). Notes to this book also make up a good bibliography on the dependencia school. Dependencia views (and other views as well) are carefully summarized in R. J. Biersteker, *Distortion or Development: Contending Perspectives on Multinational Corporations* (Cambridge, Mass.: MIT Press, 1978).

5. For very promultinational approaches, see Arthur McCormack, *Multinational Investment: Boon or Burden for the Developing Countries?* (New York: W. R. Grace, 1980); and Orville L. Freeman, *The Multinational Company: Instrument for World Growth* (New York: Praeger, 1981).

6. For a balanced appraisal of various views, see Raymond Vernon, *Storm over the Multinations* (Cambridge, Mass.: Harvard University Press, 1977). The best summary of the literature on multinationals to date is very careful in its interpretation of the research. See Richard E. Caves, *Multinational Enterprise and Economic Analysis* (Cambridge: Cambridge University Press, 1982).

7. There are many country studies. Some of the best are the following early ones: Helen Hughes and P. S. You, eds., *Foreign Investment and Industrialization in Singapore* (Canberra: Australian National University, 1969); Donald T. Brash, *American Investment in Australian Industry* (Cambridge, Mass.: Harvard University Press, 1966); Albert E. Safarian, *Foreign Ownership of Canadian Industry* (Toronto: McGraw-Hill, 1966); W. P. Hogan, "British Investments in Australian Manufacturing: The Technical Connection," *Manchester School of Economics and Social Studies* 35 (May 1967); B. Sepulveda Amor et al., *Las Empresas Transnacionales: Expansion a Nivel Mundial y Proveccion en la Industria Mexicana* (Mexico: Fondo de Cultura Economica, 1976).

8. The results are published in Sanjaya Lall and Paul Streeten, *Foreign Investment, Transnationals and Developing Countries* (Boulder, Colo.: Westview, 1977).

9. The results are published in Grant L. Reuber, *Private Foreign Investment in Development* (Oxford: Clarendon, 1973).

10. This work has not been previously published.

11. Michael Roemer and Joseph J. Stern, *The Appraisal of Development Projects* (New York: Praeger, 1975). See also Michael Bruno, "The Optimal Selection of Export-Promoting and Import-Substituting Projects," in *Planning the External Sector: Techniques, Problems, and Policies,* Report on the First Interregional Seminar on Development Planning, Ankara (New York: United Nations, 1967).

12. I. M. D. Little and James A. Mirrlees, *Project Appraisal and Planning for Developing Countries* (New York: Basic Books, 1974).

13. Lall and Streeten.

14. Ibid., p. 174.

15. Reuber.

16. See Dennis Encarnation and Louis T. Wells, Jr., "Sovereignty en Garde: Negotiating with Foreign Investors," *International Organization*, Winter 1985; and Encarnation and Wells, "Competitive strategies in Global Industries: A View from the Host Country," in Michael Porter, ed., *Competitive Strategies in Global Industries* (Boston: Harvard Business School, 1985).

APPENDIX

The Sample

Fifty applications were selected, for all practical purposes at random, from the files in the host country's investment agency. We accepted files that had been considered for action within a five-year period and that were sufficiently complete for our analysis. We excluded timber and plantation proposals, projects that were heavy users of timber or other inputs that had export restrictions, and mining projects.

The industry mix of the sample is shown in Table A.1; the nationality mix of the sample is shown in Table A.2; the market orientation for the proposals is shown in Table A.3.

Table A.1

Industry	Number of Projects
Automotive	9
Chemicals	13
Electrical and electronic	4
Fishing	4
Food procesing	2
Garments	2
Pharmaceuticals	3
Textiles	6
Misc. (only one firm in industry)	7

Table A.2

Nationality	Number of Projects
European	10
Unites States	2
Japanese	12
Other industrialized	2
Developing country	22
Unknown	2

Table A.3

	Percentage of Output to be Exported					
	0	1–25	26–50	51–75	76–99	100
Number of projects	28	11	2	0	0	8

Methodology

The economic effects of the proposed projects on the host economy were measured by subtracting the costs from the benefits for each of twenty years of assumed project life and then determining the internal rate of return.

The benefits were assumed to be the output of the proposed projects, valued at the alternative costs of importing the equivalent goods (without tariffs) or the value of the exported product. These figures were determined from data submitted by the investor in the application. The costs were those indicated on the investor's projected income statements, with the following adjustments:

1. Depreciation was added back in as a noncash cost.
2. Capital costs were included as follows:
    a. for foreign capital: dividends, interest, and repayment of principal abroad.
    b. for domestic capital: the amount of capital put into a project was charged against the project in the year in which the capital was invested.

Calculations were made for each project under the following assumptions:

1. First, it was assumed that the prices paid by private investors for all inputs reflected the value of the inputs to the economy (market prices = shadow prices).
2. As in (a), but labor was shadow priced at 70 percent of market prices to reflect the assumption that some of the workers to be employed by the project would otherwise be unemployed or underemployed.
3. As in (1), but with energy shadow priced at twice market prices, under the assumption that investors paid only half of world market prices for energy during the period under study.
4. Labor shadow priced at 70 percent of market prices, energy shadow priced at twice market prices, and the exchange rate priced at 20 percent above official rate.

5. As in (1), but assuming that the value of the raw materials reported by the investor included a 20 percent tariff.

6. As in (5), but with shadow prices of inputs and foreign exchange as in (4).

Chapter Three

Government Regulation of Foreign Investment: Emerging Lessons from Latin America

Moises Naim

In Latin America, as elsewhere in the developing world, the attitudes held and policies applied toward foreign direct investment (FDI) have varied widely over time. From the end of World War II through the early 1960s, for example, FDI was viewed as an "engine of development." Accordingly, host country governments employed a variety of incentives to attract such investment. Thereafter, the benevolent nature of FDI began to be questioned and doubts emerged concerning its contribution in advancing the cause of economic development. Over the years, these initial doubts gradually escalated, giving way to intense and systematic criticisms of FDI by academics, journalists, politicians, government agencies, and even international organizations.

Foreign firms, it was now argued, drained capital from host countries by exporting, over the long run, more funds than were brought in. Other charges leveled at foreign investors included generating distorted consumption patterns, transferring inadequate technology, absorbing or displacing established local firms, contributing to the creation and consolidation of small, powerful, foreign-oriented sociopolitical elites, intervening in local politics, altering income distribution patterns, and generally eroding the living conditions of the majority of the population. The ensuing debate showed that some of these allegations were exaggerated, and that the same empirical evidence could yield varying conclusions and policy implications.[1] Nonetheless, the generalized perception among Latin American academics and policy makers was that foreign firms and their investments merited careful and specialized treatment.

By the early 1970s in Latin America, granting explicit incentives and other forms of preferential treatment toward foreign firms became almost unthinkable. Allowing the free entry of foreign firms into the national economy was no longer considered sound policy. Instead, foreign investment was barred from entering "reserved" sectors and limits were imposed on new foreign firms wishing to operate in the local economy. Constraints on the autonomy of both new and existing foreign firms were introduced in order to mitigate the socioeconomic "costs" attributed to their operations, an aspect that led host governments to monitor closely the firms' financial, commercial, technological, and managerial behavior. Also, joint ventures with local firms were regarded as mechanisms that could generate more appropriate behavior on the part of foreign firms. Obliging a foreign firm to divest after some years was considered a way of resolving some of the inherent tensions and problems that were now associated with foreign investment.

Not suprisingly, scholars labeled the 1970s as a "time of trouble" for international business (Robinson, 1981:15). The new attitude toward FDI was soon reflected in public policy across the continent. Argentina began enacting a set of legal guidelines regulating foreign investment in 1971; Bolivia, Colombia, Ecuador, Peru, and Chile formed the Andean Pact in 1971. When Venezuela joined the group in 1983, a common restrictive policy toward foreign investment was adopted. Similar restrictions were introduced by Mexico in 1973 and by the Dominican Republic in 1978. Legislation concerned with technology transfer was enacted by Argentina in 1971, by the Andean group in 1971, by Mexico in 1973, and by Brazil in 1975. Although Chile withdrew from the Andean Pact in 1976, the countries where restrictions continued in force accounted for 90 percent of FDI in all of Latin America.[2]

What "lessons" can we glean from this experience? Before stating them let me caution that experience in Latin America concerning the regulation of FDI is as varied as the countries themselves, and that our assessments may sometimes do very little justice to the actual circumstances and practices of some specific country at a specific point in time. Also, even as we take into account the available research on the subject of foreign investment regulation in Latin America, much of what follows is based on emerging impressions and is offered largely in the spirit of tentative insights.

THE ELASTIC QUALITY OF FOREIGN INVESTMENT POLICIES

Surprisingly enough, when one compares the official documents and the general policies adopted by Latin American countries some ten years ago with those currently in force, comparatively few significant changes may be noted. If, on the other hand, one compares the *actual decisions* being made by the regulatory agencies today with decisions that the same agencies made years ago under the same policy framework, the differences can be astonishing.

Essentially, the major legal instruments governing the regulation of foreign investment (e.g., laws and codes) have exhibited considerable stability; whereas substantial changes can be noted in the intermediate legal and administrative instruments[3] (decrees, *reglamentos, resoluciones,* rules, guidelines, administrative decisions, etc.) used to implement the general policy. The point of the matter is that even if officially and symbolically, the regulatory systems of most Latin American countries have remained unchanged during the past decade, in practice the rules employed by some of the countries have been significantly modified through a series of not very visible but highly influential changes in the procedures, guidelines, and specific criteria used to administer legislation concerned with foreign investment and technology.[4] Obviously, the stability of the underlying legislation concerned with foreign investment is related to the high political cost and cumbersome process implicit in openly promoting change in so sensitive a policy domain.

Overall policy stability has also been abetted by the fact that the adjustments, adaptations, and modifications that the system periodically requires can be much more effectively, easily, and discreetly achieved through changes in administrative mechanisms. Modifying the weights and factors included in the equations used by a regulatory agency to assess a new foreign investment proposal or technology contract may, under certain circumstances, alter the country's foreign investment code. Placing the regulatory agency under the development ministry, for example, instead of having it report to the treasury or central bank, can change its performance in ways equivalent to amending its basic charter. Varying the interpretation of a rule that regulates the supply of foreign exchange can do more to attract or discourage foreign investors than modifying the tax structure imposed on foreign firms. In the words of an MNC executive with operating experience in several Latin American countries: "A mere change in the regulatory agency's ranking officials can generate as much change in the application of specific norms as restructuring the entire legal framework concerned with regulating foreign firms."[5]

Not surprisingly, therefore, every piece of research focusing on the actual functioning of foreign investment and technology regulatory systems in Latin America has identified a significant gap between stated policy and effective practice, the former tending to be more severe than the latter (Rose 1975; Robinson 1976; Naim 1978; Lombard 1978; Bennett, Blachman, and Sharpe 1978; Allen 1975; Rosenn 1983). Unfortunately, no light has been shed on the effects this pattern of policy making and implementation may have had either on the host countries or on the firms concerned. It could be hypothesized, for example, that this pattern raises transaction costs and discourages such potential investors as may lack access to mechanisms through which they would obtain a realistic view of how this dual (restrictive-lenient) legal system actually works. Presumably, such investors abandon project analysis following a naive assessment of the costs, benefits, and risks that emerge from examining formal documents, and ignore the fact that subtle exceptions can radically alter the effects of the code on project profitability. On the other hand, firms that possess knowledge and experience of how policies are actually implemented presumably become more strongly entrenched in a particular setting.[6]

For the sake of clarity, it should be emphasized that changes in the conditions actually imposed on foreign firms need not result from illegal or dishonest behavior, but from deliberate changes in a government's position vis-à-vis foreign investment that are expressed by altering the way a policy is implemented. Of course, this does not mean that illegal and dishonest behavior could not play a part in such a system; but our point is that, under the circumstances discussed here, the distance between the law and its practice is not necessarily illegal, given the extremely general wording of foreign investment codes and the ample discretion assigned to the implementing actors. Consider now the origins of this bureaucratic discretion.

THEORETICAL INADEQUACIES AS SOURCES OF BUREAUCRATIC DISCRETION IN FOREIGN INVESTMENT POLICIES

In all countries, almost every public policy is permeated by a certain degree of vagueness. Such vagueness imposes the need for specific interpretations by public officials, thereby transforming their personal judgments, values, and skills into important determinants of policy consequences (Pressman and Wildavsky 1973; Pressman, Rein, and Rabinovitz 1976). In less-developed countries (LDCs) the personal input of public administrators in shaping the policy outcome has been found to be particularly frequent and intense. Accordingly, the regulation of foreign investment and technology by LDCs presents one of the extreme examples of a type of public policy where the outcome depends enormously on the behavior of the officials and organizations in charge of policy implementation.

A number of researchers who have examined the issue report substantial levels of discretionary authority on the part of the implementing agencies concerned: Robinson, in every one of the 15 countries he studied (1976); Naim in Venezuela (1978); Lombard in Colombia (1978); Grosse in the Andean Pact countries (1983); and Rossenn in Brazil (1983). De La Torre (1981) cites discretionary authority as one of three central issues in discussing national controls on FDI (the remaining two being policy severity and stability). Hence the question: Why so much discretion in so sensitive a policy arena?

Some answers to this question were already suggested in the preceding section. We now submit that the wide level of discretion also owes something to the nature of the theories concerned with FDI, multinational corporations, and technology transfer that prevailed at the time these policies were formulated during the early 1970s, and, to some extent, to the inadequate theoretical base of the subject at present.

Although the growth of large multinational operations dates from the mid-1950s, scholarly attention to the rate of international penetration of such firms emerged only in the late 1960s (Servan-Schreiber 1968; Vernon 1971). The middle and late 1960s was also a time when the so-called *dependencia* approach for analyzing the condition of development and underdevelopment, together with FDI and technology as paramount dependence issues, began to gain popularity among social scientists and policy makers in Latin America and elsewhere.

As already noted, the widespread adoption of restrictive measures on foreign investment generated a heated debate. One of the positive effects of this debate was that the views held by specialists everywhere concerning the determinants and consequences of foreign investment were revised and some premises were even substituted by new, more realistic hypotheses. A good example of this was the gradual shift in the literature on FDI away from the neoclassical assumptions that viewed foreign investment as mainly determined by differences in the rate of return among countries, toward the more empirically grounded notions of oligopolistic behavior and market imperfections, originally suggested by Hymer (1960) and subsequently refined by Kindleberger (1969), Caves (1971), Vernon (1966), and others. Significantly, the basic conclusions emerging from the market imperfections approach for explaining FDI were shared by the nationalistic and dependency writers who were critical of FDI. Notwithstanding such converging conclusions, the policy implications that the latter group of writers derived from their conceptual framework were not generally shared by proponents of the market imperfections approach.

It is against this backdrop of theoretical doubts concerning the efficacy of the market mechanism to resolve, freely and spontaneously, the problems that FDI posed to the host countries, that the new foreign investment regulations and policies were formulated. Simply put, the basic idea stemming from these discussions was that LDC governments had to intervene to compensate for the market imperfections that were associated with foreign investment. This conviction naturally led to the enactment of the general legislation that, in essence, banned the entry of new foreign firms in some sectors, imposed entry conditions in others, and generally sought to monitor and intervene in the transactions occurring between a local subsidiary and the rest of its multinational network of affiliated firms (see Robinson, 1980; Correz 1984; Cheroll and Zalduendo, 1984).

Very soon, the monumental difficulties of this grand task started to become apparent. For one, foreign direct investment could assume more varied and complicated forms than the newly spelled out policies seemed to anticipate. If foreign investment were banned from the retail trades, for example, should an immigrant-owned grocery store be treated with the same rules as Sears? What is "reasonable" compensation for x man-hours of a technical specialist loaned by a foreign affiliate of an MNC subsidiary? Is a trade mark royalty payment equal to 3 percent of sales high, low, or or adequate? How should the price of the shares of a foreign firm that is forced to divest be valued? What if no local buyers are found for those shares? How should "appropriate" or "fair" prices be estimated for a host of intermediate goods and services that are never exchanged through a market but only through channels internal to the firm? These and a multitude of other similarly difficult questions confronted the recently created regulatory agencies that, throughout Latin America were expected to deal with foreign investment.

The government technocrats charged with providing precise answers to these questions discovered that no one—either at home or abroad, in other state agencies or even among the international organizations, who enthusiastically supported the enactment of FDI regulation—possessed knowledge of the practical guidelines required to make such decisions.

In our view, the vague character of foreign investment and technology legislation has been and continues to be the concrete manifestation of insufficiencies and inadequacies in the state of knowledge concerned with the nature and the determinants of FDI, with technology usage, transfer, and generation, and with the structure, motives, and behavior of firms conducting business across international boundaries.

MISSING LINKS IN THE COMPLEX MODEL OF INTERNATIONAL CORPORATE BEHAVIOR

At the time that Latin American dependency theory and its foreign investment and technology public policy implications were being formulated into a legal framework, and to a certain extent even today, the central areas of attention concerned with international corporate behavior have been FDI and the MNC. This emphasis muddled the recognition of at least three important points:

1. FDI and the controlling equity it entails is only one of the many instruments simultaneously available to a firm for conducting business activities across national borders. Exports, licenses, barters, joint ventures, and an amazing variety of contractual arrangements combining and complementing all other available instruments are utilized by corporations to achieve their international strategic objectives. Furthermore, in many cases, the equity associated with FDI is not expected by the firm to generate a return but only to serve as the condition that makes viable the use of these other mechanisms. This fact partly explains why the reasons and processes, through which an investor decides to move his capital to a given country, are quite different from the ones through which a firm decides to expand its operations to another country.
2. The motives and incentives firms have in expanding abroad are extremely varied (natural expansion, oligopolistic chain reactions, international diversification, export market defense, access to resources, etc.) and give rise to very different

restrictions, bargaining positions, and propensities to comply with the different regulations. Furthermore, these incentives, motives, and behaviors differ from sector to sector and, over time, within a given sector, or even within a given firm.

3. The corporate structures and business arrangements that firms employ to undertake their international activity and the operating behaviors that emerge from these structures are also extremely varied; and these too carry different implications in terms of the impacts and effects that national regulations and norms on foreign investment may have on specific firms. Again, these differences in structural arrangements of foreign firms can vary from sector to sector and through time.

The contingent nature of these assertions and their situationally dependent, ad hoc policy implications are mere reflections of the lack of a general, unified theory about FDI and corporate international activity,[7] out of which robust, all-encompassing generalizations can be used to guide public policy. When this theoretical insufficiency is combined with the political realities that generate the incentives to maintain a high level of generality and abstraction in government policies toward foreign investment, the result is none other than ample discretionary powers of regulatory officials and consequent implementation problems.

The difficulties of implementing the type of foreign investment policies generally adopted during the 1970s by Latin American countries have become even more obvious in light of recent theoretical advances concerning the nature of FDI and of MNCs. These contributions (Buckley and Casson, 1976; Magee, 1977; Teece, 1976; Dunning, 1979, 1980; Caves, 1982) essentially point (a) to the intangible nature of the "special advantages" that allow a foreign firm to compensate for the added costs of operating at a distance in an unfamiliar environment; (b) to the difficulties associated with transacting these assets through the market mechanisms;[8] and (c) to the fact that the combination of these two conditions gives rise to the type of international multiunit enterprise commonly known as the MNC.

Legislation enacted for the purpose of regulating foreign investment and acquiring foreign technology sought to "unbundle" the package of "intangible assets" that MNCs presented as an integrated amalgam of capital, technology, management, and other assets. It also attempted to intervene generally in the transactions of these intangibles. Little attention was paid to the fact that the essential trait of the business organizations that conducted these transactions was the competitive advantage they gained by "internalizing" the international transfer of assets inherently unsuited for the kind of arms-length transactions that the regulations tried to address. This reality, plus the enormous maneuvering possibilities associated with an organizational structure designed to internalize international transactions, provided the firm both with the incentives to avoid the impact of these regulations and the possibilities of doing it very effectively. Furthermore, as we see next, the nature of the regulatory agencies in charge of the policies also contributed to entangle their implementation of public policy.

WHEN ASSUMPTIONS ARE ILLUSIONS: THE NOTION OF ORGANIZATIONAL SYMMETRY BETWEEN FOREIGN FIRMS AND PUBLIC AGENCIES

As everyone knows, the very nature of public-sector organizations everywhere inhibits the emergence of flexibility, rapid response, information processing and utilization skills, systematic follow-up and feedback orientation, and high levels of managerial continuity and organizational learning. Public organizations in LDCs are even more handicapped in terms of these characteristics. Furthermore, as much research on the subject of government regulation of economic activity has demonstrated, public agencies in charge of the regulation tend to develop close relationships with the regulated sectors and industries; relationships in which "clientelism" and the cooptation of the regulators by the regulated frequently occur (Huntington 1952; Stigler, 1971; Wilson, 1980).

Surprisingly, however, many if not most of the official studies used to support the drafting of national policies, as well as academic research projects recommending what a country's policies toward foreign investment should be, and, worst of all, the policies themselves, appear to have been completely blind to the effects of these institutional characteristics in shaping the eventual outcome of the policies. Instead, with rare exceptions, much of the thinking and action (both in terms of research and policy) has implicitly assumed that the actors in the process of foreign investment regulation—foreign investors and local regulatory agencies—are basically equivalent, or symmetrical, in terms of their management and organizational capabilities. As odd as it may seem, the thinking in this area has failed to take into account the basic fact that the agencies expected to perform the highly sophisticated tasks entailed by the regulation of foreign investment are public-sector organizations. Furthermore, these organizations are found in those countries where the public sector has experienced great difficulties performing such ordinary and presumably simple tasks as delivering mail, removing urban garbage, or regulating the behavior of its own state enterprises.

This neglect is explained partly by the influence, in the analysis and design of foreign investment policies, of traditional normative welfare economic models, where the basic assumption is that the government acts in ways that maximize the real income of its citizens (Caves, 1982:286). Therefore, the intriguing question for analysts, and consequently their central theoretical preoccupation, has been with the definition of a host country's appropriate policy toward foreign investment and technology; *not* with what happens *after* the policy is enacted or with the institutional and other conditions needed for the policy to be effective.

In sum, Latin American experience clearly shows that the nature of the regulatory agencies as public-sector organizations represents an important determinant of policy implementation, perhaps ranking in importance with the character of the policy itself. A list of some of the organizational characteristics that have tended to emerge among Latin American foreign investment regulatory agencies includes: congested routine operations, inappropriate and unstable staffing patterns, bureaucratic rivalry, vulnerability to external pressures, information overflow, inadequate monitoring, and limited enforcement capabilities. Consider these deficiencies in greater detail.

Congestion. As has occurred with many public organizations, the demands made on regulatory agencies have grown at a much faster pace than their capacity to process and respond adequately to the business at hand, thus congesting their organizational routines. Not surprisingly, such congestion has made the agencies more reactive than proactive, and slowed their capacity to identify and adapt to changes in their external environment.

Inappropriate and unstable staffing. The literature tends to assume that regulatory agencies are generally staffed by experienced, multidisciplinary professionals, who are fluent in second and third languages; familiar with project evaluation, technology appraisal methods, and international corporate finance; proficient in bargaining and managerial skills; and possessing the versatility to deal with different sector and industry managers on a one-to-one basis. Government officials with such a profile can certainly be found, but they tend to be the exception rather than the rule. Political appointments, public-sector salary levels, and personnel policies render it difficult to attract and retain a sufficient number of qualified professionals.

Bureaucratic rivalry. While the norm has been to centralize all foreign investment decisions in a single government agency, in practice a constellation of public agencies end up participating and influencing a country's policy toward foreign investment and technology. Such agencies include the central bank, congressional committees, as well as public offices concerned with planning, the treasury, foreign trade, industry, agriculture, foreign affairs, regional development, science and technology, and in some cases even the military and the office of the president. Such offices interact in complex and sometimes conflicting ways as they try to influence the general implementation of poicy or the treatment accorded to a specific project. In some countries, the foreign investment agency must devote as much time and resources to its dealings with other government bodies as it devotes to the screening and control of foreign investors and local importers of technology. Such rivalries reflect natural competition for power, resources, and prestige that arises between bureaucratic organizations everywhere, but they also illustrate the particular ways in which an LDC's dilemmas toward foreign investment tend to be resolved in practice. Each agency pursues objectives that, presumably, are of importance to the government, regardless of the fact that some of these objectives may be difficult to reconcile and that trade-offs between them have to be made. In some cases, instead of making these trade-offs explicitly they are made implicitly, through the pulling and hauling of the different agencies, which in turn see their relative bargaining power vis-à-vis other government agencies as significantly determined by the political priority of the objectives they are expected to pursue. Such shifting intragovernmental influence has frequently shaped the decisions made by foreign investment agencies throughout Latin America.

High vulnerability to external pressures. Foreign investment regulatory agencies have tended to be particularly vulnerable to external influences, which may lead an agency to modify its norms and procedures, grant exceptions, accord differential treatment to a "special" foreign investment proposal or technology acquisition contract, or even to reverse a decision already taken. These influences originate both from the government and from the private sector, from domestic as well as from foreign actors, through legal, visible, and explicit means, and through under-the-table payments and other corrupt practices. In general, however, the regulatory agencies have not had the political clout to buffer the external pressures to which they are commonly subject. Special projects are a good example of this extreme vulnerability. These are projects that, because of their investment size, employment generation, export potential, sensitivity or priority of the sector involved, interdependence with some other government program, or involvement of the personal interest of a cabinet member or the president, are channeled outside the established system. In such case, the regulatory agency acts in a rubber-stamp capacity once all the important conditions have been negotiated.

Information overflow. Regulatory agencies tend to collect more information than they can effectively use. Much of their staff time is assigned to obtaining and processing such information; yet the agencies lack the organizational mechanisms and processes through which this information can be appropriately analyzed and used to support and learn from their decisions. In many instances, and partly because of the organization's congestion and the effects of bureaucratic politics and external influence, the dynamics of decision making tend to be disconnected from such organizational processes as the collection and evaluation of information. This inadequacy in the use of information is further compounded by theoretical confusion surrounding the regulation of foreign investment, as discussed in the previous section.

Inadequate monitoring. In the initial years and to some extent continuing, regulatory agencies devote an inordinate amount of time and effort at estimating "correct" prices for goods and services exchanged mainly, or only, through a firm's internal channels. In this task they encounter the enthusiastic assistance of private consulting firms that provide—in exchange for handsome fees—data banks, sophisticated information retrieval systems, and other information systems. Little attention is paid to the fact that a laboriously reached decision to lower the price at which a firm was trying to register a contract may be offset by an unnoticed increase in the price of another internal transaction not subject to the agency's scrutiny. In short, regulatory agencies generally have failed to give proper attention to the fact that the dynamics of the situation require permanent and detailed audits to detect deviations from the parameters originally defined. Such situations require a strong monitoring capacity on the part of the agency. The development of such capacity has not been a priority among Latin American regulatory bodies. The effects of this neglect are cumulative, insofar as the failure to make timely use of available information inhibits organizational learning by limiting the possibilities to build on knowledge gained from examining past decisions and their consequences.

Limited enforcement capabilities. The general strategic orientation of the foreign investment regulatory agencies has been toward the entry phase, at the time of the initial drafting of an investment or technology transfer agreement. Inadequate monitoring of post-entry behavior has been even more acute in the case of technology contracts, where very little, if anything, is done to check if the spirit or even the letter of the laws and the signed contracts are being followed. This should be no surprise, as a lack of follow-up capability is a common trait of public organizations, particularly in LDCs. For all practical purposes this has meant that once a foreign company is granted permission to operate in the country or the technology contract has been signed, ample possibilities exist for gradually drifting away from the stated conditions. Nonetheless, from time to time (and this also conforms to the patterns frequently exhibited by the public sector) a specific enforcement "spasm" arises, thereby generating frenzied supervisory activity on the part of the regulatory agency, which might be focused either on a specific sector or on a specific firm or on a specific clause or issue (employment or local content incorporation, for example). In general, however, such "enforcement spasms" are short-lived, since they have to be implemented at the expense of attention to the agency's day-to-day operations.

Many other problem features could be added to this list of organizational characteristics of agencies regulating foreign investment. The ways in which these characteristics shape the implementation of policy, significantly defining its actual outcome, can also be refined and specified. At this stage, however, the important point to emphasize is that these long-neglected factors should be incorporated systematically in any discussion of the regulation of foreign investment and technology import, and that improved mechanisms should be sought to diminish the impact of these implementation difficulties on policy outcomes. Otherwise, even if progress is made at the conceptual level, by better clarifying what LDCs should do about foreign investment and technology transfer, we would continue to be plagued by blurred ideas about *how* that should be done.

THE REGULATION OF FOREIGN INVESTMENT AND TECHNOLOGY: EXPECTATIONS AND REALITIES

Latin American legislation concerned with the regulation of foreign investment and technology was enacted with great expectations. Not only was it anticipated that the new laws were going to serve as an antidote for the eventual problems and economic distortions that could arise out of foreign investment and technology imports, but it was also hoped that such laws could somehow compensate and correct the pernicious social and economic effects caused by the mistakes and omissions of past public policies toward such foreign inputs. Several attempts have been made to appraise the effects of these policies both on the countries concerned (Banco de la República, 1975, 1976; Robinson, 1976; Lall and Streeten, 1977; SIEX, 1984), as well as on the firms (Robinson, 1976:280; Grosse, 1980, 1983). Nonetheless, the conclusions reached have been severely impaired by the lack of appropriate and reliable data and by the immense methodological difficulties raised by the counterfactual nature of many of the hypotheses and analytical frameworks that have to be utilized.

Despite these limitations, general patterns of effects, possibilities, and limitations of some specific aspects of regulatory policies toward FDI and technology have emerged with sufficient clarity as to allow a number of plausible working hypotheses. Consider some of the emerging lessons concerning such regulation drawn from Latin American experience.

The Effects of Regulatory Policies on Foreign Investment on the Host Country's Attractiveness to Foreign Investors

Both the findings of available research and the practical experience of several Latin American countries suggest that a restrictive regulatory system toward foreign investment does not seem to act as a significant barrier to new foreign investment. Conversely, a liberal legal framework coupled with incentives and other promotional schemes is also not a significant means for attracting foreign investors if other, more important, conditions are not present. At a time when Venezuela, for example, employed one the region's most restrictive approaches for implementing foreign investment rules (1973 to 1978), that country was still able to attract strong interest on the part of foreign investors. Chile, on the other hand, withdrew from the Andean Pact and liberalized foreign investment laws, and yet was unable to attract much new foreign investment. More recently, a widespread liberalization of foreign investment policies by Brazil, Mexico, Colombia, Argentina, and Venezuela has not significantly aroused the interest of foreign investors. The apparent lack of significance of foreign investment regulation in shaping a country's investment climate is confirmed by statistical surveys of the long-term effects of government policies on FDI. Root and Ahmed (1978) examined as many as 41 LDCs, testing the statistical significance of 44 different variables, and noted that "the overriding conclusion of this study is that government policies are not likely to be decisive determinants of foreign investment climates . . ." (p. 90).[9] To conclude our statement on this lesson, we emphasize two points, one pertaining to the purpose of foreign investment and the other to the actual determinants of investment climates.

First, for policy purposes, it is important to recognize that the reasons that lead a firm to initiate operations in another country are not the same as those that cause a firm to *invest* in that country.[10] As noted earlier, undertaking to invest abroad and establishing a foreign subsidiary are structurally different processes. These differences go much beyond the simple differences between foreign portfolio investment and foreign direct investment.[11] Accordingly, it becomes necessary to approach the issues of regulation by host countries from different perspectives.

Second, host governments should visualize their foreign investment policies as only one component of a highly complex and often not well understood *system* of interdependent laws, regulations, and business conditions that influence the investment climate as a totality, that simultaneously create incentives and disincentives both for the establishment of business operations controlled by foreign firms and for foreign investment as such. It is the resulting balance of incentives and disincentives that creates the motivation for foreign firms to select or ignore a given country.

Bargaining with Foreign Investors

As Kindleberger (1965, 1969) noted years ago, the relationship between host countries and foreign firms tends to be—or frequently ends up be-ing—one of bilateral monopoly.[12] Initially, the country boasts monopoly control over access to its markets or resources and, subsequently, over taxa-tion and expropriation. The firm, in turn, controls the supply of its "knowledge based" goods and services (or intangible assets). The lower bound of the price to be paid for these goods and services is determined by the amount required by the foreign firm not to invest or withdraw. The up-per bound is determined by a price beyond which the country would rather do without the services of the foreign firm. Kindleberger also argued (1965:334) that any price in between these two limits—which are likely to be very far apart—cannot be objectively praised or criticized. We would also add that, in practice, these two limits are exceedingly difficult to opera-tionalize.

During the 1970s this framework was elaborated by a group of writers (Streeten, 1976; Lall, 1974; Vaitsos, 1973a, 1973b, 1974) who stressed the need for LDCs to bargain with foreign firms, thus driving the terms of the arrangements between countries and firms closer to the end of the negotiating range more favorable to the country. How near that end the countries would arrive at depended on "bargaining power." Such bargain-ing power was seen essentially as a function of the degree to which three conditions existed. In Streeten's words (1976:227): "The ability of the host country to strike a good bargain will depend on three sets of factors: (i) solidarity among countries offering similar faculties, (ii) fragmentation among companies eager to invest, and (iii) information available to the host government."

As many case studies have demonstrated, however, the presence of these three conditions is not enough to permit a country to strike "a good bargain" (see Mikesell, 1971; Tugwell, 1975; Moran, 1974; Muller and Moore, 1978; Gereffi, 1978; Evans, 1979; Bennett and Sharpe, 1984; Fleet, 1984). These conditions generate, at best, the *potential* to obtain better con-ditions for the host country, if other factors permit the transformation of such potential bargaining power into *effective* power. As Bennett and Sharpe (1984:222–223) conclude in their study of the Mexican automotive policy and the negotiations it entailed with the MNCs concerned:

Whether a resource can serve as a source of potential power depends on the context, particularly the structure, of domestic and international relationships in which each actor is enmeshed. . . . An actor may have sources of power on which it does not draw effectively. In this conflict the [firms] drew more effectively on their potential power than did the Mexican state. . . . Understanding why the state did not fully use its potential power requires that this host government not be treated as a single unified entity. *Conflicts within and especially between various agencies and the lack of central direction from the President weakened the Mexican state's ability to draw fully on its potential power* (emphasis added).

Again, the importance of taking into account the above-noted implications of the character of public-sector organizations as sectors involved in negotiations between countries and foreign firms, and the limits such implications impose on the exertion of a host country's potential bargaining power, is crucial. It is our contention that this reality has affected the relationships between foreign firms and host countries in more fundamental and systematic ways than the available literature tends to suggest.

It is commonly assumed, for example, that a government's potential opportunity to influence a foreign firm and obtain better conditions increases *after* the firm's entry. Indeed, as Kindleberger (1973) noted, once the investment is made the firm becomes a quasi hostage of the government, which may now exert its influence through higher taxes or even expropriation. This condition was and still is commonly the case in natural resource industries. In the manufacturing sector, however, as Bennett and Sharpe (1984:221) and others have established, this tends not to be the pattern emerging from the dynamics of bargaining power. Instead, manufacturing firms tend to *increase* their bargaining power vis-à-vis the state, insofar as their relationships with suppliers, distributors, unions, and consumers reinforce the host country's need for their presence and generate local allies for their cause. We would add that foreign firms often develop close, and not always antagonistic, relationships with public regulatory agencies. Also, such agencies generally do not possess the strong monitoring and supervising capacity required to guarantee compliance with the conditions negotiated by a former staff group with the foreign firms at the time of their entry. These realities, plus the extreme vulnerability to external interferences exhibited by foreign investment agencies, can become very significant constraints on a country's actual possibility to negotiate effectively with a foreign investor, and what is even more important, to maintain and expand the country's influence once the firm is allowed to operate within its borders.

"Unbundling" the Foreign Investment Package: The Elusiveness of Equity and Technology

As mentioned earlier, another concept that gained popularity among academics and policy makers in Latin America during the 1970s was that of "unbundling" the package of capital, technology, and management with which MNCs confronted host countries. Presumably, it was both convenient and possible to separate the component elements of this package and negotiate each one separately, thus obtaining better conditions.[13] This notion fits nicely with the assumption that the presence of domestic investors in an MNC's ownership structure would lead the firm to be more responsive to national needs and exert a countervailing force against the natural tendency of MNCs to extract "higher-than-normal" economic rents from host countries. These were the views underlying the legislation that forced existing foreign firms to spin off to local investors specific parts of their equity, prohibited the entry of new wholly owned foreign firms and, in general, gave preferential treatment to joint ventures among foreign and domestic firms.

Unfortunately, no comprehensive and systematic appraisal of this policy is available and the data on this subject are incomplete and unreliable. Direct observation, together with interviews with informed analysts, government officials, and foreign executives tends to suggest very strongly that the divestment policies have proven unsuccessful. The number and economic importance of foreign firms that have complied with the divestment clauses does not seem to be very significant. In some cases where partial divestments have apparently occurred, the national "investors" are frequently domestic lawyers or financial entities with merely a representational function and no significant managerial influence whatsoever. In other cases, where equity has been divested partially to local industrialists, the foreign headquarters often continues, in practice, to retain control of the operation. Nor does local ownership of former wholly owned foreign subsidiaries seem to have led to a more desirable, nationally oriented behavior on the part of the firm (through, for example, improved performance in terms of employment, exports, quality, prices, transfer of funds, rigorous compliance with local taxes, etc.).

Last, it is worth noting that the presence of local entrepreneurs as minority stockholders of foreign subsidiaries tends to *increase* the MNC's bargaining power by incorporating, in the defense and management of its interests vis-à-vis the government and its regulatory agencies, actors with special insight, as well as the political and personal contacts required to intervene very effectively on the firm's behalf. Such division of labor between foreign and local owners is, of course, a natural consequence of their respective comparative advantages: the foreign owners dealing with the technical and managerial aspects of the operation and the locals with needed relationships in the host country, particularly those dealing with the political and regulatory aspects of the business (see Evans, 1979).

Assessing the impact of the "unbundling" efforts in technology imports by regulatory agencies is also difficult, given the lack of relevant studies or reliable data. The agencies have confronted exceedingly complex problems with the definitional aspects associated with technology and its international transfer. Initially, a more general approach was employed, in an attempt to include many of the subtleties and intangible facets of the technology acquisition process. A narrower focus emerged once agency operations were organized in terms of routine procedures that, understandably, came to center on the more explicit, tangible, and formal aspects of the transfer process. As a result, agency attention and screening efforts have tended to focus almost exclusively on the type of technology that is more amenable to be patented and suitable for arms-length, contractually based exchanges. In all likelihood this approach has been useful to support the bargaining position of local technology importers. On the other hand, by placing so much emphasis on the formal, legal, and financial aspects, the approach ignores or neglects the less tangible and explicit dimensions of the technology transfer process that, as we now know, can be quite important.

Such less-tangible transactions associated with the international transfer of technology, which are difficult to conduct through the market, are crucial (see Teece, 1976, 1981; Magee, 1977). The fact that regulatory agencies have neglected to focus on these transactions does not mean that they do not play a significant part in complementing and supporting the links between local and foreign firms operating in a given country and the foreign owners of these "soft," nonpatentable technologies. It is also quite possible that prohibiting payment for such tangibles, as some countries have done, does not mean that the owners of such intangible assets fail to obtain the rents associated with ownership. Even if we grant that the legal labels and contractual conditions associated with such rents are not *formally* related to the exploitation of the intangible assets, certainly the essential reality upon which such legal arrangements are based is none other than the economic exploitation of these assets. Indeed, it is possible that laws and regulations that forbid payment for such intangibles simply serve to increase transaction costs and create an illusion of effective government intervention in a process that, by its very nature, is extremely difficult to be intervened directly by national governments.

In sum, there is little that can be said empirically about the "unbundling" approach, except to stress that it does not appear to be a viable or practical alternative in light of the policy implications derived from theories concerned with MNC behavior and technology transfer that emphasize the transactional and organizational implications of the ownership and exchange of intangible assets (see Caves, 1982:279; Magee 1977; Teece, 1981).

The Positive Effects of Foreign Investment Regulation

Despite the considerable difficulties experienced in regulating foreign investment in Latin America, significant positive outcomes have nonetheless emerged. Admittedly, the exact nature and magnitude of these outcomes are as difficult to ascertain as are the negative outcomes and for the same reasons—namely, the absence of systematic research and reliable information.

Paradoxical as it may seem, an obvious contribution has been the generation of new information. Despite some shortcomings, improved estimates are now available with respect to the number and origin of foreign firms operating in a given host country, the nature and size of their investments, and even a record of certain aspects of their behavior and performance patterns. Unfortunately, this information has not been used sufficiently in research, which effort could lead to more refined and effective policies.

Another positive outcome emerging from foreign investment regulation has been the relative strengthening of the position of local firms in their bargaining with MNCs, and especially with foreign technology suppliers. In some cases, the laws provide local firms with advantages and possibilities unacceptable to foreign firms (e.g. the right to use a technology obtained under license in producing for export) and that are not necessarily sought or needed by the local firm, thus obliging the former to devise methods and schemes that avoid alienating the MNC concerned. In general, however, the laws contain restrictions that have proved quite profitable to the local firms. Perhaps as a result, the attitude of local business people and government officials has changed in favor of a more affirmative negotiating posture vis-à-vis foreign firms. As an experienced Colombian government official noted in a personal interview:

We have learned that almost everything is open to negotiation. We no longer accept unexamined assumptions about an investment project and nonnegotiable clauses. All clauses and conditions are negotiable in principle, and we now know that. Actually, sometimes we even become surprised at the conditions we end up obtaining from foreign firms; conditions which years ago would have been unthinkable even to suggest.

The new affirmative attitude has undoubtedly helped encourage behavior on the part of foreign firms more in keeping with national objectives. It is possible, for example, that, thanks to the regulations in place and to an improved bargaining posture, the extent of forward and backward linkages of foreign firms with the national economy may have increased at a faster rate. It is also possible that the external debt problems that Latin American countries now face might have been worse had the MNCs enjoyed a more flexible framework regulating their financial behavior. On the other hand, in this area MNCs have enjoyed ample room to maneuver, regardless of the regulations; and the slippery and fungible nature of capital (especially when in flight) makes it almost impossible to establish precise answers to such questions.

Another positive outcome of foreign investment regulation has been the emergence of some training and organizational learning. To be sure, the corps of professional and technical staff with the knowledge and experience to deal effectively with foreign firms is far from sufficient. On the other hand, it is substantially larger than ten years ago. If government agencies in charge of the policy implementation do indeed exhibit all the limitations that we have noted, there is no doubt that they are now more experienced and knowledgeable about the problems with which they deal. If agency staff suffers from high turnover, the knowledge and experience gained is presumably not lost to the country when staff members move to another agency or even to the local private sector. Also, the fact that many Latin American countries have established specialized public agencies focusing on the regulation of foreign investment has created an international network of institutions and individuals that, at times, has served to coordinate policies and reduce competition among host countries in attracting FDI. This network, and the periodic exchange of views, knowledge, and experience among regulatory officials of different countries has been useful to counter some of the difficulties posed by the multinational character of the actors being regulated.

CONCLUSIONS

In this chapter, we have identified some of the lessons that may be derived from the experience of Latin American countries in their decade-long attempt to regulate and control foreign investment and technology. These are:

1. The policies that most Latin American countries adopted a decade ago have not suffered major changes in their essential scheme, even though many domestic and international changes, revisions, and modifications of relevant knowledge have occurred, and pressures to alter the countries' standing vis-à-vis foreign investment have emerged.

2. Latin American countries have responded to these changes through subtle and not always visible modifications in ways that policies are effectively implemented. Frequent administrative changes and modifications in the way policy guidelines are interpreted and carried out by implementing agencies have, for all practical purposes, implied significant modifications in host country relationships with foreign firms.

3. Foreign investment policies presently in force feature inherent design limitations that provide enormous power and latitude to government officials in charge of their implementation. The extreme discretionary powers of implementing officials granted by the present policy framework is hypothesized to be related to the inadequacies of the main theoretical views on FDI, MNCs, and technology flows on which policy formulation was based originally.

4. National regulatory agencies set up to implement the policies have not escaped many of the problems associated with public-sector bureaucracies and have, therefore, faced important performance constraints. Public-sector traits that may be noted among foreign investment regulatory agencies and that have had a negative effect on their behavior and performance are, among others:

congestion, inadequate and insufficient staff, bureaucratic rivalry, vulnerability to external influences, information mishandling and overflow, and limited monitoring and enforcement capabilities.

5. National policies toward foreign investment—both promotional and restrictive—do not seem to be significant factors in shaping a country's degree of attractiveness to foreign firms. Local and international business conditions, the competitive situation of a firm's industrial sector, and the political risk perceived by the MNC are much more influential than foreign investment regulations in determining a firm's interest in a given country.

6. Countries, in principle, enjoy substantial bargaining power vis-à-vis foreign firms. In practice, however, such bargaining power has proved to be exceedingly difficult to exert effectively. External interferences, bureaucratic infighting, lack of expert personnel and personnel turnover, ill-defined bargaining objectives, and frequent modifications of these objectives have significantly limited the exercise by government agencies of their potential power. Furthermore, changes in agency staff and policy orientation, the vagueness of the conditions agreed upon with a firm at the time of entry, and the lack of a systematic capacity to monitor and follow up the agreements, have also played a part in reducing bargaining power by allowing the conditions actually fulfilled by the firms to depart from those originally negotiated.

7. Government efforts aimed at "unbundling" integrated "packages" of capital, technology, and management offered by foreign firms have not proven particularly effective. Foreign companies have forcefully resisted these attempts, and government agencies have not had the resources or the organizational incentives and technical support to achieve such unbundling effectively. Again, these policies exhibit significant design flaws in that they are aimed at imposing arms-length, market-oriented transactions in economic exchanges that have originated because of the inherent inadequacy of the market to mediate such transactions. Furthermore, the "unbundling" approach has been severely constrained in its effectiveness because important local conditions that are required if the efforts are to be successful (substantial local absorption capacities for foreign technology, efficient local markets for securities, for example) are not present in the majority of Latin American countries.

8. Foreign investment regulation has, nonetheless, also generated positive outcomes. Although difficult to estimate, it is clear that regulatory efforts have helped Latin American countries to improve greatly the information now available to governments concerning foreign firms and their activities, has strengthened the bargaining position of local firms vis-à-vis foreign firms, has generated a more assertive attitude among local entrepreneurs and government officials in their dealings with foreign firms, has contributed to increase the backward and forward linkages of foreign firms, and has created generally a capacity to interact in a more systematic and informed way with foreign firms and technology suppliers.

It should be clearly evident from this review of regulatory policies on foreign investment in Latin America that even if important issues concerning their implementation and actual consequences are not yet well understood, there is evident need for reform. Unfortunately, the lack of more precise knowledge about the consequences of foreign investment legislation, and about the ways regulatory agencies actually end up implementing the policies, limits the possibilities of discussing alternative regulatory frameworks that would serve national interests more effectively. New efforts to improve the ways host countries deal with foreign firms will have to be based on more realistic assumptions about the nature, possibilities, and constraints of the actors—the firms and the government agencies. Also, governments will have to be more realistic about what to expect from firms, and to develop a better understanding of the "costs" associated with the presence of foreign firms in their respective national economies.

A recognition that even the most technically sound and effectively implemented policies relating to foreign investment and technology transfer will not eliminate completely some of its "costs" is perhaps the first step toward a more realistic and effective policy. It can also be a step toward a mcre stable treatment of foreign investment and technology. After all, as the sociologist Max Weber noted many years ago (1930), the most important institutional requisite for private investment is a legal system that offers security and predictability.

NOTES

1. Several syntheses of the arguments and counterarguments utilized by the contrasting views on the effects of FDI and MNCs (multinational corporations) may be cited. Following a pioneering effort by Lall (1974), the works of Gilpin (1975), Moran (1974), Foster-Carter (1976), and Kobrin (1977) constituted interesting attempts at clarifying the main contending issues and arguments. The most comprehensive and systematic effort was that of Biersteker (1981). Naím (1978, 1980) provides a discussion of the policy consequences and analytical prerequisites for successful implementation that are implicit in the different views concerning the effects of FDI and MNCs on host countries.

2. Bitar (1984). White (1982) offers a discussion of the evolution of the legal framework toward foreign investment in Latin America. Correa (1984) presents a detailed comparative description of foreign investment regulation in Latin America and the Caribbean while Cheroll and Zalduendo (1984) do the same for Central America and the Caribbean.

3. For a descriptive analysis of these different legal instruments, see Villalba (1981).

4. For convenience we will in general also include policies regulating the acquisition and payments for foreign technology as part of foreign investment policies. Also, the terms MNC and foreign firm are used interchangeably even if the first is only one specific type of foreign firm.

5. Personal interview.

6. Other hypotheses concerning the possible effects of this dual pattern of policy implementation might include a potential bias in favor of more speculative or volatile types of foreign investors, who employ a shorter time horizon, a lower level of commitment, fewer or less qualified expatriate managers, less advanced technology, and so on.

7. Several surveys on the available theories about the determinants of FDI reached this conclusion. See, for example, Ragazzi (1973), Dunning (1977, 1979, 1980), Rugman (1980), Naím (1985). Calvet (1981) has also surveyed the literature, reaching the same conclusion and arguing that a theory of the multinational corporation as a more specific and somewhat different phenomenon than FDI was also needed. See also Buckley and Casson (1976) and Caves (1982).

8. As Caves (1982:4–5) notes, "intangible assets are subject to a daunting list of infirmities for being put to efficient use by conventional markets." Among these are public good nature, the fact that transactions in intangibles suffer from information impactedness and that such information impactedness is amplified by opportunism. For a presentation and discussion of these concepts and terminology, see Williamson (1975); and for an application of these notions to MNCs in LDCs see Calvet and Naim (1980).

9. Grosse (1983) studied the impact of the Andean Pact foreign investment Code (Decision 24) on FDI and noted that "the data tended to show a reduction of FDI into the ANCOM (Andean Common Market) countries during the first five years of the Code's existence—*but no enduring impact beyond that*" (p. 131, emphasis added). Grosse also notes, however, that this conclusion must be interpreted with great caution, given the methodological difficulties in separating the influence of the foreign investment code on FDI from other very influential events occurring at the same time in the countries included in his analysis, which also have had a negative effect on FDI (p. 124). A different conclusion was reached by the Junta del Acuerdo de Cartagena, the main official body of ANCOM, which undertook a study to evaluate the impact of Decision 24 and found that the data showed that the Code did not have a negative influence on FDI in the region (see JUNAC 1979). It is also interesting to note that the data based on interviews of MNC managers in general suggests a much greater impact of foreign investment laws on FDI than the evidence suggested by the statistical analysis actually shows. See Robinson (1976:280), Meeker (1971), Pincus and Edwards (1972:89), and Grosse (1983:127–129), and compare with the data presented by Calcagno (1980), Bitar (1984), and Junta del Acuerdo de Cartagena (1984). Sourruville et al. (1984) surveyed through interviews and questionnaires 234 foreign subsidiaries in seven Latin American countries and found that foreign investment regulation was ranked by their respondents as the sixth most important factor (out of 18) in influencing their investment.

10. By analyzing FDI as a sequential process, Kogut (1983:38) suggests that models of FDI have tended to ignore the role played by the advantage of a coordinated multinational system in facilitating additions to the flows of FDI. From this perspective, the possibilities generated by such coordinated systems of firms operating internationally constitutes an important and frequently neglected determinant of FDI.

11. Traditionally, the difference between foreign portfolio investment and FDI was essentially assumed to be the fact that the first did not entail the ownership of

sufficient equity as to grant the control and management of the firm, while FDI required such controlling equity (see Ragazzi 1973). In reality, however, it is possible, and under some circumstances quite common, to have managerial control without having the controlling amount of equity (see Robinson 1973).

12. Niehans (1977) calls this "the horrors of bilateral monopoly." Williamson (1975) has plausibly argued that market situations that initially involve multiple agents tend to evolve rapidly toward a "small number exchange" in which the transaction is bound to occur only among a specific and very limited number of economic actors regardless of the fact that many more potential actors may have the possibility of participating.

13. For an analytic discussion favoring such an approach, see Vaitsos (1970, 1973b, 1974). Vernon (1977:172–173) presents a critique of this idea.

REFERENCES

Allen, T. W. *The Asean Report.* Hong Kong: Dow Jones, 1975

Banco de la República. *El Efecto de las Inversiones Extrajeras sobre la Balanza Comercial Colombiana.* Bogota: Banco de la República, 1975.

_____ . *El Efecto de las Inversiones Extrajeras sobre el Empleo en Colombia.* Botoga: Banco de la República, 1976.

Behrman, J. "Actors and Factors in Policy Decisions on Foreign Direct Investment." *World Development* 12:8 (1974), 101–123.

Bennett, D., M. Blachman, and K. Sharpe. "Mexico and Multinational Corporations: An Explanation of State Action." In J. Grunwald (ed.), *Latin America and the World Economy: A Changing International Order.* Beverly Hills, Calif.: Sage, 1978.

Bennett, D. and K. Sharpe. "Agenda Setting and Bargaining Power: The Mexican State vs. Transnational Automobile Corporations." In R. Kronish and K. Mericle (eds.), *The Political Economy of the Latin American Motor Vehicle Industry.* Cambridge, Mass.: MIT Press, 1984.

Biersteker, T. J. *Distortion or Development? Contending Perspectives on the Multinational Corporation.* Cambridge, Mass.: MIT Press, 1981.

Bitar, S. "Corporaciones Transnacionales y las Nuevas Relaciones de America ·Latina con Estados Unidos." *Economia de America Latina* 11 (1984).

Buckley, P. J. and M. Casson. *The Future of Multinational Enterprise.* London: Macmillan, 1976.

Calcagno, A. E. *Informe sobre las Inversiones Extranjeras en America Latina,* E/CEPAL/G. 1108. Santiago de Chile: CEPAL 1980.

Calvet, L.A. "Foreign Direct Investment Theories and Theories of the Multinational Corporation." *Journal of International Business Studies* 12 (Spring/Summer 1981) 43–59.

Calvet, L. A. and M. Naim. "The Multinational Firm in Less Developed Countries: A Markets and Hierarchies Approach." Paper presented at the ELBA-AIB Joint Conference in Barcelona, 1980.

Caves, R. E. "International Corporations: The Industrial Economics of Foreign Investment." *Economica* 38 (1971), 1–27.

———— . *Multinational Enterprise and Economic Analysis*. Cambridge: Cambridge University Press, 1982.

Cheroll, R. L. and S. Zalduendo. "El Marco Legal de la Inversion Extranjera en el Caribe y Centroamerica." *Integracion Latinoamericana*, December 1984, 32–46.

Correz, C. M. "Characteristics y Tendencias de la Regulacion de las Inversiones Extranjeras en America Latina y el Caribe." *Integracion Latinoamericana*, December 1984, 20–31.

De la Torre, J. "Foreign Investment and Economic Development: Conflict and Negotiation." *Journal of International Business Studies* 11 (Fall 1981) 9–22.

Dunning, J. J. "Trade, Location of Economic Activity and MNE: A Search for an Eclectic Approach." In B. Ohlin et al. (eds.), *The International Allocation of Economic Activity*. London: Macmillan, 1977, 385–418.

———— . "Explaining Changing Patterns of International Production: In Defense of the Eclectic Theory." *Oxford Bulletin of Economic Statistics* 41 (November 1979), 269–296.

———— . "Toward an Eclectic Theory of International Production: Some Empirical Tests." *Journal of International Business Studies* 11 (Spring/Summer 1980). 9–31.

Evans, P. *Dependent Development*. Princeton, N.J.: Princeton University Press, 1979.

Fleet, M. "Bargaining Relations in the Colombian Motor Vehicle Industry." In R. Kronish and K. Mericle (eds.), *The Political Economy of the Latin American Motor Vehicle Industry*. Cambridge, Mass.: MIT Press, 1984.

Foster-Carter, A. "From Rostow to Gunder-Frank: Conflicting Paradigms in the Analysis of Underdevelopment." *World Development* 14:3 (1976).

Gereffi, G. "Drug Firms and Dependency in Mexico: The Case of the Steroid Hormone Industry." *International Organization* (Winter 1978), 237–86.

Gilpin, R. *U.S. Power and the Multinational Corporation*. New York: Basic Books, 1975.

Grindle, M. S. (ed.), *Politics and Policy Implementation in the Third World*. Princeton, N.J.: Princeton University Press, 1980.

———— . "Public Policy, Foreign Investment and Implementation Style in Mexico." In A. Dominguez (ed.), *Economic Issues and Political Conflict: U.S.-Latin American Relations*. London: Butterworths, 1982.

Grosse, R. *Foreign Investment Codes and Location of Direct Investment*. New York: Praeger, 1980.

———— . "The Andean Foreign Investment Code's Impact on Multinational Enterprises." *Journal of International Business Studies* 14 (Winter 1983), 121–123

Huntington, S. "The Marasmus of the ICC: The Commission, the Railroads and the Public Interest." *Yale Law Journal* 52 (1952).

Hymer, S. H. "The International Operations of National Firms: A Study of Direct Foreign Investment" (Cambridge: unpublished PhD dissertation, Massachusetts Institute of Technology, 1960).

———— . *The International Operations of National Firms: A Study of Direct Foreign Investment*. Cambridge, Mass.: MIT Press, 1976.

Junta del Acuerdo de Cartagena (JUNAC). "Evaluacion de la Inversion Directa Extranjera en el Grupo Andino y de la Administracion de la Decision 24," JUN/di. 360, March 30, 1979.

_____ . "Inversiones Extranjeras," J/UI.ES/025, March 29, 1984.

Kindleberger, C. P. *Oligopolistic Reaction and the Multinational Enterprise.* Cambridge, Mass.: Harvard University Press, 1973.

_____ . *American Business Abroad: Six Lectures on Direct Investment.* New Haven: Yale University Press, 1969.

_____ . *Balance-of-Payments Deficits and the International Market for Liquidity.* Princeton, N.J.: Princeton University Press, 1965.

Kobrin, S. J. "Multinational Corporations' Socio-Cultural Dependence and Industrialization: Need Satisfaction or Want Creation?" Working paper, Sloan School of Management, MIT, 1977.

Kogut, B. "Foreign Direct Investment as a Sequential Process." In C. P. Kindleberger and D. B. Audretsch (eds.), *The Multinational Corporation in the 1980s.* Cambridge, Mass.: MIT Press, 1983. 38–56.

Lall, S. "Less Developed Countries and Private Foreign Investment: A Review Article." *World Development* 2:4–5 (1974),

Lall, S. and P. Streeten. *Foreign Investment, Transnationals and Developing Countries.* London: Macmillan, 1977.

Lombard, F. J. "Screening Foreign Direct Investment in LCD's: Empirical Findings of the Colombian Case." *Journal of International Business Studies* 9 (Winter 1978), 61–80.

Magee, S. P. "Multinational Corporations, the Industry Technology Cycle and Development." *Journal of World Trade Law* (1977), 297–321.

Meeker, G. "Fade-Out Joint Venture: Can It Work for Latin America?" *Inter American Economic Affairs* (Spring 1971), 25–42.

Mikesell, R. V. (ed.). *Foreign Investment in the Petroleum and Mineral Industries: Case Studies of Investor Host Country Relations.* Baltimore: The Johns Hopkins University Press, 1971.

Moran, T. H. "Multinational Corporations and Dependency: A Dialogue for *Dependentistas* and *Non Dependentistas.*" *International Organization,* Winter 1978, 79–99,

Muller, R. E. and D. H. Moore. "Case One: Brazilian Bargaining Power Success in Befiex Export Promotion Program with the Transnational Automotive Industry." New York: United Nations, Center for Transnational Corporations, 1978.

Naím, M. "The Political Economy of Regulating Multinational Corporations." Ph.D. dissertation, Sloan School of Management, MIT, 1978.

_____ . "Transfer Pricing by Multinational Corporations and Its Regulation by Host Countries." *Interciencia* 5:3 (1980),

_____ . "Por que una Firma invierte en otro pais: Teorias Acerca de los determinantes de las inversiones extranjeras." *El Trimestre Economico* (1985).

Niehans, J. "Benefits of Multinational Firms for a Small Parent Economy: The Case of Switzerland." In T. Agmon and C.P. Kindleberger (eds.), *Multinationals from Small Countries,* Cambridge, Mass.: MIT Press, 1977.

Pincus, J. and D. E. Edwards. "The Outlook for U.S. FDI in the Andean Pact Countries in the Seventies." *Journal of International Business Studies* (Spring, 1972), 89–108.

Pressman, J., M. Rein, and F. Rabinowitz. "Guidelines." *Policy Sciences* 4 (1976),

Pressman, J. and A. Wildavsky. *Implementation*. Berkeley: University of California Press, 1973.

Ragazzi, G. "Theories of the Determinants of Direct Foreign Investment." *IMF Staff Papers* (July 1973),

Robinson, R. D. *International Business Management—A Guide to Decision Making*. New York: Holt, Rinehart and Winston, 1973.

————. *National Control of Foreign Business Entry*. New York: Praeger, 1976.

————. *Foreign Investment in the Third World: A Comparative Study of Selected Developing Country Investment Promotion Programs*. Washington, D.C.: Chamber of Commerce, International Division, 1980.

————. "Background Concepts and Philosophy of International Business from World War II to the Present." *Journal of International Business Studies* 12 (Spring/Summer 1981), 13–21.

Root, F. R. and A. Ahmed. "The Influence of Policy Instruments on Manufacturing Direct Foreign Investment in Developing Countries." *Journal of International Business Studies* 19 (Winter 1978), 81–93

Rose, S. "The Andean Pact and Its Foreign Investment Code: Need for Clarity?" *Tax Management International Journal* (January 1975),

Rosenn, K. S. "Regulation of Foreign Investment in Brazil: A Critical Analysis." *Lawyer of the Americas* 15 (Fall 1983),

Rugman, A. M. "Internalization as a General Theory of FDI: A Re-appraisal of the Literature." *Weltwirtschaftliches Archiv* 116:2 (1980), 365–79.

Servan-Schreiber, J.-J. *The American Challenge*. New York: Atheneum, 1968.

SIEX (Venezuelan Superintendency of Foreign Investment). "Documento Base." *Seminario Inversiones Extranjeras y Desarrollo Economico*. Caracas: Ministerio de Hacienda/SIEX, 1984 (June).

Sourrouille, J. V., F. Gatto, and B. Kosacoff. *Inversiones Extranjeras en America Latina*. Buenos Aires: BID-INTAL, 1984.

Stigler, G. "The Theory of Economic Regulation." *The Bell Journal of Economics and Management Science* 2 (1971), 3–21.

Streeten, P. "Bargaining with Multinationals." *World Development* 4 (March 1976),

Teece, D. J. *The Multinational Corporation and the Resource Cost of International Technology Transfer*. Cambridge, Mass.: Ballinger, 1976.

————. "The Market for Know-How and Efficient International Transfer of Technology." *Annals of the American Academy of Political and Social Science* 458 (November 1981), 81–96.

Tugwell, F. *The Politics of Oil in Venezuela*. Palo Alto, Calif.: Stanford University Press, 1975.

Vaitsos, C. V. "Bargaining and the Distribution of Returns in the Purchase of Technology by Developing Countries." *Bulletin of the Institute of Development Studies* (University of Sussex, 1970), No. 3.

————. "Policies on Foreign Direct Investment and Economic Development in Latin America." *IDS Communication* 106 (University of Sussex, 1973a).

_____ . "Foreign Investment Policies and Economic Development in Latin America." *Journal of World Trade Law* (November-December 1973b), 607–18.

_____ . *Intercountry Income Distribution and Transnational Enterprises*. Oxford: Clarendon Press, 1974.

Vernon, R. "International Investment and International Trade in the Product Cycle." *Quarterly Journal of Economics* (May 1966), 190–207

_____ . *Sovereignty at Bay: The Multinational Spread of U.S. Enterprises*. New York: Basic Books, 1971.

_____ , *Storm over the Multinationals: The Real Issues*. Cambridge, Mass.: Harvard University Press, 1977.

Villalba, J. O. "Equivocal Perceptions of the Andean Code: An Explanation Based on Conflicting Legal Traditions." Unpublished manuscript, Sloan School of Management, MIT, 1981.

Weber, Max. *The Protestant Ethic and the Spirit of Capitalism*. New York: Scribner 1930. (German original published in 1904).

White, E. "Evolution and Recent Trends in Host Developing Countries Policies vis-à-vis TNC's." Buenos Aires: Centro de Estudios Juridicos-Economicos Internacionales, 1982.

Williamson, O. E. *Markets and Hierarchies: Analysis and Antitrust Implications*. New York: The Free Press, 1975.

Wilson, J. Q. *The Politics of Regulation*. New York: Basic Books, 1980.

Chapter Four

European Practices and Policies

John M. Stopford

Any discussion of European experience with international investment must start from the perspective of European attitudes and policies toward big business in general and foreign firms in particular. Government policies have in the main reflected concerns about scale, concentration, efficiency, and national protectionism. Very little explicit policy has been developed in respect to ownership as a separate instrument for achieving national ends. Rather, joint ventures have been used as but one of the many means of achieving commercial objectives. A few numbers make the point. Of all the foreign investments in the United Kingdom at the end of 1981, over 80 percent were wholly owned by the foreign parent, and less than 10 percent were in the form of minority (i.e., less than 50 percent) equity holdings. In France, over 90 percent were majority-controlled by the foreign parent in the mid-1970s. Similar figures are believed to hold true for other European countries.

This chapter reviews the main lines of development of policy and practice toward inward foreign direct investment in the major European countries over the past forty years. The focus is primarily on the experience of France, West Germany, and the United Kingdom, for which most of the available data pertain. Some reference is made to developments in other European countries and to European Economic Community (EEC) policy where it affects the behavior of firms and their choice of ownership policy.

Over this long period of postwar recovery and sustained growth, followed by the current conditions of faltering adjustments to the two oil shocks of the 1970s, the role of foreign investment has continued on a path of steadily increasing importance. By the mid-1970s, the latest period for which reasonably reliable statistics are available, foreign investments had risen to command the shares of European manufacturing industries shown in Table 4.1. In very general terms, their shares of industry, as measured by production, value-added, and capital investment, were higher than their shares of employment. Their shares of particular industries varied widely, as Table 4.2 shows. They tended to have above-average shares of advanced industries, notably electronics and pharmaceuticals, and below-average

Table 4.1 Foreign-Owned Firms' Share of Manufacturing Industries, in Selected European Countries (in percentages)

Host Country	Year	Employment (percent)	Production (percent)	Value Added (percent)	Investment in Gross Capital Formation (percent)
Austria[a]	1976	22	23	22[b]	20[b]
Belgium[a]	1978	38	44[c]		
France	1975	19	28	25	25
West Germany	1976	17	22		
Italy	1977	18	24		
Sweden[a]	1977	6[d]	7[d]	7	4
United Kingdom	1981	15		19	26

[a]Percentages based on majority-owned subsidiaries only.
[b]Data for 1973.
[c]Data for 1975.
[d]Data for 1976.

Source: United Nations Center on Transnational Corporations, Organization for Economic Cooperation and Development, and national governments.

shares of Europe's mature industries. Added to these bare statistics are others to show that foreign-controlled investments tend to have higher export propensities and productivity levels than do national firms. These measures of performance generally hold true when measured on an industry-by-industry basis.[1] Data are not available for service sectors, but here too the international dimension is of increasing importance. Indeed, foreign direct investment in services has been growing much faster than in manufacturing.

Such a general depiction of foreign investors, the so-called multinational corporations, as agents of growth and efficiency fits a common perception of the role of MNCs in advanced countries. Yet the generality belies the worries of many critics of the MNCs. It also begs the question of how governments have acted to control the inflow of foreign capital and the behavior of the MNCs once they have established local operations. If MNCs are so effective in increasing growth, efficiency, and employment—key items on the agenda of most governments—why then are they not universally welcomed within a framework of minimal controls?

Official concerns about the role of foreigners have depended primarily upon the views taken on the role of state planning and on the need to maintain indigenous firms that possess strategically important technologies. National positions on these issues have varied considerably, though there have been signs recently that past differences have eroded. The issues at stake are extraordinarily complex in the European environment, for a variety of reasons. *First*, the major European countries are important exporters of capital as well as importers. Thus, policies to control the inward flow of capital are conditioned by fears of retaliatory actions. *Second*, most European economies are highly interdependent, and those interdependencies have increased as a result of the formation and subsequent enlargement of the EEC. Frequently it is difficult if not impossible to consider a national industry in isolation from the rest of the continent. *Third*, European industries are subject to growing interdependencies with those in the United States and, more recently, in Japan. Especially in those industries where technology is important, attempts to create national policies that are at odds with the dynamics of the industry have proved largely self-defeating. *Fourth*, there are high proportions of state enterprise in many industries. Thus, some sectors are proscribed to foreigners and, in others, the foreign role is severely curtailed. *Finally*, it should be noted that the EEC remains far from an integrated market. Not only are internal trade flows constrained by customs and other border costs, plus nontariff barriers, but also investment flows (most notably in financial services) are inhibited by differences in national regulation.

To capture some of the subtleties involved in this patchwork of often conflicting needs, the paragraphs that follow provide a resumé of national approaches to planning as applied to direct foreign investment. With those

Table 4.2 Foreign-Owned Firms' Share of Selected Manufacturing Industries in Major European Countries (for varying years in the mid-1970s; in percentages)

Host Country	Food, drink tobacco (ISIC No. 31)	Textiles and clothing (ISIC No. 32)	Chemicals (ISIC No. 351/2)	Drugs (ISIC No. 3522)	Non-Electrical Machinery (ISIC No. 382)	Electrical and Electronics (ISIC No. 383)	Motor Vehicles (ISIC No. 3843)
Austria	19		33				
Belgium and Luxembourg	22					40	
France			21		32		
West Germany	26	8	33	52(P)	37(A)	71(S)	21(A)
Sweden	10	4	27	20(P)		51(A)	
United Kingdom	11	3	27	45(P)	18	20	

Note: Percentages based on employment unless indicated by: (P) Production; (A) Asset data; (S) Share capital.

Sources: J. M. Stopford and H. H. Dunning, *Multinationals: Company Performance and Global Trends* (New York: Macmillan, 1983), based on a variety of sources plus share capital percentage from J. Savary, *The French Multinationals* (New York: Macmillan, 1984).

statements as background, the more particular issues affecting ownership policy are addressed.

NATIONAL POLICIES

France

France, generally regarded as the European country most resistant to foreign investors, has had a long tradition of statism and government intervention going back to Colbert and the First Empire. It has also been marked by the assumption of the state's superiority over other economic entities in the determination of the national interest.[2] Until roughly the mid-1960s, the mechanisms and purposes of state intervention had been the traditional and widely used blunt instruments of monetary and fiscal controls and incentives, all designed to promote a stable economic environment, basically favorable to private enterprise. Subsequently, the means and objectives of intervention shifted toward greater selectivity.

These shifts were induced partly by the consequences of the then-nascent EEC and partly by a drive for growth to pull France out of its economic problems.[3] Reaction to crisis rather than a coherent strategy seemed more important in shaping action—for example, the need to arrest the decline of such industries as coal, steel, shipbuilding; plus the need to support sectors affected by rapidly changing technologies and enterprises international in scope. Support to arrest the rate of decline was primarily a domestic affair and need not be discussed here. Support for industries such as aircraft, atomic power, and computers was designed to promote a "national champion." The case of computers is discussed later on as part of a wider review of the industry. Support for the internationally based enterprises was varied in its nature and effect. In industries such as chemicals, it took the form of passively blessing mergers that created stronger home companies. In petroleum, electrical machinery, and automobiles, ultraprotectionist moves were taken to reduce, or specifically to exclude, foreign interests. Thus, Westinghouse was prevented from acquiring Jeumont-Schneider; the prospective Fiat-Citroën merger was stopped after Fiat had acquired 40 percent of Citroën; and so on. Elsewhere, as in foods and machine tools, state intervention took the form of little more than stirring speeches and vague promises that resulted in action only when firms fell into real difficulty.

The mid-1960s was a period when France, like the United Kingdom, believed that as production became more international in character it was essential to create larger and thus stronger home groups capable of withstanding foreign competition. An Institut de Developpement Industriel (IDI) was set up to facilitate domestic restructuring. Moreover, foreign investment was to be encouraged where it would enhance export development.[4] Given China's current desire to move in the same direction, it is worth noting that the French policies failed when policies of autarky conflicted with the dynamics of international competition, and purely domestic restructuring could not achieve the minimum scale needed for supply competitiveness.

For inward investment, these changes in attitude had profound consequences. Whereas previously foreigners had met with a generally defensive regulatory stance, they became subject to explicit criteria governing their entry to France. The period 1963–66 was one of extreme hostility to foreigners as the authorities worked out their policies. In 1967 a new decree spelled out the rules to govern all investments involving 20 percent or more of a French company.[5] All investments of over 1 million francs had to be investigated by the Committee of Foreign Investment. Once defined as "foreign," little note was taken of where the proposed investment lay on the scale of 20-100 percent foreign participation. In essence, there were four basic criteria: (1) Acquisitions were regarded less favorably than the creation of new enterprises. (2) Acquisitions were seldom allowed if the company to be acquired was profitable or could be regrouped with others to form a "national champion." (3) New enterprises were welcomed unless an overly high degree of dependence on foreign technology would result. (4) Balance-of-payments effects, especially upon exports, were examined in detail.

These criteria, though by no means precise, had the effect of delaying decisions and discouraging many investors who might otherwise have tried to enter. In such a strategically important sector as automobile components, Lucas (of the United Kingdom) was prevented from adding to its long-standing 40 percent holding in Ducellier, thus creating a powerful continentwide network of components, on the grounds that Ducellier was a "national champion" and a key supplier to the nationalized automobile assemblers. The new rules, which were primarily designed to cover terms of entry, were gradually extended in the late 1960s and in the 1970s to affect existing foreign investment. Yet despite such nationalism, foreigners still managed to invest in many industries.

With the mounting economic woes after the second oil shock and with the election of Mitterrand's socialist government, the tendency toward investment protectionism was intensified. Many of the key industries such as chemicals were nationalized and the foreigners displaced, or, where they had important technologies, allowed to continue but under more stringent controls. In the last two years, however, these policies have been relaxed in those sectors where foreign technology is needed for the country to be modernized with sufficient rapidity. Even Japanese investors, previously excluded or at least severely discouraged from entering, are now actively being wooed. Japanese investments in 1983 rose to about $80 million, more than six times the 1979 flow. Most have been in the form of wholly owned ventures with high (over 75 percent) targets for their export ratios. A few state-owned firms have been setting up joint ventures in areas of high technology, such as carbon fibers. Policies of autarky have been substantially modified in the light of past failures.

United Kingdom

The United Kingdom's policies have been more consistent and less subject to formally calculated rules. A generally welcoming stance has been tempered with some caution in specific areas, notably in oil and financial services. The general policy emerges implicitly and in an uncoordinated manner from central British institutions, such as the Department of Trade and Industry, the Treasury, the Monopolies and Mergers Commission, and the Bank of England. They have all become rather more relaxed about inward investment as the years have gone by, though the new wave of Japanese investment has reinvigorated those who doubt the benefits. Yet, underneath this placid surface, there has been a sharpening of attitudes. The welcome mat is still out and many foreign investors, including the Japanese, are positively wooed. There is, however, a greater emphasis on the need to ensure that Britain gains its full share of any available returns, especially where discretionary funds are offered.[6]

Economic nationalism affected the workings of the 1960s planning machinery, when such bodies as the national Economic Development Council and the Industrial Reorganization Corporation worked to foster national champions in automobiles, computers, electrical machinery, ball bearings, and elsewhere. Lacking the drive and the power of the equivalent French machinery, these efforts were largely ineffective, were reliant on special deals, and concentrated more on propping up "lame ducks" than on supporting the more dynamic sectors. As much of the foreign investment was in the newer, more technologically progressive sectors, the relatively short-lived attempts at national planning had little impact on the foreigners.

The current official policy, after the lifting of exchange controls in 1979, is that foreigners receive equal treatment to that accorded domestic enterprises. Yet there are limits to equal treatment. Foreign ownership is officially proscribed in industries under public ownership. The recent moves to "privatize" some of the erstwhile nationalized industries have also been limited by considerations of national security, most notably in British Aerospace and British Telecom. In both instances, the government reserves a substantial block of shares to itself. Though there are other limitations in such sectors as ITV franchise holders, they are much less restrictive than those imposed in many other developed countries such as France. Even in such a sensitive area as nuclear technology, a British-at-all-costs approach is breaking down, with, for instance, an acceptance of the need for international collaboration in the German-Dutch-British uranium enrichment project, Urenco.

In the North Sea oil and gas province, there has always been some nationalism in the British approach. Legislation, for instance, lays down that oil and gas from the British sector must first be landed in the United Kingdom (even if it is immediately reexported). The British National Oil Corporation was created to hold the rights to 50 percent of all the oil produced in the British sector. Further, an Offshore Supplies Office was set up to increase the proportion of North Sea-related business that went to British industry. In the 1980/81 licensing round, French interests were excluded because it ws felt they were not cooperating with official British attempts to develop a coherent North Sea gas pipeline policy. In the early 1980s, the allocation principles were changed to favor smaller British companies and modified further to include foreign companies willing to carry out a certain amount of research in Britain.

By the standards of the oil industry, this has not been a particularly nationalistic policy. The Offshore Supplies Office was created only in reaction to the initially feeble response by British industry to the opportunities afforded it by the North Sea. Its terms of reference were, however, limited only to ensuring that companies in the North Sea gave British suppliers a full and fair opportunity to quote for any business going. Where British suppliers failed to compete on price, quality, or delivery dates, oil companies have been under no pressure to place the order in Britain. Moreover, the government had been reducing British National Oil Company's role before announcing, in early 1985, its abolition.

British intentions were not always as outward looking as this analysis might imply. Many members of the Labour governments of 1974–79 would have preferred a much more nationalist approach. Indeed, their pressure led to the creation of the British National Oil Corporation. Theirs was a minority view, for it was clear to others that an overly nationalistic approach here would rebound on British interests elsewhere. There were American threats—for instance, that nationalization of American companies would lead to retaliation against British Petroleum in the United States (a potent threat, given its Alaskan interests). Countries such as Britain, whose companies have gone multinational, can seldom afford to discriminate against inward investors. The threat of retaliaton blunts nationalistic urges.

Financial services are another sector, where, despite the current moves toward deregulation, the fears of foreign domination have preserved some elements of nationalism. London has developed as the premier center for Eurocurrency dealings, largely due to the deliberate policy of reducing official intervention to a minimum. Wholesale banking has become a global industry par excellence, in which London plays a major role, and most large banks of whatever nationality have local representation. Acquisitions of the large clearing banks has been prohibited, though foreigners have been allowed to buy smaller banks. In insurance, Lloyds tried to limit outside holdings to a mere 20 percent, though that limit was broken when the large American firm March & McLennan bought out C. T. Bowring after a bitterly contested fight. Recent legislative changes have allowed banks to buy up to 29.9 percent of brokerage houses, thus opening the way for foreigners to gain access to the London Stock Exchange, a sector hitherto restricted to local nationals. As these developments unfold, the abilities of the authorities will be severely tested by the search for an appropriate balance among incentives, economics, and regulation. Greater foreign involvement will bring the benefits of greater liquidity and trading volume. But, as in other sectors, there are fears that the national interest could be harmed. The present governor of the Bank of England recently stated: "We would not contemplate with equanimity a stock exchange in which British-owned member firms played a clearly subordinate role, any more than we would like to see Lloyd's or any other City market dominated by overseas interests."[7] Current moves to strengthen domestic firms may not be enough, especially if they rely solely on information regulation. Yet were domestic interests to be overly supported by restrictive regulation, London would be vulnerable to competition from other financial centers that might adopt lower regulatory requirements.

Apart from a few *causes célèbres* of acquisitions by foreigners being blocked by the Monopolies and Mergers Commission, no further moves to restrain foreign interests effectively have been made in the financial or any other sector. On the contrary, the present government seems determined to increase British competitiveness by means of removing constraints from the working of free market forces. Nationality of ownership of indigenous assets seems less important than the firms' ability to create growth.

West Germany

Germany is more similar to Britain in its approach to foreigners than it is to France. Postwar recovery was built on the general philosophy of the "social market economy." Its basic elements were private ownership of the means of production (with some exceptions), free entrepreneurial initiatives, unrestricted competition, and the guarantee of a certain social stability. This was later adapted to that of the "enlightened market economy" as adjustments to internal economic difficulties and to the growing effect of the EEC became necessary. The adaptation took the form of attempts to create greater social integration and greater control of established power structures in the economic and political fields.[8]

Beginning in the late 1960s and continuing throughout the 1970s, there were moves to create some "national champions" in oil, aerospace, nuclear energy, and a few other sectors. These were, by comparison with the French, fairly modest efforts. Of more significance was the rising power of the Cartel Office. By the late 1960s German industry was the most concentrated in Europe, and the government came to recognize that the increases in concentration brought about by the drive for enhanced competitiveness on international markets could be overdone.[9] The Cartel Office was given wider powers to prohitit cartels and mergers among very large companies. though the granting of many exemptions diminished the impact of those powers. The result has been a clearer focus on competition as an instrument of national planning. In addition, the officially sanctioned concentration process "provided the basis for the development of more and more powerful enterprises, through which cooperation between government and large enterprise could be extended and intensified."[10] The Cartel Office as the arbiter of this essentially nationalistic process later found itself at odds with the EEC Commission in the interpretation of Community competition regulations (see below) and usually took a much tougher line when foreign transactions were involved.

For foreign firms that had come in at the ground floor of the early days of reconstruction or earlier, these developments had little impact. Firms like Shell, Ford, IBM, and ITT had become assimilated within the social and economic structures and could grow untrammeled. For newcomers trying to enter in a big way later on, though, the Cartel Office could be found in the doorway. Thus, for example, in automobile components, GKN's major bid for the Sachs Group in the mid-1970s was blocked on the ground of restraint of competition, even though many observers considered the bid to be in accordance with the EEC's generally avowed support for increasing continent-wide competition. For smaller acquisitions, however, relatively few obstacles have been strewn in the bidders' path. The prevailing doctrine of free enterprise has, within some very broad limits, ensured that foreigners were welcome, provided that they could fit within the complex and interrelated structures of banking interests, of extraparliamentary committees, and of the various alliances between business and the labor unions in various industries.[11]

Other European National Policies

Elsewhere in Europe, official policy was the familiar mixed bag of approaches.

In Italy much reliance was placed on creating and reinforcing public enterprises as a response to growing competition from the rapidly growing foreign presence (mainly American) in the 1960s. After some spectacular business failures, when, for example, some Americans pulled hastily out of Sicily leaving large debts behind, official and union attitudes hardened. These, combined with general economic difficulties, caused many multinationals to withdraw from Italy. More recently, however, there have been signs of a resurgence of investor interest, notably in the pharmaceutical industry.

Scandinavian countries and Spain have pursued more *dirigiste* policies of limiting the foreign presence to a relatively few sectors. Spain also has strong regulations requiring joint ventures for almost all foreign investments, except for highly export-oriented facilities such as the recent Ford and General Motors assembly plants. Belgium has generally welcomed foreigners, whereas the Dutch have been more cautious and have reserved for government wide discretionary powers to control the foreign interests.

Competing Incentives

There is, however, a growing phenomenon, sometimes labeled "dowry chasing," that has raised doubts in some quarters about the wisdom of allowing European governments to act independently in their drive to attract new job-creating investments. Dowry chasing is the phenomenon whereby multinational investors play off national and regional authorities against one another to gain the largest possible investment incentive. The game is an old one, but as the competition among potential "brides" has increased, so too has the generosity of the "dowries" offered. The competition is now so intense that the generosity of incentives offered can on occasion be so great as to wipe out any of the expected future benefits to the host.

Countries possessing the inherent advantages of a large domestic market have not had to offer quite so generous a set of incentives as those offered by the smaller countries. The Republic of Ireland, for example, has attracted "footloose" export-oriented investors by virtue of its generous cash grants and tax exemptions. Ireland runs the risk that those lured in will leave when the benefits expire. Indeed, it was forced a few years ago to extend the time horizon on tax concessions when firms did start to leave. In other words, the incentives needed to attract export-processing investment can be costly.

Most European countries, following the lead of the Irish Development Authority, are attempting to reduce the administrative complexities involved in gaining the incentives. The attempt is to create "one-stop shopping" at the national level, so as to reduce the confusion incurred when regional authorities compete against one another. Germany is an exception, in that grants are still administered at the regional level. For the Japanese especially, the resulting confusion has turned many would-be investors away from Germany and toward Britain where the rules are simpler and the national welcome warmer.

Such summary statements hardly do justice to the complexities of the national policies and attitudes held in Europe. Yet, with the exception of France, Scandinavia, and Spain, there are now relatively few discriminatory regulations that handicap foreigners relative to local investors, and even there incentives are used to attract newcomers who can add to national strengths. Where discrimination exists it is generally restricted to certain sectors where national champions are being fostered or where state enterprises have local monopolies. There are, to be sure, many obstacles facing foreign investors, especially newcomers, but they have more to do with local custom and practice and social institutions than official policy. Under such circumstances, it is hardly surprising that where foreigners can operate they can do so with few official guidelines that constrain their options on ownership policy. Thus, the choice of whether or not to enter a joint venture is conditioned primarily by commercial considerations. Only under special circumstances do EEC-level legal regulations affect the choice.

OWNERSHIP CHOICES

The basic strategic issues affecting ownership policy in MNCs are well known and will not be discussed at length here.[12] For the purposes of this review, three basic operating motivations favoring joint ventures over available alternatives can be distinguished: (1) those involving vertical supplier-customer relationships, (2) those involving horizontal linkages with competitors, and (3) those concerned with diversification strategies. These motives can apply at both a national and an international level.

Vertical Joint Ventures

For vertical joint ventures, natural resource companies provide the classic cases. The aluminum industry is dominated by a few vertically integrated producers, yet there are numerous joint ventures at the smelting stage of the chain of production. Why this should be so is illustrated by the case of the Norwegian smelting company, A/S Ardal og Sunndal Verk. The smelter was originally started during World War II by the Germans, who saw the advantages of cheap hydroelectric power. Incomplete in 1945, it was inherited by the state because no private company had the resources to complete and operate it. Originally it was dependent upon a barter supply agreement with Alcan (Canadian) under which alumina was exchanged for aluminum metal. As the original agreement neared its end, there was no certainty of renewal. To secure guaranteed access to its raw materials, the company could either expand to become vertically integrated itself, or it could become part of an established producer. The latter course was chosen, and the company ended up as a 50/50 joint venture between the government and Alcan,[13] thereby lessening dependence on outside suppliers.

The majority of European smelters are jointly owned by local interests and the integrated MCNs for similar reasons. There are also added incentives for sharing the heavy research and investment costs and market opportunities among competitors, who still today retain some of the characteristics of a cartel. In France and Switzerland, however, the smelters are wholly owned by home-based MNCs, Pechiney and Alusuisse. In the United Kingdom, where three smelters had been set up, largely at government initiative though in private hands, two of the three joint ventures failed because of adverse economic conditions. The survivor has recently been wholly absorbed by Alcan, as the local partners could not sustain the investments required for continuation. Such conditions in Europe are very similar to those prevailing elsewhere in the world.

Similar pressures for joint ventures exist in oil refining, and in some segments of the paper and chemical industries, where issues of security of supply and scale are important. In North Sea oil exploration and production, joint ventures between two or more parties are also common, though here the main motivations are those of sharing of risks and of responding to government pressures.

Horizontal Joint Ventures

Horizontal joint ventures occur between firms that decide to collaborate rather than compete (subject to the stringent legal obstacles described later on) or that conclude they have complementary skills and resources best exploited together. The simplest case is that of a foreign company possessing technology or production skills joining forces with a local company possessing access to end markets. The joint-venture route provides the former with speedier penetration for its products than it could achieve alone (and also perhaps some advantages in winning government procurement contracts), and the latter saves the investments necesssary to match the former's technology or product. For example, Fiat has sought joint ventures (mainly with American firms) for its diversified activities in off-highway equipment and tractors, while maintaining a wholly owned policy for its mainstream automobile business.

Horizontal joint ventures can be stable and extremely successful as long as the territory to be served is the local one. As soon as one partner wishes to develop an internationally integrated network, problems arise. For many years Ford owned only a majority of the equity of its British subsidiary, the rest of the shares being widely distributed through its quotation on the London Stock Exchange. The subsidiary expanded and developed as a virtually independent entity serving as the supply point for the British and Commonwealth markets. When Ford decided to lower costs by rationalizing its European network and by specializing the production in its various component factories, the interests of the parent company and the local shareholders began to diverge. To permit full integration of the British unit into the continental network, Ford had to buy out the local minority. The history of the IVECO venture in trucks and buses has followed a similar path. In 1974 Fiat, OM, and Lancia in Italy; Magirus Deutz in Germany; and UNIC in France joined forces to develop products capable of penetrating the U.S. market. Originally conceived as a joint venture among all the various parties, the difficulties of achieving integration both at the human and the corporate levels proved insuperable.[14] Fiat ended up with 80 percent of a Dutch-registered holding company, and KHD (the parent of Magirus Deutz) holds the remaining 20 percent. Fiat now operates the IVECO company as though it were in sole charge.

Diversification-Based Joint Ventures

The third type of joint venture, in diversification strategies, is really an extension of the second. The marriage makes sense if the partners have complementary skills and similar objectives. It is a common form of arrangement among local firms, usually small ventures. Success and growth of the venture can bring its problems, and often one of the original partners ends up in sole charge. How frequently this type of venture spans European borders is not known, but the indications are that it is rare; the risks of combining unknown products with unknown markets are enormous.

As alternative form for an international-level joint venture capable of establishing and maintaining a coherent and integrated system among the various national subsidiaries is that of a single joint holding company that, in turn, owns all of the equity of the subsidiaries. This approach has proved successful in specialty chemicals where Laporte of the United Kingdom and Solvay of Belgium hold equal shares of Unox, the holding company for the world's largest producer of peroxide chemicals. Other examples include the Bowater-Scott venture in paper tissues and Rank-Xerox in copiers. As for all such formulae, there can be problems. Xerox is known to be unhappy with the performance of its British partner and has taken effective managerial control, while Rank retains a share participation. From different origins, Rank-Xerox and IVECO have much in common in terms of the balance of effect between the managerial and legal structures. Whether they should be regarded as joint ventures or wholly owned subsidiaries that happen for historical reasons to have sleeping partners is a moot point.

EVIDENCE ON OWNERSHIP PRACTICES

Evidence of the frequency with which European firms choose among the various forms of ownership is scarce. Yet there are some data that, taken together, provide an outline of what has been going on. Economic theory, as it applies to foreign investment, suggests that where the investment is based upon firm-specific advantages (such as technology) and where the firm's choice is not constrained by official regulation, a firm generally prefers a wholly owned subsidiary.[15] (The exceptions, as in the vertically integrated industries, have already been noted.) By this means, the firm internalizes its advantage and is positioned to exploit to the full the market imperfections that prompted the investment in the first place. Given the fact that intra-European investment in the past 40-odd years has been relatively free of government obstacles, one might therefore expect that most of the investments made would have been wholly owned.

Table 4.3 provides some evidence to support the theory. Data on the ownership structure of the major foreign subsidiaries of 118 leading European manufacturing MNCs in 1981 were drawn from the *World Directory of Multinational Enterprises*.[16] Not all the parent companies included in the Directory could be used for these purposes, owing to the lack of publicly available data. Reporting practices vary widely among companies and what some consider a major subsidiary is a minor one for others. Moreover, some identify the particular activities of subsidiaries, while others are silent on the subject. Thus, the data in Table 4.3 must be treated with some caution. Though efforts were made to exclude all sales, financing, holding, and other nonmanufacturing subsidiaries, some inevitably slipped through the net. The focus is on manufacturing facilities, for which the ownership choice is most critical both to the firm and the local government. Sales subsidiaries are an extension of the export structure and subject to other considerations.

Contrary to widely accepted notions about national differences in behavior, British MNCs are no more prone to seek wholly owned positions than their neighbors.[17] Indeed the Swiss and Scandinavians top the list and there is very little difference among British, German, and Dutch practice. Only the French and Benelux MNCs seem to have a slightly greater propensity to enter joint ventures. Of the 1,826 subsidiaries, 76 percent were wholly owned and only 10 percent were minority-owned. Even though oil and mining companies were excluded, other natural resource companies were included.[18] Had they also been excluded, the wholly owned proportion would have been even higher.

The data in Table 4.3 refer to all EEC and EFTA (European Free Trade Association) countries with the exception of Spain, where there are important restrictions on ownership. Even so, as the separate line in the table shows, nearly one-third of the 165 subsidiaries in Spain, owned by the same group of MNCs, were wholly owned. Regulations cannot be ignored, but they can be circumvented if the MNC possesses adequate bargaining strength. Most likely a number of the manufacturing subsidiaries in Spain were excluded from the original data set because they were too small. Had they been included, the proportion of joint ventures probably would have been higher.

Table 4.3   Ownership Practices of 118 European Multinations in EEC and
             EFTA Countries, 1981

Parent Company	Number of Companies[a]	Number of Subsidiaries	% of subsidiaries that were owned		
			(percent)	(percent)	(percent)
Switzerland	5	143	85	10	5
Sweden & Norway	15	332	83	7	10
United Kingdom	53	525	77	13	10
Netherlands[b]	7	186	75	15	10
West Germany	20	389	74	17	9
Italy	2	25	72	12	16
France	13	143	67	22	11
Benelux	3	83	53	19	28
Total	118	1,186	76	14	10
Subsidiaries in Spain	118	165	53	18	29

[a]Excludes oil and mining and nonmanufacturing companies; sales, financing, and other non-manufacturing subsidiaries excluded where possible; subsidiaries in home country and Spain excluded.
[b]Includes Estal (50 percent Dutch, 50 percent German) and Unilever (50 percent Dutch, 50 percent British).

Source: J. M. Stopford, The World Directory of Multinational Enterprises (New York: Macmillan; 1982).

Given the imperfections of the data in Table 4.3, some cross-bearings are needed to check whether the picture is reasonably accurate. Table 4.4 provides one such check for all foreign investments in manufacturing industries in the United Kingdom, the country for which the most complete data seem to be available. Note that the table includes sales subsidiaries, so that the test is not a complete one. The general sense of an overwhelming preference for complete ownership is confirmed, both by a head count of the subsidiaries and by the book value of the assets involved.

To place this preference in perspective, Table 4.5 shows the ownership record of British direct foreign investments in all countries. In high-income countries a similar pattern is revealed, but in lower-income countries, where the most stringent controls on foreign ownership exist, joint ventures are much more common. The trends that led to this position in 1981 provide some clues as to firms' preference. In 1965, the proportion of wholly British-owned subsidiaries in the more developed countries was only 47 percent. That percentage has risen steadily since then, thereby suggesting that the drive to internalize firm-specific advantages has intensified. In developing countries, the equivalent figure was 41 percent in 1965. It subsequently dropped to 23 percent on 1976, but since then has risen to 47 percent. Thus

Table 4.4   Foreign investment in the United Kingdom, by Country of Investor and Ownership, 1981

Nationality of Parent Company	Total		Wholly Owned		Majority Holdings (51–99.9%)		Minority Holdings (50% or less)	
	No. of Subsidiaries[a]	Value £ million	No.	Value	No.	Value	No.	Value
Western Europe	1,315	4,387	1,025	3,554	181	442	109	391
(as % of total)	(100)	(100)	(78)	(81)	(14)	(10)	(8)	(9)
USA	998	8,866	880	7,439	59	1,098	59	330
(as % of total)	(100)	(100)	(88)	(84)	(6)	(12)	(6)	(4)
Canada	92	882	79	812	7	24	6	46
(as % of total)	(100)	(100)	(86)	(92)	(8)	(3)	(7)	(5)
Japan	67	292	48	250	12	34	7	8
(as % of total)	(100)	(100)	(72)	(86)	(18)	(12)	(10)	(3)
Other	179	1,438	131	870	23	145	25	421
(as % of total)	(100)	(100)	(73)	(61)	(13)	(10)	(14)	(29)
Total	2,651	15,865	2,163	12,925	282	1,743	206	1,196
(as % of total)	(100)	(100)	(82)	(81)	(11)	(11)	(8)	(8)

Notes: The table excludes oil, banking, insurance, and branch holdings. Row and column totals do not all add precisely due to rounding errors.

Source: Business Monitor, M4A, 1981.

Table 4.5 Ownership Policies of British Multinational Corporations, by Area, 1981

Nationality of Parent Company	Total		Wholly Owned		Majority Holdings (51-99.9%)		Minority Holdings (50% or lesss)	
	No. of Subsidiaries[a]	Value £ million	No.	Value	No.	Value	No.	Value
Western Europe	3,429	6,472	2,698	4,955	407	1,150	324	367
(as % of total)	(100)	(100)	(79)	(77)	(12)	(18)	(9)	(6)
USA	837	7,892	724	6,830	61	839	52	223
(as % of total)	(100)	(100)	(87)	(87)	(7)	(11)	(6)	(3)
Other developed	1,638	7,664	1,209	5,008	237	2,037	192	619
(as % of total)	(100)	(100)	(74)	(65)	(14)	(27)	(12)	(8)
Rest of world	2,442	5,767	1,284	2,735	472	1,901	686	1,131
(as % of total)	(100)	(100)	(53)	(47)	(19)	(33)	(28)	(20)
Total	8,346	27,795	5,915	19,529	1,177	5,927	1,254	2,340
(as % of total)	(100)	(100)	(71)	(70)	(14)	(21)	(15)	(8)

Notes: The table excludes oil, banking, insurance, and branch holdings. Row and column totals do not all add precisely due to rounding errors.

Source: Business Monitor, M4A, 1981.

even where controls exist, British MNCs have shown a marked desire to concentrate their efforts where they could exert control and to avoid or deemphasize activities where they could not. No such trends seem to exist in respect to French MNCs. A recent study indicated that the preference for majority-controlled subsidiaries was just as strong in the mid-1970s as it was in 1981.[19] Equivalent data are not available for other European investors, but there are many signs that much the same is happening for them as for the British.

Taken together, Tables 4.3, 4.4, and 4.5 shed some light on the relationship between size and ownership. Many observers have considered smaller investors to be more prone to seek joint ventures, if only because they lacked the competitive muscle to go it alone.[20] Yet Table 4.3 applies to the largest MNCs, whereas Tables 4.4 and 4.5 cover *all* investors. There is no discernible difference, at least in the European theater, between the two sets of figures. The implication is that smaller investors are equally anxious and equally successful in asserting unambiguous control via ownership.

Data of this type can shed no light, of course, on the investors' precise motivation, nor can they distinguish among the various types of joint ventures or illuminate the differences among industries. A further problem is that the statistics apply only to joint ventures that are embodied in separate legal entities. Changing competitive pressures at the global level are prompting more and more companies to enter into what has been dubbed "contractual" joint ventures.[21] Here the firms involved enter into long-term agreements to collaborate in specified ways without forming separate companies. Contractual joint ventures can take many different shapes and sizes. Some concern supply agreements for products; others involve the provision of technical services, such as quality control or, for airlines, maintenance; some have to do with technology transfers. The latter form is of growing significance in Europe and very frequently involves the Japanese. BL (formerly British Leyland), for example, has such an agreement with Honda whereby Honda provides designs for part of BL's model range, as well as some of the components. In computers, ICL depends upon Fujitsu in a similar fashion. The list of such agreements continues to lengthen despite the fact that not all the experience has been happy. The fear is that the importer of the technology becomes overly dependent upon the supplier, loses competitiveness, and sooner or later becomes vulnerable either to takeover by the supplier or to commercial extinction by market forces.[22] The full significance of all these forms of nonequity joint venturing is extremely hard to measure. One may suspect that under conditions of rapidly changing technology they will prove to be devices that merely slow down the rate of decline of already weak competitors.

REACTIONS TO EXTERNAL THREATS

The worries about the contractual form of technology sharing are part of a wider concern about how best European industries should be reconstructed so as to regain the last decades' losses of competitiveness. Three basic options have been explored, all of them involving some form of joint venture and all meeting considerable difficulty. One is to develop a "national champion," the second is to create a "European champion," and the third is to permit large-scale restructuring and rationalization of existing national competitors on an continental scale.

Developing a national champion usually involves both merger of existing competitors and the use of joint ventures as a stepping stone on the way toward creating a monolithic structure. Such temporary joint ventures have been common in computers, chemicals, automobiles, steel, and other industries. Whether the process is efficient and whether the very notion of a national champion is tenable in contemporary European conditions are important questions. The example of European computers suggests that the answers to both questions is negative.

France was the first of the major European countries to develop a champion, under the aegis of its Plan Calcul. The first moves occurred in the early 1960s when French sensibilities were aroused, first by the partial takeover of a major national competitor, Bull, by General Electric of the United States (and later by Honeywell) and, second, by the U.S. government's refusal in 1966 to grant export license for two of Control Data's largest computers. A national "solution" would probably have emerged later even without these events in response to the growing domination of IBM. In any event the Plan Calcul was designed to channel public money, first into CII (the product of a shotgun marriage of two small competitors) and later into Honeywell-Bull as the government gradually forced Honeywell to cede more of the equity of the joint venture to French interests. Since Plan Calcul was first formulated, the investments have yielded little and market-traded shares (despite public procurement bias) have slipped increasingly into foreign hands. Indeed, IBM executives are fond of pointing out that the taxes IBM (France) has paid since 1966 exceed the total of the French investment. In the United Kingdom, the national champion that emerged from a series of mergers over the 1960s was ICL, whose current dependence upon the Japanese has already been mentioned. In Germany, the two champions, Nixdorf and Siemens, have made some progress as second-tier competitors, but both have their problems.

The need for a European policy has long been realized, but action has been minimal. In 1973, Unidata was created as a consortium among Philips of Holland, Siemens of Germany, and CII of France. Its purpose was to foster cooperation in marketing, planning, and R&D. It was short-lived, as European governments could not agree on the necessary common technical standards and were unwilling to dismantle their own national procurement requirements. More recently, the EEC Commission has sponsored the ESPRIT program to fund basic and cooperative research at the "precompetitive" stages. Many observers feel that this initiative will go the same way as Unidata. Until there is a far greater political will among all European governments to ensure the success of such initiatives and to make the necessary adjustments, there seems little chance of success for any political solution to a competitive problem.

French interest in all electronics sectors has heightened in recent years, most notably since 1981 when its Plan Filiere Electronique was announced. This program involves the spending of 140 billion 1982 francs over the period 1983-87 and is the exlusive preserve of four nationalized French firms. To the extent this plan succeeds for France, it will further delay any moves toward a European solution.[23]

While national computer champions have largely failed and continent-wide agreements seem elusive, there has been success in aerospace. The Airbus consortium joint venture among state companies in France, Germany, and the United Kingdom has shown that cooperation can produce world-beating technology and commerical success, albeit, as the Americans would argue, at the price of government-subsidized loans to ensure competitive prices. Some of the European defense collaborations, as for the Tornado jet and the 155 mm gun, are also rated successes, but most other cooperative efforts at the governmental level have proved to be sadly disappointing. The obstacles to real integration of effort are immense, and few if any politically inspired European champions are likely to emerge.

The third alternative, that of creating private-sector pan-European mergers or joint-venture structures, seems equally uncompromising. The record of major cross-border mergers has been dismal in recent years. In tires, the Dunlop-Pirelli Union with its elaborate scheme of cross-holdings in jointly owned subsidiaries has been disastrous. After canceling the Union, Pirelli remains unprofitable, and Dunlop has sold its European tire factories to Sumitomo of Japan. The Estel Dutch-German merger in steel is unprofitable. The problems seem as much behavioral as economic. To cross cultural barriers to create tightly integrated structures of management, as in the IVECO case (mentioned previously), takes a long time, and the objective can seldom be achieved without someone having unambiguous power to control the future course of the enterprise. Mergers contracted within framework of joint ownership do not seem to be the answer.

Although there are few successfull cross-border mergers of entire companies, examples abound of success in linking specialized units in different European countries, either by merger or by joint venture. The number of joint ventures included in the tables is appreciable and includes many profitable, healthy enterprises. The scope for further rationalization is considerable in many industries, and many firms continue to explore possibilities. Here, however, they meet serious legal obstacles as the next section shows.

Not all Europeans are convinced that rationalization purely within Europe is an adequate response to the demands of rapidly changing technology. Carlo de Benedetti, chairman of Italy's Olivetti, takes the view that the ingredients for a successful joint venture in such a process of rationalization—the trading of technology for market access—do not exist within Europe, where the established companies already have good market access. He considers that joint ventures must be at an international level. Recently, Olivetti has signed an agreement with the American firm AT&T, whereby AT&T has subscribed 25 percent of Olivetti's capital as part of a comprehensive commercial, industrial, and R&D agreement. As de Benedetti put it, "creation of a network of integration and collaboration at European and international levels permits us to develop a global range of products covering the most innovative and integrated areas of data processing, office automation and telecommunications. In other words, it allows us to be a global competitor."[24] Rather than being defensive, Olivetti is on the offensive; its objective is to be in many markets simultaneously. As few firms can have the inside track in all markets, joint ventures at the global level become important. Though few others have taken such bold steps, there are signs that more joint ventures with non-Europeans are on the way. The recent Philips/AT&T joint venture in digital switching, where the development costs could exceed $1 billion, is a recent example. And Philips, like Olivetti, is including European partners in a growing network of technical collaborations.

LEGAL OBSTACLES

Cross-border agreements of various kinds to enhance economies of scale and to lower overall costs are influenced by EEC law. Mergers, manufacturing joint ventures, R&D joint ventures, and other forms of collaboration among independent firms are all covered. The main provisions of the law are embodied in Articles 85 and 86 of the Treaty of Rome.

In very general terms, Article 85 is designed to outlaw all agreements or concerted practices that prevent, distort, or otherwise restrict competition within the EEC. Article 86 regulates the affairs of a single company so as to guard against the abuse of a dominant market position. Generally speaking a market position is considered dominant if it exceeds 65 percent, though the question of defining the relevant market is open to debate. In the Continental Can Case it was established that the concept of abuse refers not solely to restraint of trade but also to changes in the structure of competition.[25] Thus Article 86 became applicable to mergers between competing companies.[26] Both Articles 85 and 86, similar in many respects to the U.S. antitrust provision of Sections 1 and 2 of the Sherman Act, affect the establishment of joint-venture agreements of all kinds. A joint venture is typically prevented when the parent companies involved continue to compete in the relevant markets, unless exemption is specifically granted under Article 85(3).

Case law has been established for a variety of types of joint-venture agreements. Three cases are reviewed below to indicate the range of considerations. For a full appreciation of the complex issues, consultation of the complete legal documentation is required. Nevertheless, the impact of the law on economic considerations can be interpreted fairly readily.

Manufacture and sale agreements that allow for specialization of production across EEC frontiers are an obvious way for companies to reduce costs. A landmark case was the 1975 agreement between ICI of the UK and WASAG AG (part of the German Bohlem Group) to create conditions of equal ownership and control of existing German production of black powder.[27] Briefly stated, ICI was to purchase 50 percent of WASAG's powder subsidiary and to shut down its own production facilities in the United Kindom, thereby allowing the U.K. market to be supplied exclusively from Germany. ICI was the sole U.K. supplier, with a near-100 percent market share. The agreement was seen by the courts to be designed solely to eliminate existing competition between the two companies and effectively to block all others from entering the United Kingdom market. Moreover, there was an issue of a related product, namely, safety fuses. Combined, the two companies would produce double the number of safety fuses made by all other EEC manufacturers together. The EEC Commission decided that it was inconceivable that the two companies would resist the temptation to align prices and to share markets for safety fuses. Exemption under Article 85(3) was thus denied, and the agreement was canceled with the companies' concurrence.

Other types of specialization agreements have been allowed by the Commission when better consumer prices result from rationalized production, especially when small or medium-sized manufacturers are involved. Even large firms can be granted exemption from Article 85(1) if their special circumstances warrant it. A case in point was the 1975 decision relating to the Bayer/Gist-Brocades agreement on long-term specialization in penicillin manufacture.[28] The two large firms, German and Dutch respectively, produced raw penicillin and an intermediate product (6-APA acid). In 1969 both had been faced with decisions about expansion. They agreed that Gist-Brocades would expand its raw penicillin plant and Bayer its 6-APA plant, and each would supply the other with the increased offtakes required. Various licensing and financial provisions were also included in the deal. In 1971 a further agreement was concluded to transfer the expanded plants into two jointly owned subsidiaries.

The EEC Commission objected to the formation of these subsidiaries as a means of establishing joint control of production and investment, and the 1971 agreement was terminated. However, after much deliberation, the earlier specialization agreement was allowed to continue, provided that the supply and licensing conditions were changed so as to ensure that no exclusive provisions were retained.[29] The arguments turned on the evidence that the agreement had led to an improvement of production at lower prices for sale to others who competed with Bayer and, to a lesser extent with Gist-Brocades, in penicillin specialities. Thus, consumers had benefited and economic progress had been assisted. In other words, most of the economic benefits of specialization were allowed to be gained, but the form of agreement could not be embodied within a structure of operating joint ventures.

Another kind of joint venture of increasing significance applies to agreements for joint research on a scale too great for a single company to justify independently. Joint research up to the stage of industrial application is not held to affect competition.[30] But when such agreements carry forward into application, the Commission has ruled that they can be approved only when the results can be used freely by the companies involved without any geographical or other restrictions on production or marketing within the EEC. The implications of this ruling were tested in the Beecham/Parke Davis decision in 1979.[31] Here, two large pharmaceutical multinationals, one British and the other American, had agreed to collaborate in the development of a new class of therapeutics so as to promote technical progress and to speed up the development process above the rate likely to be achieved by independent research. These desirable objectives were allowed only after restrictive clauses in the cross-licensing and profit-sharing clauses had been removed. The 1984 agreement between Philips and Siemens to share a $560 million development contract for the next generation of microchips has been subject to similar reviews, though the active support of the Dutch and West Germany governments no doubt helped to smooth the way for eventual approval.

The implication of these and other similar cases is that joint ventures, whether in an operating or a contractual form, will be allowed if they meet the tests of (1) providing a unique solution to difficult problems, (2) increasing competition, and (3) producing benefit to consumers. As one legal expert has recently concluded, "judging from the cases decided to date, the creation of joint subsidiaries will be allowed only on an exceptional case."[32]

One should note that this judgment of the likely restrictive impact of legislation upon the establishment of future joint ventures applies only to those affecting cross-border transactions within the EEC. Joint ventures that in the first instance affect only national conditions are treated by local regulations. Given that the phenomenon of dowry chasing is increasing and that many of these new ventures are highly export-oriented, with other EEC markets as the prime export targets, they add further threat to already beleagured indigenous competitors. One reaches the troubling conclusion that EEC law has been developed so as to restrict seriously the range of possible competitive responses other than in exceptional circumstances.[33] Thus, though the purpose of the laws is to increase competition and consumer benefit, the effect is to assist non-EEC producers to penetrate European markets with perhaps only short-run gains to consumer interests.

NOTES

1. For a general review of relative performance, see H. Gunter, *Employment Effects of Multinational Enterprises in Industrialised Countries* (Geneva: International Labor Office, 1981).

2. For these purposes, the state can be regarded as the combination of the usual offices of government together with the rest of the administration, including the Commisariat du Plan, as well as the public enterprises directly under the control of the administration. For thoughtful reviews of this approach to the power and the practice of the state, see C.-A. Michalet, "France" in R. Vernon, ed., *Business and the State* (New York: Macmillan, 1974); J. M. McArthur and B. R. Scott, *Industrial Planning in France* (Cambridge, Mass.: Harvard Graduate School of Business Administration, 1969); and A. Barrere "La Coherence de l'Economie publique, le plan et le marche," *Economic Publique* (CNRS, 1968, pp. 449–482.

3. This paragraph draws heavily on Michalet.

4. See, for example, Commission on the General Economy and Finance, Sixth Plan, *Rapport* (Paris: La Documentation Francaise, 1971).

5. Twenty percent was effectively the French definition of the boundary separating portfolio from direct investment.

6. For a fuller account of contemporary British policies, see J. M. Stopford and L. Turner, *Britain and the Multinationals* (New York: John Wiley, 1986.

7. Robin Leigh-Pemberton, "Changing Boundaries in Financial Services," *Bank of England Quarterly Bulletin* 24, no. 1 (March 1984).

8. For a general review, see George H. Kuster, "Germany," in Vernon. See also Andrew Schonfield, *Modern Capitalism* (Oxford: Oxford University Press, 1965).

9. The Federal Chancellor, *Bundestag Papers*, Period V, No. 4236 (Bonn: Hegner, 1969), p. 3.

10. Kuster, p. 82. See also H. O. Lenel, "Haben Wir Noch Eine Soziale Markwirtschaft?" *Ordo* 22 (1971).

11. The 1983 attempt by GEC of Britain to buy 40 percent of the ailing electrical giant AEG was blocked more by the concentrated action of the bankers and unions than by any governmental intervention.

12. For a review of the issues, see J. M. Stopford and L. T. Wells, *Managing the Multinational Enterprise* (New York: Basic Books, 1972); L. G. Franko, *Joint Venture Survival in Multinational Corporations* (New York: Praeger, 1971). For a more recent review of changing practices, see K. R. Harrigan, "Joint Ventures and Global Strategies," *Columbia Journal of World Business* 19, no. 2 (Summer 1984).

13. The story has its complexities. For details, see O. H. Jensen and J. E. Sandvik, "Samarbeidsforetak—Joint Ventures i Norsk Industri" (Bergen: Foretaksokonomisk Institutt, Norges Handelshoyskoke, 1971).

14. For fascinating details of some of the managerial adjustments and development efforts needed to create a unification of purpose, see D. McAllister, "A Strategy for Organisational Learning: The IVECO Experience," in B. Garratt and J. M. Stopford, *Breaking Down Barriers* (London: Gower, 1980).

15. See, for example, J. H. Dunning, "Changes in the Level and Structure in International Production: The Last One Hundred Years," In M. H. Casson, ed., *The Growth of International Business* (New York: Macmillan, 1983); and P. J. Buckley

and M. Casson, *The Future of the Multinational Enterprise* (New York: Macmillan, 1976).

16. J. M. Stopford, *World Directory of Multinational Enterprises* (New York: Macmillan, 1982).

17. L. G. Franko, for example, argues that continental firms actively seek joint ventures in contrast to British and American practice. See his text, *European Multinationals* (New York: Harper & Row, 1976).

18. This was mainly because many of them were highly diversified and it proved impossible to separate out which subsidiaries were exclusively active in a resource-related sector.

19. J. Savary, *French Multinationals* (London: Frances Pinter, 1984).

20. See, for example, Franko.

21. W. G. Friedman, "The Contractual Joint Venture," *Columbia Journal of World Business*, January-February 1972.

22. For a provocative review of the implications of new forms of competition for such agreements, see G. Hamel and C. K. Prahalad, "Creating Global Strategic Capability," *Harvard Business Review* (July/August 1985, 139–148).

23. For details, see C. Stoffaes, "French Industrial Strategy in Sunrise Sectors," in A. Jacquemin, ed., *European Industry: Public Policy an Corporate Strategy* (Oxford: Clarendon Press, 1984).

24. Carlo de Benedetti, "Multinationals and the Future of Europe," a speech given at an IRM Conference, *Multinationals and the Future of Europe* (London, April 1984).

25. Continental Can v. Commission, Case 6/72, Judgment of February 2, 1973, CCH * 8171, p. 8301.

26. For an excellent summary of the legal considerations affecting the application of these laws, see Utz P. Toepke, "Legal Aspects of International Investments," in Ingo Walter, ed., *Handbook of International Business* (New York: John Wiley, 1982). This section draws heavily on Toepke's analysis.

27. For the Commission's decision, see *Official Journal of the European Committees*, No. L322/26 of November 16, 1978, CCH * 10,089.

28. For details, see *Official Journal of the European Committees*, No. L30/13 of February 5, 1976, CCH * 9814.

29. The exemption under Article 85(3) was granted for eight years, subject to periodic performance reviews.

30. Commission Notice on Agreements, Decisions and Concerted Practices Concerning Cooperation between Enterprises, July 29, 1968. *Official Journal of the European Committees*, No. C 75 corrected by OJ No. C84, August 28, 1968, CCH * 2699.

31. For details, see *Bulletin of the European Communities* 1979/1, point 2.1.32, CCH* 10,121.

32. Toepke, p. 25.23.

33. One such exception was the recent Philips purchase of Grundig, allowable under EEC law only as a last resort to retain some indigenous competition against the Japanese invasion in consumer electronics. Earlier joint-venture proposals that at one stage had involved French interests had been barred.

Chapter Five

Japanese Intervention with Respect to Direct Foreign Investment

Noritake Kobayashi

BASIC POLICY AND NEW PROBLEMS

Japan was a late starter in the world economy, and for a long time the primary goal of the Japanese was to catch up with the Western industrialized countries.

For the catching-up process, the Japanese needed both capital and technologies of the advanced world. However, there was also a deeply rooted fear that if Japan accepted foreign resources too easily, it might result in economic overdependence on foreign influence and the domination of the national economy by foreign interests. Accordingly, the Japanese government and business have long shared the same basic attitude and policy toward the receipt of foreign investment, preferring the import of technology to that of capital. For the funds needed to build and construct modern industry and business, it chose loans rather than direct investment.

This policy seems to have worked very well. By the effective utilization of imported technology, the Japanese economy has developed into the world's second largest market economy.

In the meantime, the impact of foreign direct investment on the national economy was kept at an appropriate level. By the end of the 1983 fiscal year, foreign investors had committed approximately $5 billion in Japan, and more than 2,220 foreign capital-affiliated firms were operating in Japan. However, the weight and impact of the foreign investors in and on the Japanese economy was rather small. In terms of assets, those owned by foreign capital-affiliated firms contributed only 1.4 percent of total corporate assets in Japan. Their contribution in terms of sales, net profits, and employment remained also relatively small: 1.5, 2.1, and 0.4 percent, respectively.

The reasons for the success of the Japanese economy and business are attributed not only to the reliance on foreign technology but also to vigorous corporate efforts to achieve the goal of catching up with the Western industrialized countries in accord with the national objective established by the Japanese government. A close cooperative relationship existed between the Japanese government and business for the realization of this common goal. This system of cooperation is sometimes called "Japan Incorporated." The system worked very well until recently, as will be explained in more detail.

By the 1980s, the Japanese have found that their catch-up process is more or less completed. In many business fields, the Japanese realize that their level of progress has surpassed that of their Western counterparts, thereby causing substantial trade conflict all over the world. Now, for many Japanese businesses, how to develop their overseas activities (including direct investment) more smoothly has become of more immediate concern than how to defend their domestic market against the inroads of foreign direct investments. In a major transformation of attitude triggered by expanding international activities, the Japanese have come to realize that if they want to be freer in doing business abroad, they must also allow foreign investors to act more freely in Japan. The new international imperatives of business do not necessarily correspond with those perceived by the Japanese government, which may feel, more strongly than private interests, the responsibility to protect the stability of the domestic market in the turbulent world situation.

The rationale of Japan Incorporated was a national consensus based on the life-style and value of the comparatively poor Japanese. Subsequent economic development, however, has made the Japanese feel that they are richer than ever before, and the old rationale for cooperation with the government no longer has as strong an appeal as before. Without a new basis of national consensus, the government seems to be suffering considerable difficulty in maintaining the Japan Incorporated system in a working condition as effectively as before.

The change of the Japanese position in the international marketplace from one of follower to one of leader caused another new problem. First, the Japanese feel that it is becoming more difficult to find new useful technologies abroad and, even if they exist, the foreign holders of such technologies are not as willing, as formerly, to make them available to the Japanese because they are afraid of intensified competition as a foreseeable result. Second, Japan, as a leading technological nation, is now often asked to share its know-how with others, particularly people in the developing world. However, many Japanese firms seem to be very cautious in that they worry about the boomerang effect they themselves once enjoyed.

As a reflection of the recent change in the position of Japan in the world economy and, consequently, in that of Japanese business and industry, the Japanese government went through a major overhaul of the Foreign Exchange and Foreign Trade Control Law (Law No. 228 of 1949) in 1979, an amendment known as Law No. 65 of 1979. By this enactment, the government changed its basic policy to deal with inward foreign direct investment from that of "prohibition as a general rule and permission as an exception" to that of "permission as a general rule and prohibition as an exception." The result was a 100 percent liberalization of control over foreign direct investment. However, in view of the state of flux in the international economic situation, the government reserved the right to suspend this liberalized control in case of a critical emergency with respect to the nation's economy.

My aim in this chapter is to discuss Japanese corporate reactions to government intervention with respect to direct foreign investment. As already explained, Japan has a long history of foreign direct investment control. The direction and content of the control have change in the course of the history, depending on the situation both at home and abroad. For each phase of the history, the reactions of business and industry were different. Also important is the fact that the implications of corporate reactions likewise varied. Sometimes they were positive and favorable and at other times, negative and unfavorable. In the former case, business looked at government control as a form of protective assistance and in the latter, as unwelcome intervention. The perception of business was strongly affected by the balance of power existing between government and business during the several phases in the development of the control policy.

In this presentation, what I wish to do is to take several phases of the economic development in a post-World War II Japan, and the related changes in foreign investment control, and to relate these to changes in the relationship between the government and business.

CHANGES IN THE GOVERNMENT–BUSINESS RELATIONSHIP AND THE CONTROL OF FOREIGN DIRECT INVESTMENTS

The development of the postwar Japanese economy can be divided into several phases, each characterized by a different pattern of relationship between government and business and, accordingly, by the degree of government control over foreign direct investment.

War Reconstruction Period: Dependence for Survival

First was the war reconstruction period between 1945 and 1951. When the war was over, the Japanese economy had to start afresh; little survived the destruction of the war. During this period the private-sector economy depended heavily on the government for recovery.

The government controlled prices for economic stabilization and assisted basic industries, including electric power, steel, coal mining, and shipping, by allocating to them scarce resources necessary to satisfy the government's planned reconstruction. The balance of power was clearly in favor of the government. Also, business found it advantageous to rely on strong government leadership for recovery under difficult conditions.

In the area of foreign direct investments, the government enacted two laws during this period: the Foreign Exchange and Foreign Trade Control Law (Law No. 228 of 1949) and the Law Concerning Foreign Trade (Law No. 163 of 1950). The primary purpose of the first was to protect the fragile Japanese economy and the national balance of payments from possible negative impact of stronger foreign investors. Accordingly, only foreign investors who could satisfy certain conditions prescribed by the law were validated by the Japanese government and allowed to invest in Japan. In addition, certain benefits were received by such validated investors. These benefits meant an unconditional government guarantee that the foreign investors had the right of remittance, in the currency of investment, for the investment, dividends, interest on capital invested, and/or for royalties, service fees, of other compensation for technological services.

The conditions for validation consisted of two kinds, affirmative and negative. The affirmative conditions were that the investment should directly or indirectly contribute to the improvement of the nation's balance of payments or to the development of essential industries or public enterprises. The negative conditions were such that validation would not be accorded to arrangements that were considered unfair or in contravention of the law, and which were not freely and voluntarily entered into by the Japanese party. Validation could be refused if the arrangements applied for were deemed likely to have an adverse effect on the rehabilitation of the Japanese economy. These terms, particularly the affirmative, were very restrictive to foreign investors.

Rehabilitation Period

The second phase of Japanese economic development covers a rehabilitation period between 1952 and 1960. By this time, many Japanese industries had succeeded in overcoming the danger of collapse. However, they were fully aware that if they were going to grow in an increasingly competitive postwar market, they needed to make further effort in the direction of rationalization.

To this end, the government met with the representatives of several industry associations and business leaders in the steel, machinery, electronics, automobile, synthetic fiber, and rubber and petrochemical industries and jointly developed plans to meet the requirements of industrial rationalization.

To illustrate the typical course of planning, the government would, for instance, make long- and medium-term projections of demands. It then developed an appropriate investment plan for the industry. It tried to show the industry how to achieve an optimum scale of production and at the same time how to cut production costs directly. The government also, in many cases, provided incentives for industrial growth and rationalization by extending loans through government-sponsored financial institutions and by recognizing accelerated depreciation for tax purposes.

People say that in the second phase, the system of Japan Incorporated came into full bloom. This was a period in which groundwork was laid for the forthcoming period of high-speed recovery. As Japan's economic and international balance-of-payment situations improved, the government's strict attitude toward validating foreign investment applications began to be relaxed. The first relaxation came in 1956 when the government decided to recognize an important exception to the general rule of the validation requirement. Namely, if a foreign investor waived his or her right for the remittance of investment and its proceeds, he or she would be permitted to make investment without going throught the validation procedure that was prescribed by the Foreign Investment Law. This measure led to what became known as "yen-based operations." It was adopted to facilitate the introduction of foreign capital and technology necessary for Japanese rehabilitation. Major foreign firms (e.g., Coca Cola, Esso Standard Oil, Mobil Oil, Olivetti, and Hoechst) invested in Japan under this system with the hope that the progress of liberalization would eventually free them from the existing restrictions with respect to the remittance of earnings in foreign currency.

Preparation Period for the Progress of Liberalization

The third phase of the development was the period between 1961 and 1970, during which government and business were busily preparing to expand the liberalization of both trading and capital transactions.

Thanks to government cooperation, Japanese business started to grow very rapidly in this period. As a result, the power balance gradually shifted from government to business. However, business realized that its growth had been achieved only behind the protective wall the government had maintained against the foreign business. But as the Japanese economy grew more affluent, and particularly after Japan joined the Organization for Economic Cooperation and Development in 1964, a strong foreign pressure was exerted on the Japanese government to open the domestic market for freer entry of both goods and investment. However, there was uncertainty. If this protective curtain were lifted, could Japanese business compete successfully against foreign business in open markets, both domestic and international? A strong xenophobia prevailed in Japan. Again, Japanese business and government found a mutual interest and a basis for continued collaboration.

The government took two approaches to meet the requirements of business. First, it took a firm stand to slow down the progress of liberalization of trading and capital transactions. Second, it tried to reorganize Japanese industries by corporate mergers in order to increase their international competitive strength.

The government was successful in delaying the progress of liberalization until the end of this third period (1970), as will be explained more fully later. During this phase, however, the government found it increasingly difficult to persuade those industries growing in self-confidence to follow government guidelines for reorganization. Therefore, in this third phase of economic development, the government had to face the reality that, though it might still protect and serve business and industry by inaction, it could no longer exert the same degree of influence over them through guidelines calling for positive response.

The first relaxation of the validation requirements in this period was announced by the Japanese government in 1961, when it was officially declared that, henceforth, reliance would be primarily on negative rather than affirmative conditions for screening validation applications. By 1964, the government had made clear, by action through the screening process, that it would approve foreign ownership in joint ventures established in Japan up to 50 percent, rather than 49 percent, which had been the limit previously.

As already explained, after Japan joined the OECD, strong pressure built up to accelerate the liberalization process, the result of which was a so-called five-year program for liberalization in 1967. The launching of that program was announced in a cabinet order prescribing the basic logic to be followed by the government in the course of the subsequent liberalization effort.

In the cabinet order, the government emphasized its conviction that in view of the increasing interdependence of the economic communities of the world, it was necessary, in the interest of the long-range development of the economy, to make efforts for creating firm relationship and cooperation between our economy and those of other countries, and for maintaining and expanding the freedom of capital movements as well as of current invisible operations. However, the government went on to point out, many of Japan's enterprises did not yet have strength to compete against foreign rivals on equal terms. Therefore, the government contended that it should protect "the order and interest" of Japanese industry by taking positive actions in order "(1) to prevent confusion of industrial order which may accrue from foreign enterprises coming into Japan, (2) to create a basis on which our enterprises and foreign enterprises can compete on equal terms, and (3) to strengthen . . . the quality of the enterprises and reorganize the industrial structure so that Japanese enterprises and industries can fully compete against their foreign rivals." In addition, the government made explicit reference to foreign investors and requested them to be bound by the following ten commandments:

1. They should seek coexistence and coprosperity with Japanese enterprises by preferring, for the time being, joint ventures on a substantially equal basis.
2. They should avoid concentrating their investments in specific industries.
3. They should not unduly suppress Japanese small and medium-sized business by entering industries in which most enterprises are small in scale.
4. They should cooperate with Japanese enterprises in their efforts to maintain order in their respective industries.
5. They should avoid unduly restrictive arrangements with their parent companies abroad, and they should not resort to unreasonable restrictions concerning transactions, or to engage in unfair competition.
6. They should try to contribute to the promotion of technology in Japanese industries, and not to hamper efforts by Japanese enterprises to further their own technological development.
7. They should cooperate with Japan in the improvement of the nation's balance of payments by such means as the promotion of export trade.
8. They should employ Japanese nationals as officers, and they should try to offer shares on the open market.
9. They should avoid closure of plants or mass dismissal, and they should avoid unnecessary confusion concerning employment and wages by paying due regard to prevailing practices.
10. They should cooperate with the government in its economic policy.

Given these general guidelines, what were the specific steps taken by the government to implement the liberalization program?

First, it made a distinction between cases in which a foreign investor would acquire the shares of an already existing firm and those in which it would establish a new joint-venture firm by liberalizing only in the second case. Acquisitions remained under control. Even at the end of this period, the foreign acquisition of equity of an existing firm was limited to 25 percent.

Second, the government divided Japanese industry into hundreds of categories, almost on a product-by-product basis, and liberalized individual categories of industry only after it was satisfied that such industry possessed sufficient competitive strength vis-à-vis Western rivals. Liberalized industries were further divided into two kinds: (1) those in which 100 percent foreign ownership was permitted, and (2) those in which only 50 percent foreign ownership was permitted.

Between 1967 and 1970, three steps were taken by the government to expand the scope of the liberalized categories (i.e., in which 100 percent foreign ownership was possible). As a result, by 1970, 77 industries were

100 percent liberalized, while 445 categories remained in the 50 percent category. This process was slow and was very much restrained by perceived national interests.

Oil Crisis and After: The Completion of Liberalization and the Decline of Effectiveness of Government-Business Cooperation

The process of liberalizing foreign direct investment was finally completed only in the fourth phase of economic development, which started in the early 1970s and still continues.

In 1971, *all* categories of industries were liberalized at least up to 50 percent foreign ownership. In the meantime, the number of industries included in the 100 percent category increased from 77 to 228, including the automotive industry.

There was an indication that the Japanese government thought that the 50 percent liberalization, with some exceptional cases in which 100 percent foreign ownership would be permitted, was the final step to be taken. However, the nation's economy continued to grow during the 1970s and, as a result, trade imbalances expanded, thereby causing problems for many of Japan's trading partners. To restore the equilibrium, foreign pressure on Japan to open up its domestic market more broadly for foreign direct investments intensified.

Consequently, the Japanese government felt compelled by 1973 to liberalize further. This time, the government declared that all industries, except for a limited number of restricted categories, were liberalized, thereby allowing foreign investors to own 100 percent of firms with but few exceptions. At the same time, the 50 percent liberalized category was abolished. It was also announced that a foreign investor could acquire in most instances any percentage of the equity of existing firms, provided that such acquisition was approved by the management of the acquired firms.

For the first time, the rule of "permission as a general rule and prohibition as an exception" was realized. The change in the basic rule necessitated a major revision of the Foreign Exchange and Foreign Trade Control Law (Law No. 65 of 1979) in 1979, as already explained.

The limited category of restricted industries, in the beginning, included such important industries as integrated circuits, pharmaceuticals, electronics, precision machines, computers and information, and photo-film materials. But by 1980 all such restricted industries had been liberalized. Still remaining exceptions are agriculture, forestry, fisheries, mining, and leather and leather goods industries. The reservation of these industries could be explained easily in terms of national security and protection of minority groups.

Why did the Japanese government and business surrender so easily to the foreign pressure for liberalization in the fourth phase of economic development? In my opinion, there are several valid reasons for this phenomenon.

First, as Japan had grown into a major economic power, government and business realized that the implementation of the liberalization obligation became necessary in order to fulfill the nation's international responsibility.

Second, some Japanese firms in such fields as electronics and automotives were finding improved opportunities for growth overseas rather than domestically, as already explained. They were, in fact, becoming multinationals and were no longer one-country-based firms. If they wished to have freedom of operation in overseas markets, as a matter of reciprocity, they had to recognize a similar freedom for overseas competitors who might choose to operate in Japan. In some cases, great advantage was found by Japanese firms in their cooperation with overseas partners when they entered into either horizontal or vertical divisions of labor in a complementary way. The benefit from such cooperation could be doubled if transacted in nonregulated free markets.

Third, Japanese firms in certain other fields might prefer government protection, it being easier for them to survive behind a protective wall. However, neither government nor business continued to be as confident as formerly in forming a common front against foreign pressure, based on a so-called national consensus.

The last point relating to the loss of confidence in sharing a common objective may need a further explanation, for it illustrates the changing pattern of relationship between Japanese government and business in recent years. During the most recent phase of the economic development, the oil crisis hit Japan, which, in my opinion, changed the Japanese government-business relationship and caused a decline in the effectiveness of the cooperative relationship. Until that crisis, the concerted efforts of government and business had generated tremendous economic growth and, as a result, affluence. As long as the growth and affluence continued, it was safe to assume that the majority of people living within the system of Japan Incorporated were more or less content. There had been a national consensus to support the joint efforts of the politicians, the government bureaucrats, and business leaders—the three constituents of Japan Incorporated. The object was survival in the first phase of Japan's economic development, and catching up with the Western business and industry in the second and third phases.

However, after the oil crisis hit Japan, the situation changed greatly. Economic growth went down sharply. When the economic growth no longer supported improvement of living conditions, people began to lose confidence in the concept and system of Japan Incorporated. Simultaneously, many dilemmas hidden by the rapid economic growth surfaced. People came to realize that the rapid growth not only produced serious "pollution" but also broadened the "welfare gap" within the Japanese community. They started to criticize the three constituents of the system for the extremity of their economic rationalism and began to search for a life worthier of living. Quality of life became a principal issue.

The major constituents of Japan Incorporated were shocked by this development, and tried to win back popular confidence by implementing new policies for a resurgence of economic growth. But they soon found their power to do so restrained by worldwide recession.

Even today, the government, together with business representatives, continues to work on major economic programs. These programs include dispersion of industries to the countryside, prevention of further spread of pollution, restructuring of industries, conservation of energy and other resources, and promotion of research and development in advanced technologies.

It is difficult, however, to find mutual interest between business and government except for the last item above,—the promotion of advanced research. Moreover, none of the above-mentioned goals is broad enough to win national consensus to the extent that the former goals of "survival" or "catching up with the Western business and industry" did. Under the circumstances, business began to make an alliance with the government only when convenient.

If a system similar to that of Japan Incorporated is to survive as an important element in Japanese economic dynamism, it will be necessary for the major constituents of the system—the politicians, government bureaucrats, and business leaders—to find another objective by which they can win back the confidence of the people, both inside and outside the system.

It is obvious that further delay in the progress of liberalization relating to foreign direct investment is not a national goal that will find support by the majority of Japanese, who live in a world of international interdependence and who have already realized the limitation to growth.

A FEW AFTERTHOUGHTS

For a long time after World War II, the Japanese economy suffered from the shortage of foreign exchange, the backwardness of its technological development, and a dearth of capital. All these problems could have been solved much faster if Japan had adopted a more open-type system for the inducement of inward foreign direct investment. However, the Japanese government relied on a closed, rather than an open-type, system. It was very selective, indeed, in making choices with respect to volume, kinds and types of foreign capital, and technology to be introduced into the country. The screening tended to be a somewhat arbitrary, time-consuming procedure. The broad range of "administrative guidance" exercised by the government in connection with the validation process became notorious, as it seemed to represent an abusive use of bureaucratic discretion.

Nevertheless, the end result was remarkable. Very few Japanese after the war could have dreamed of the economic and business success that would be achieved and realized 40 years later. Within the Japanese economy, the influence of powerful foreign rivals was kept to a minimum. More recently, Japanese business has become an exporter, rather than an importer, of many kinds of managerial resources.

In the past 40 years, Japanese business reaction to the government policy with respect to inward direct foreign investment has been split between support and opposition. Also, it has been true that those who were in opposition as a general rule changed their attitude when their immediate interests were involved directly. In such cases, they formed an alliance of convenience with the government in order to win from foreign investors more favorable terms for tie-ups than originally proposed.

However, the end perhaps justified the process and means. At present, the majority of people involved in business seem to find satisfaction, in retrospect, in the way their government dealt with inward foreign direct investment. But does that mean that the adoption of a closed and selective type of system is to be recommended for another country anxious to promote such investment? The answer to that question is conditional, in that it depends on the existence of certain environmental factors.

First, foreign investors whom one wishes to invite to invest may have become wiser and more prudent than before in making the investment decision, given the past 40 years of experience. They may no longer be willing to accept strict restraints imposed on their investment by a host country government. In the world of increasing economic interdependence, investors may easily find many alternatives for profitable investment. Also, the type of technology involved may be more complicated and sophisticated than that available 40 years ago. The more complicated and sophisticated the technologies are, the more advantages may be recognized by investors in a total package type transfer. By "total package type" transfer we mean a transfer of technology together with the management methods and culture out of which the technology in question developed, that is, direct foreign investment rather than a contractual transfer.

Second, for an effective selection of direct foreign investment, a country must be equipped with a group of government officials foresighted enough to see the long-term requirements of the country's business and industry and who have expert knowledge and sufficient wisdom to make a distinction among available resources—capital and technology—as to which are appropriate and useful (with respect to timing and sequence) for the country's business and industry and those that are otherwise. Japan is very fortunate to have had a long tradition of an excellent bureaucracy consisting of many officials possessing good foresight and judgment.

Third, the business and industry receiving foreign direct investment must have the motivation and capability to digest, use, and develop the imported resources for their independent growth. Japanese business and industry have been successful because they did not stop simply with the receipt of valuable foreign resources. They worked hard to digest them, use them gainfully for their own independent development, and, in many cases (as has been observed in connection with the development of the management system known as "total quality control"), improved upon them in practical application. In the meantime, they have employed a large portion of the earnings accrued from their foreign tie-ups in the improvement of corporate management and in research and development undertaken upon their own initiative. Without these types of untiring self-propelled efforts, Japanese business and industry would have become increasingly dependent on foreign direct investors and, as a result, more subjected to foreign influence than, in fact, they are.

History may or may not be repeated. The successful experience of Japan is possibly unique because of the particular situation in which it was placed after World War II and because of several factors discussed in this chapter.

For a country anxious to promote foreign direct investment, it is necessary to make a careful assessment of its situational and factor endowments, compare them with those of Japan, and then develop its own strategy deemed to be most appropriate and gainful, given its particular situation and endowment.

BIBLIOGRAPHY OF USEFUL WORKS

Abeggien, James C. *Business Strategies for Japan*. Tokyo: Sophia University Press, 1971.

Fukui, Hiroo (ed.). *A Commentary on the Foreign Exchange Law*. Tokyo: Kinyu Zaisei Jijo Kenkyukai, 1981. In Japanese.

Johnson, Chalmers. *MITI and the Japanese Miracle*. Palo Alto, Calif.: Stanford University Press, 1982.

Kobayashi, Noritake. *Joint Venture in Japan*. Tokyo: Toyo Keizai Shimposha, 1967. In Japanese.

————— . *The World of Japanese Business*. Tokyo: Kodansha International, 1969.

————— . "Foreign Investment in Japan." In I. A. Litvak and C. J. Maule (eds.), *Foreign Investment: The Experience of Host Countries*. New York: Praeger, 1971.

————— . "Japanese Experiences and Prospects for International Joint Ventures." In Cameron (ed.), *Private Investments and International Transactions in Asia and South Pacific Countries*. Tokyo: Mathew Bender, 1974.

————— . *Japanese Multinational Enterprises*. Tokyo: Chuo Keizaisha, 1980. In Japanese.

_____ . "The Present and Future of Japanese Multinational Enterprises." *The Wheel Extended* 11:3 (1981). Published by the Toyota Motor Sales Company.

Komiya, Tyutaro et al. (eds.). *Japanese Industrial Policy*. Tokyo: Tokyo University Press, 1984. In Japanese.

Ministry of International Trade and Industry. *The Movements of the Foreign Capital Affiliated Companies*. Tokyo. MITI, 1984. In Japanese.

Vogel, Ezra F. *Japan as Number One*. Cambridge, Mass.: Harvard University Press, 1979.

Yoshida, Fujio. *Capital Liberalization and Foreign Investment Law*. Tokyo: Zaisei Keizai Kohosha, 1967. In Japanese.

Part Three

COSTS AND BENEFITS

Chapter Six

A Survey of the Theory of Direct Investment in Developing Countries

Richard S. Eckaus

OBJECTIVE AND SCOPE

The objective of this chapter is to provide a survey and assessment of the economic theories of foreign investment in developing countries. For the most part the perspective of these theories is that of the economy receiving the investment, not the problems of the firm making the investment. In some analyses, however, both sets of issues are treated to assess the overall impact of the investment.

I will make a number of references to the possible relevance for China of the theories of foreign investment, but I will not concentrate on these implications. There are, in any case, relatively few immediate consequences of the theories for policy in China or in any other country. Rather, the theories suggest issues that require individual attention in each country receiving foreign investment. Moreover, my knowledge of the Chinese economy is quite limited. When I can draw some practical lessons, I will assume that the Chinese economy has many of the features of other developing economies, being distinguished by its unique history and institutions and its size.

This survey will focus on direct investment, that is, investment carried out directly by producing firms. However, most of the rigorous theory of foreign investment, as part of the real theory of international trade, does not make a clear distinction between the conditions and consequences of direct as compared to equity investment. Since that theory does provide useful insights, it will be surveyed briefly.[1]

It is assumed that the focus of this volume is on investment in production units, so this chapter will not consider lending by international agencies or commercial banks to government authorities. The macroeconomic issues related to the latter type of investment will, therefore, also not be considered.

The perspective on China as a developing country has immediate implications in the assessment of direct foreign investment issues. Many developing countries, because of their poverty and small size, have limited markets for new products and new technologies. Their labor force, for the most part, possesses only traditional skills. Goods and services, which are required as complementary inputs to modern production establishments, are, locally, quite scarce, so foreign firms have to produce many of these goods themselves, rather than purchase them.

China's large size, in terms of its population and geography, will offset some of these conditions. Although the domestic market for some goods that are common in the developed countries will be small, relatively speaking, the total market may, nonetheless, be large enough in absolute size to support a wide range of new production facilities. The wide geographical dispersion of the markets may justify more than one or just a few plants. Likewise, because of its size and diversity, as well as its previous history of industrialization, some of its labor force, if not already skilled in the necessary techniques, will be more adaptable to new methods and also more capable of local production than is true in many developing countries.

China's size is also, to some extent, a determinant of the significance of foreign investment and the potential impact it can have. An example of this point can be demonstrated by the following approximate calculation. China's gross domestic product (GDP), which is roughly the same as its gross national product (GNP), is listed in the World Bank's *World Development Report, 1984*, at $260 billion in 1984.[2] Its investment rate was recorded at 28 percent of its GDP. This implies a total investment of about $73 billion. That is a large number in absolute terms and one that will undoubtedly continue to grow in the future.

In some developing countries, foreign investment accounts for 30 percent or more of total annual investment. For China that would correspond to a foreign capital inflow of $22 billion. While there have been flows of this size to a single country for a single year, as in the case of Mexico in 1981, they are highly unusual. In the current state of retrenchment in the international markets, lending at this level appears unlikely in the near future. International financial market conditions can, of course, be expected to change in the future, but such changes are especially difficult to predict. Nonetheless, foreign investment is unlikely to have the same relative significance in China as in many other developing countries in providing foreign saving, simply because of the magnitude of China's economy. However, even if the foreign investment were much less than 30 percent of total investment, it could be quite important for the new products and technologies that it carries. Thus, the composition of foreign investment in China may be more important than its magnitude.

Another aspect of the importance of the sheer size of China in assessing the potential role of foreign investment is related to the generation of exports. Again a simple comparison will be helpful. In 1982, according to the World Bank's *World Development Report, 1984*, the exports of South Korea, for example, were 39 percent of its GNP. The absolute size of those exports was $27 billion, according to the World Bank *Report*; China's exports in the same year were roughly equal to South Korea's. If China's exports were the same fraction of its GDP as was true in Korea, those exports would have to be more than $100 billion, which is, in absolute terms, large indeed. To maintain the ratio as China grows, as it surely will, exports would have to climb at the same rate. This implies that foreign markets would be penetrated by Chinese exports to an almost unprecedented degree. Given the pressures already being exerted by the developed countries on the newly industrializing countries to limit their exports, it would be difficult for China to do this. Therefore, while foreign investment can be expected to help in generating exports, it can not, in relative terms, be expected to perform the same role in this respect in China as it has in other developing countries.

These comments are meant only to suggest the kinds of pragmatic issues that must be kept in mind, and to provide perspective, as the theory of foreign investment is taken up.

THE GENERAL CHARACTER OF THE THEORY OF FOREIGN INVESTMENT

The "real" theory of foreign investment, which will be the subject of this chapter, should be distinguished from the analysis of the financial and balance-of-payments effects of foreign investment, which is a separate and equally elaborately detailed area of investigation. The real theory, in turn, falls mainly into two categories. The first might be called the "pure" theory and is an aspect of the more general subject of the theory of factor mobility in international trade. This type of analysis is, for the most part, carried out formally in the conventional 2 × 2 model, that is, with the convenient assumptions that there are only two countries, producing and trading only two goods. The second type of foreign investment theory is generally less formal. It is specifically concerned with the activities of multinational corporations and is, characteristically, more a set of stories than theories. It is in some ways closer to current realities, but there can be less assurance of its scope and generality, simply because it is less rigorous.

As will become clear, there are important insights to be gained from both types of foreign investment theories that emphasize different problems and potentials associated with foreign investment. Yet the theories of foreign investment are far from complete and provide, directly, only a few clear prescriptions and details for the formation of policy. In order to evaluate particular investment projects in terms of their contribution to national welfare and development, specific analyses have to be undertaken for which the general theory provides some guidelines. This means that, in this area as in others, China will have to find its own way.

It should be noted that both the formal and the less rigorous theories are alike in presuming that it is at least potentially possible to evaluate the social as well as the private costs and returns to foreign investment. It would divert this chapter too far from its subject to take up the subject of social cost/benefit analysis. But the ideas of social cost/benefit analysis will always be in the background.

It will help to follow the discussion to understand the character of the economic theory of direct foreign investment. There is no general theory beyond the proposition that, if not impeded, there is a tendency for capital to flow to the area in which it has a higher return. Beyond this, the theory of direct foreign investment consists of a set of separate hypotheses and examples of particular circumstances that can give rise to such investment and, in some cases, analyses of its welfare consequences.

The next section of the chapter will survey the theory of foreign investment as a part of real international trade theory. The relevant insights will be pointed out. The third section will turn to discussions of international investment by multinational corporations. These discussions, for the most part, exist separately from the theory that is discussed in the section that follows. Again the relevant insights will be pointed out.

THE THEORY OF CAPITAL MOBILITY
IN INTERNATIONAL TRADE

The theory of international factor movements, which includes the movement of capital, or foreign investment, is an intensively cultivated area of international trade theory, as indicated by the devotion of an entire recent issue of the *Journal of International Economics* to the subject.[3] The theory concentrates on the welfare effects of such movements and the consequences of various types of policy interventions. The movement of capital is the result of differential returns in different countries, with some differences in the explanation of such differentials.

The Hecksher-Ohlin-Samuelson Model

The most thoroughly worked version of the theory of international trade is that which is based on the Hecksher-Ohlin-Samuelson (HOS) model. In this theoretical model the basic technological assumptions are that the production technologies are equally well-known in all trading countries and are characterized by constant returns to scale. It is also assumed that there are no transportation costs and that productive factors are internationally immobile. As noted, the theory is worked out in a world of just two trading countries, which may be a "home" country and the "rest of the world." The most detailed results are developed for static conditions, such as a timeless equilibrium, and for comparative statics, which is a comparison of two such equilibria.

The conventional assumption of this type of theory with respect to economic structure has been that there are perfectly competitive markets for all outputs and inputs. However, an intensively worked branch of the theory consists of analyses of the consequences for trade and welfare of specific types of market imperfections and interventions.

The basis for mutually advantageous international trade in the HOS model is the different proportions in which the primary production inputs are available in the different countries. That is the source of the familiar explanation that a country with a large labor force relative to its capital endowment will export goods produced with relatively labor-intensive technologies and import goods produced with relatively capital-intensive technologies.

While immobile productive factors are the starting point for the theory of international trade, it has been extended to analyze the implications of capital mobility on the assumption that capital moves toward the location that maximizes its expected return. The conventional assessment of the effects of the addition of capital to the endowments of one country, without a reduction in the capital of the source country, is that there will be an increase in the aggregate welfare of both countries. It is, in general, simply better for everyone if there are more productive resources in the world than if there are fewer.

However, it has been demonstrated with considerable ingenuity that, while aggregate welfare would be improved by foreign investment, the welfare of the nationals in the country receiving the investment might not change or might even decline.

The first possibility of no effect arises when the foreign investment is so small relative to the entire economy that it has no discernible effect on the composition or magnitudes of trade and there are no "distortions" in the efficiency with which resources are allocated. Under these assumptions the foreign capital would receive a "rental" that would be exactly equal to the value of its private marginal product and that would be the same as its social marginal product. On the other hand, if the foreign capital inflow is "large," then in the absence of "distortions" or "imperfections," to be defined and described later, it could normally be expected that there would be a gain in welfare. That would arise because the rate of return to capital, which would be equal to the value of its marginal product, would be the same whether evaluated from a private or social point of view.

The distortions that are of concern are those conditions that would make it impossible for markets to work as if perfectly competitive—or for government authorities to simulate the perfect allocations of a market. Such distortions or imperfections arise from economies of scale, external economies, monopoly power, imperfect information, and government interventions that are not, themselves, perfectly designed.

These results appear to be straightforward extensions of the conventional theory of resource allocation without distortions. Yet the conditions under which they are valid are actually quite strict and the formal real theory of foreign investment has been preoccupied with demonstrating those conditions and the limits to the theoretical results. Several different types of circumstances in which foreign investment could be "immiserizing" for the receiving country have been demonstrated. This is an apparently paradoxical result and might be worrisome to a country contemplating the encouragement of substantial capital inflows, so it is desirable to understand how it might come about. The paradox has several alternative sources and sorting them out carefully requires a more detailed theoretical exposition than would be appropriate here. The exposition will, therefore, be heuristic and intuitive, with apologies to those who would prefer to see the formal structure of the arguments.[4]

One possible source of immiserization due to foreign investment can be explained in the following way. Suppose that foreign capital is introduced into a country engaged in trade with perfect markets for outputs and inputs. Suppose also that the consequence is a change in the patterns and terms of trade. With perfect factor markets each factor would receive the new value of its marginal product. That would imply a shift in the relative incomes of labor and capital because of the different intensities with which they are used in production of the two goods. Suppose, furthermore, that this shift is so biased and large that the income of labor actually declines. Since the labor is wholly national and the capital is at least partly foreign, the national income could decline even though gross domestic product would rise. The result requires a change in international trade patterns and results from the relations between relative returns to inputs and the relative prices of the goods in which they are relatively intensively used in production.

Perhaps a quotation from Bhagwati will help:

To understand the possibility of a fall in national welfare despite a rise in aggregate welfare, it might be tempting to go no further than the following simple observation. Whenever the national aggregate endowments exhibit different capital/labor ratios, the domestic relative distribution of income might deteriorate for nationals, as a change in relative commodity prices alters the wage/rental ratio for reasons expounded by Stolper and Samuelson (1941). It is important to recognize, however, that generally this income-redistribution effect will not be strong enough to produce the differential responses in national and aggregate welfare if the relative factor-endowment discrepancy is too small to create either the differential trade-volume or the differential trade-pattern phenomenon. Even when either of these phenomena arises, moreover, a fall in national welfare despite a rise in aggregate welfare can occur if and only if certain specific conditions . . . are satisfied.[5]

As suggested by Bhagwati, the capital movement can induce changes in both the patterns of trade and the volume of trade and it is these combined with changes in relative factor prices that can create a loss in national welfare, even when there are perfect markets. As he notes elsewhere, and in other contexts, conclusions of this type are the result of some type of "imperfection" that may not be immediately obvious. In this case the "imperfection" is the failure of the capital-receiving country to impose an optimal tax on the income of the foreign investment. The clear example is the case in which the capital investment is supplied completely inelastically, that is, a fixed amount would occur regardless of the associated rewards. Then a 100 percent tax could be imposed without discouraging any of the investment and the difference between the national and the aggregate welfare results of the capital movement would disappear.[6]

Before going on to still other theoretical analyses, it might be helpful to stop and consider whether there are practical implications for China in these theoretical results. This is a difficult question to answer as it is well known that dropping even one of the simplifying assumptions of the theory can reverse results. First, it must be recognized that the technological and market assumptions of the theory do not accord with reality. The technological issues can be set aside at this point and taken up later. The market assumptions can be utilized if they are not taken literally. We can conduct the discussion as if there were such perfect markets, if, alternatively, it is assumed that there exists some other type of allocation system for goods and factors that generates economic efficiency. In this latter interpretation, the "prices" to which reference is made can be interpreted as shadow prices reflecting accurately the real relative scarcities in the economy.

The theoretical analyses use differential calculus and require the evaluation of differential changes. In the world of theory this is an appropriate procedure. In the world of policy it is necessary to ask whether those differentials are likely to be large enough to be significant. As noted above, China's size makes it different from nearly all other developing and developed countries. Perhaps it is not correct to assume that China constitutes a single supplying source of productive inputs rather than consisting of a set of separate sources that are not fully interconnected. Even so, the goods and factor supplies and demands that are interconnected are quite large. It seems unlikely that the foreign investment that will take place in China, even if concentrated in export industries or import substituting industries, will, in the near future, be sufficiently large to change relative factor prices, even taking into account changes in trade patterns and volumes. This immiserization effect, therefore, seems practically unlikely within any short period.

The theory does suggest some issues that are relevant to policy, however. In particular the question of the optimal taxation of foreign investment is raised. There are, presumably, benefits to foreigners from investing in China and it is desirable for China and foreign investors to consider how those benefits will be shared through taxes and/or other conditions.

Market Imperfections and Their Impact

The theory of the effects of foreign investment takes several different directions once the assumption is dropped of perfect markets without policy interventions. Foreign investment with monopoly power, with increasing returns to scale, and in the presence of tariffs and other market imperfections have all been subjects of analysis.

It is recognized that when there are perfect markets all around or some equivalently efficient means of allocating resources, aggregate welfare cannot be improved by the imposition of an export or import subsidy to encourage trade or an export or import tax to discourage trade. When there is foreign investment that earns income that accrues to foreigners, there is a difference between aggregate welfare and national welfare. In this case, which is of interest here, the previous ranking of free trade versus subsidized or taxed trade may be reversed. Tariffs or subsidies that would reduce aggregate welfare may possibly improve national welfare. The key to this result again lies in the possibility that such policy interventions may result in advantageous relative changes in trade volumes or patterns and returns to national factors of production, as distinct from foreign factors of production. These might be so advantageous that they more than offset the negative effects of tariffs or subsidies. Correspondingly, a reduction in tariffs may actually lead to a decline in national welfare, if foreign capital is present in a country. To put the results in still a different way, foreign investment, which in other circumstances may be mutually beneficial, may result in a decline in national welfare if there is a distortionary tariff. The results are sensitive to particular technical conditions on the effects of relative price changes and the shares of factors in total returns, which cannot be stated readily in a nonmathematical way.[7]

Foreign investment can benefit the receiving country, in the absence of foreign "distortions," even if there are certain types of domestic conditions that would not prevail if there were perfect efficiency in the allocation of resources. Perhaps the most obvious example of this occurs when there are unemployed or underemployed resources, or when there are resources that receive a wage that is higher than the shadow value of their social marginal product. This condition is commonly alleged to be widespread in the labor force of many developing countries. I will not attempt to judge whether it is true in China, but will merely present the argument. In this case, and assuming no other distortions, an inflow of foreign capital would not only generate its additional marginal product but would raise the national product by increasing the productive employment of the otherwise unemployed or underemployed labor.[8]

By comparison, an inflow of capital can immiserize rather than be beneficial when economic growth and expansion of foreign trade would be immiserizing, whether growth results from domestic capital formation or foreign capital inflows. Immiserizing growth can have more than one source. Perhaps the easiest example and explanation of this theoretical possibility is the situation in which the demand for exports is so inelastic that an expansion of exports due to growth actually results in a decline in income.[9]

The literature reveals few clear examples of immiserization through growth, so perhaps this theoretical possibility need not be taken too seriously in the specific Chinese context. The lack of examples may, however, be due to the international trade theorists' reluctance to extrapolate the implications of their 2 × 2 models.

This last case provides a simple lesson for a country: Be cautious about accepting foreign investment that will produce so much of a commodity that, when it is traded abroad, it will change the relative price of the commodity. Perhaps it is not necessary to invoke the entire machinery of the immiserizing growth analysis to come to this conclusion, but it does reinforce the caution. It should also be noted that a good social cost/benefit analysis of a project should demonstrate whether the danger of immiserizing growth is a real concern.

Tariff policies can also create conditions under which foreign investment can be immiserizing. The simplest example is the situation in which there is a relatively small level of foreign investment that is used to produce a good that will be consumed domestically. Suppose the project can make private profits only because of a tariff barrier that protects the domestic market. Putting aside the infant industry argument, which might eventually justify the tariff and domestic production, the tariff and consequent investment would create a welfare loss for the country. That welfare loss is intensified because it is imposed fully on the nationals, if the foreign investment is allowed to repatriate profits at a normal rate.

There have been a number of studies of the effects of import substitution policies of the type just described. Although these are not completely conclusive, they do indicate that such policies have often been counterproductive in terms of overall growth.[10]

These last examples make a general point: There can be no assurance that investment projects will add to the national welfare, if they are not justified in terms of shadow prices that reflect real resource scarcities. For any particular set of social goals and resource and technological constraints, there is, presumably, only one relevant set of efficient allocations and corresponding set of shadow prices, while there are an infinity of ways to make costly mistakes. These mistakes can be compounded if the investment is foreign and receives an internationally competitive return and all the losses are borne domestically.

It is possible to imagine foreign capital inflows in some countries that are so large that they change the relative shadow prices of resources within a country. In this case it can become efficient to export goods that, prior to the capital inflows, would not have been exported. This case seems unlikely for China, given its size. On the other hand, the temptations will always be present for foreign investment to promise domestic production if it is protected by a tariff wall, even though that investment would not be justified on strict efficiency grounds and would, in effect, reduce national welfare.

MULTINATIONAL CORPORATIONS AND FOREIGN INVESTMENT

The theory of international investment surveyed above is both a positive and a normative theory. As a positive theory, which attempts to explain why foreign investment occurs, it says only that such investment responds to potential earnings differentials that have their source in goods and factor price differences, whatever their sources, including various economic imperfections and distortions. As a normative theory of the welfare effects of international capital mobility under different conditions, it points out the potential disadvantages of such capital mobility. It is, however, a theory that is divorced from the institutions that bring the capital, divorced from history, and divorced from technological change and many other conditions that affect the reality of foreign investment. Foreign investment in the previously described theory could be equity capital, debt finance, or direct investment by foreign businesses. None of the unique features of these alternative types of investment are taken into account in this type of theory of capital mobility.

Yet our most common observations of foreign investment strongly suggest that the form of the investment does in fact make a difference for the totals of capital transferred, the conditions of the transfer, and the effects on the receiving countries. Foreign investment, like other features of economic life, does not wait on theorists to explain why it exists nor for understanding of its broad social and economic implications. The last 30 years or so have seen a burgeoning of foreign private investment in developing countries by multinational corporations and, more recently, by commercial bank lending abroad. This chapter, as noted, deals only with direct investment.

The role of the multinationals in world trade and especially their effects on developing countries have been the subject of a tremendous volume of speculation and a more modest amount of careful study in the last three decades or so.[11] It has been as if foreign direct investment as economic and political phenomena were being discovered by social scientists for the first time. For a country with as intense a sense of history as China, it comes as no surprise that foreign business is different from domestic business in many important ways.

There has been a great deal of hypothesizing about the reasons for multinational investment. The "product cycle theory" with respect to the patterns of investment by multinationals, is a prominent example.[12] There is also a rapidly expanding literature as to its economic, social, and political effects in developing countries. With a few recent exceptions, this literature is seldom rigorous and even less frequently do the descriptions have a quantitative basis that can be used to test the theory. Yet the existing literature does provide a number of important perceptions and suggests areas for further investigation in the specifically Chinese context, so that a survey will be enlightening.

The alternative to foreign direct investment when there are differences in the returns to capital are debt or equity investment in production units or flows of capital to local financial institutions, which then make the funds available to local enterprise. These alternatives to MNC investment would use financial and goods markets for the transfers necessary to establish and carry out the business activities. MNCs, on the other hand, rely on integrated operations within a single firm for such transfers. This does not mean that multinationals fully integrate their overseas and home country operations, but at least some part of their total operations must be integrated, unless the multinational, in effect, performs as an overseas venture capital firm.

These observations suggest that, to explain the prominence of MNCs, it is necessary to explain why firms integrate domestic and overseas operations rather than rely on the operations of markets or their equivalents. To some degree the hypotheses presented above are reasons, both alternative and complementary, for such integration.[13]

It is useful to keep in mind that there are important potential advantages in reliance on markets—or their equivalents. Local managers and financial institutions know local institutions and laws, have knowledge of local suppliers and local markets and the problems of managing the local labor force, and, by definition, are not subject to discriminatory treatment as foreign firms. These are advantages that must be offset by other disadvantages, if MNC operations are to be justified.[14] The procedure to be followed in this section will be to present and evaluate briefly the alternative explanations of MNC investment that have been offered.

Direct Investment As Portfolio Diversification

There are different kinds and distributions of risk in foreign investment as compared to domestic investment. That makes foreign investment potentially valuable as a means of diversifying portfolios in order to reduce risk as well as increase average returns. It might be argued that the benefits of diversification could be obtained through foreign equity investment but, for various reasons, that option might not exist, especially in developing countries. There are not many developing countries with stock markets or other formal channels for acquiring business equity. Seldom are there the detailed and reliable regulations for public disclosure of business operations and specific and well-established legal procedures that are necessary to encourage large-scale transfers of business equity. Thus, in order to take advantage of the opportunities for diversification, it may be necessary for firms to undertake direct investment in developing countries especially.

There have been some tests of the hypothesis that direct investment by MNCs in the United States and Europe can be explained as a means of portfolio diversification.[15] The results of these tests suggest that the hypothesis can, at best, account for only a relatively small part of such investment. There have been few, if any, tests of the hypothesis with respect to direct investment in developing countries. A good test is likely to find some value in the hypothesis simply because the developing countries offer a different set of risks and returns as compared to investments in advanced countries.

The arguments posed against the portfolio diversification hypothesis are:

1. It does not account for the fact that some of the funds used for foreign investment are often raised in the country of destination.
2. The investment is usually in the same type of activities as in the home country, rather than in different types of production.
3. Only a limited amount of autonomy is allowed to foreign subsidiaries.
4. Multinational subsidiaries are actually geographically concentrated rather than being spread over the globe.

These counterarguments are not conclusive, however. In fact the conditions to which they allude could easily be consistent with and even supportive of multinational investment as portfolio diversification, taking into account differences in costs of funds in different countries, differences in the availability of skills, and differences in market concentration.

Before leaving the hypothesis, it is useful to raise explicitly the question as to against what types of risk MNCs might be diversifying. The usual implication is that the danger foreseen is loss of profitability and net worth associated with a decline in sales or some loss of productive capacity. Other not necessarily consistent motivations for corporate policy have also been advanced. In particular it has often been argued that maintenance of market share is an important corporate goal. This might be especially important in the Chinese context. After all, a market of a billion, even relatively poor, persons could, with a little growth, become a gigantic market.

Direct Investment in Response to
Market Imperfections and Distortions

The most conventional theoretical approach to foreign direct investment now is to regard it as a phenomenon of an oligopolistic market structure, often with differentiated products.[16] This framework can help to account for a number of the most striking features of direct foreign investment: the size of the MNCs, the emphasis on the use of brand names, on competition through quality differentials, and the intense bargaining rather than the "arm's length" transactions that often accompany direct foreign investment.

The "market imperfections" explanations of direct investment take many different forms.[17] One of these finds the reason in the superior ability of foreigners to differentiate the products sold in foreign markets. According to this theory,[18] MNCs have a special advantage in their ability to differentiate products and, by direct investment, can extract monopoly profits based on this ability. While this is a theory that may explain some cases, it is difficult to accept it as a completely general theory. It does not explain why local entrepreneurs cannot be sold or rented those product-differentiating skills, perhaps for a share of whatever local monopoly profits there are to be gained.

There is another type of theory that relies on the mere existence of a domestic market for differentiated products to explain direct investment. In such a market a new firm may be able to make a place for itself by successfully creating a niche for itself through product differentiation. If there are no restrictions on foreign investment, there is no reason why this newcomer should not be an MNC. In one of the few rigorous analyses of the welfare effects of foreign investment where there are differentiated products and economies of scale, it has been demonstrated that investment may flow in the wrong directions and that recipient countries may actually be harmed.[19]

It should not be surprising that market imperfections can make foreign investment counterproductive. Analogous results have already been described above. The problems arise from the differences between private returns and social returns to investment. These can exist not only because of monopoly power, with or without differentiated products, but also because of the existence of public goods elements and externalities in production.

MNC investment may take place because of tariffs or other less-explicit barriers to goods produced abroad, including lack of expert knowledge of the foreign market. Direct investment may also be the result of lack of technical, managerial, and marketing skills abroad that would otherwise generate goods and services desired from a particular country. Capital market imperfections that restrict access to funds or raise their cost inordinately and that constrain production may be overcome only by direct investment that carries funds along with it.

The reasons for direct MNC investment may, therefore, be the same reasons that are often given for the vertical and horizontal integration of firms within the foreign corporation's home country. The firm may, by integrating its operations, avoid the undesirable consequences of market imperfections or create and capture economies of large-scale operation that would otherwise be lost. These may or may not be primarily in production activities, as there may be several plants. They can occur in financing and the various types of management outside of production—for example, internal organization and marketing.

Without integration the firm may generate external economies, benefits that do not flow through markets and that would be lost to the firm if it did not integrate its operations to capture some or all of such benefits. Activities that generate externalities include foreign trade itself, which creates skills that could be lost if there were no direct investment. Trade also generates market acceptance of certain types of products from which local as well as foreign producers can benefit. For various reasons it may be impossible to collect through trade and markets as much of the benefits of technological information or special skills as can be collected through local production.

MNC Investment and the "Product Cycle"

As noted above, the "product cycle" stories about MNC investment, which take various forms, rely, to some degree, on the existence of "imperfections" for their explanations of direct investment.[20] The product cycle stories all describe direct investment as a means of transferring technologies to developing countries that have been developed and exploited first in more advanced countries. Yet, if there were no particular monopolistic advantage held by technological innovators, there would be no foreign investment to exploit that advantage. Without capital market imperfections, the finance necessary for foreign investment would not have to be provided by the MNC itself.

While the product cycle story is insightful in certain cases, there are many types of foreign investment for which it is unsatisfactory: for example, in primary goods production by conventional techniques, in the manufacture of conventional products, and in various service sectors in which management rather than technical skills are critical.

Direct Investment As Imperialism

The theory of imperialism is a rich interweaving of historical forces in which direct investment often has an essential role. From the standpoint of economic theory, the existence of market imperfections and distortions, in turn, accounts for the particular political role that foreign direct investment can have in the receiving country.[21]

Political power may be obtained from the economic capabilities of foreign investors, when they are large relative to local producers and local governments. Political power has been used by foreign investors to obtain special favors, in terms of monopolistic and monopsonistic positions in local markets or freedom from local taxes or access to local subsidies. Political power has also been taken by foreign governments through military actions or the threat of such actions with the objective of gaining economic power for their private firms.

There are many historical and contemporary examples of intervention by governments on behalf of their citizens' investments abroad and many examples of foreign investors using their economic power for political purposes to gain more economic power. It is only to be expected that corporations with economic power at home and abroad, which potentially gives them political power, should try to use both types of power to their own benefit everywhere. Yet it does not follow that all foreign investment must represent economic imperialism. Even if one believes that the tendency always exists, whether it is allowed to become overt and active depends in part on the government of the home country and, to a greater degree, on the government in the country receiving the investment and the success with which the latter imposes rules of conduct on foreign investors.

Direct Investment and Technology Transfer

An aspect of direct investment that has received special attention from its critics and defenders is related to the character of the technologies that are transferred and their "appropriateness" for developing countries. A common complaint is that the technologies were developed for the relative capital/labor ratios and prices and complementary supply and demand conditions of advanced countries. It is argued that the technologies transferred are, therefore, "inappropriate." That means that they do not contribute as much to the national product as similar amounts of resources using technologies without such defects. Inappropriate technologies would, in the absence of market imperfections and distortions, also result in lower profits on the part of the MNCs, so there is a puzzle as to why they would ever be chosen for transfer.

It is impossible to establish the general accuracy of the charge that inappropriate technologies are transferred by MNCs. There are many "horror stories" of clear mistakes being made in the choice of technologies sent to developing countries. Many of these are examples of initiatives by agencies of foreign governments or international institutions rather than private corporations. The clearly larger scale of operations of MNCs in developing countries and differences from traditional technologies are not clearly evidence of mistakes, except for those critics who value small-scale enterprise and traditional techniques for their own sakes.

A number of careful case studies have been carried out that find that the extent to which technologies are adapted to local conditions by MNCs depends on the effectiveness of competition.[22] In those cases in which firms have been able to differentiate their product by quality, branding, and marketing—that is, through the practices of monopolistic competition, there has also been less technological adaptation. Lack of knowledge of technological alternatives and, sometimes but not always, an engineering preference for modernity have been obstacles to technological adaptation.

Direct Investment As Intrafirm Integration in Oligopolistic Markets

It has been noted previously, and is repeated here only for emphasis, that MNC investment takes place because of a preference for integrated operations rather than reliance on market mechanisms. Market contracting mechanisms may not exist, may not operate efficiently, or may not be used by firms because avoiding them creates opportunities for firms to exploit economies of scale or differentiate their products. Or direct investment may be a means by which firms can capture a larger share of the benefits they create than through reliance on external contracts. Multinational operations consist of more than just the transfer of capital, as many analyses make clear. They typically include transfers of technical, managerial, and marketing knowledge, embodied in machines or in people. These transfers, as well as the capital movement, provide benefits to the firm.

There are also, of course, potential benefits to the receiving country in obtaining technologies and skills that would otherwise not be available. In direct investment all of these associated features of the capital flow are "bundled," that is, they are part of the package of products and human and technological capabilities that are transferred along with the capital. Oligopolistic firms prefer the bundling because it provides a means of differentiating their products, of competing with other firms, and a context for bargaining with host countries in which the prices and quantities of the various parts of the bundles are not explicit. On the other hand, these are also reasons why the host country will prefer that the components be "unbundled." This becomes an operational issue in several ways. In particular, when MNCs want to repatriate profits, they must, in effect, reveal a nominal profit rate. If, however, the various components of the investment have been bundled, it will be difficult, if not impossible, to identify the true profit rate.

If MNC investment reflects a preference for integrated operations, then it cannot be easily substituted by portfolio capital flows. Such flows would provide real capital but not the other benefits of the integrated operations of MNCs. The problems associated with bundling may, therefore, be intrinsic ones.

CONCLUSIONS

This survey of the theory of direct international investment reveals that there are potential benefits to the host country from foreign investment. It can bring not only capital but also new technologies and skills that might not otherwise be obtainable. Yet the survey also indicates the various ways in which "distortions" and "imperfections" can lead to foreign investment that may actually reduce the national product of the receiving country, or not increase it by as much as would otherwise be the case, with a different composition, technology, and management.

The theories of international capital mobility are intended to explain not only the circumstances in which capital moves abroad but also the welfare consequences of such movements. The theories of direct investment by multinational corporations, in particular, are essentially stories about the various reasons why firms prefer to integrate their operations across national boundaries. The reasons may have their sources in the riskiness associated with the enterprise, problems of assembling information and making complete contracts, as well as various distortions in the structure of the firms and the economic sectors in which they operate.

"Distortions" are common. They include the cases in which government authorities fail to follow optimal policies as well as the exercise of monopoly power on the part of the firms. There are also externalities and public good effects that result when it is impossible for firms to capture for their capital and entrepreneurial efforts the full benefits of their activities.

The theories of direct investment generate only a few immediate prescriptions for government policies with respect to magnitudes, economic sectors, technologies, and foreign and domestic markets. One general lesson to be drawn from the theories is that there is no guarantee that foreign investment will contribute to national welfare unless decisions are made with the inputs and outputs from that investment valued at prices that reflect their real social scarcities. If this is not the case, it can be expected with confidence that both domestic and foreign investment will contribute less to national welfare than typically promised, and may even subtract from it.

The different theories can also be regarded as suggesting the ways in which market prices have to be adjusted in order to give the signals that will lead to efficiency and, thus, provide accurate guidelines for the evaluation of projects. It should be noted that regional authorities may be no more likely to make accurate social cost/benefits analyses than private firms unless means are provided to insure that they identify their local interests with the national interest.

It may not be possible, and not desirable, to attempt social cost/benefit calculations for all foreign investments. The ability of most governments to carry out such calculations is, at best, limited. This does not mean that social cost/benefit accounting should never be attempted. When the investments are "large" and "critical" for the progress of other sectors, it may well be important for the host country and the investing firm to collaborate in such a calculation. In other cases, a general supervisory consideration of foreign investments may be all that is feasible and all that should be attempted.

Government policy makers and private investors can make two different types of mistakes: with respect to private interests and with respect to the social interest. It is the responsibility of the firm to avoid the former mistake and the responsibility of the government authorities to avoid the latter. For foreign investment to flourish, the exercise of both types of responsibilities must be coherent. Both types of tasks are complicated enormously when an economy is in transition due to rapid growth and structural change. The theories of direct investment suggest only general guidelines as to how to avoid social mistakes and, therefore, must be adapted to local conditions and supplemented by other theories.

NOTES

1. The injunction to focus on the theory of investment was taken seriously so this chapter does not cover all the ways of transferring technology, although that is a common and often dominating aspect of direct investment.

2. World Bank, Washington, D.C., 1984

3. *Journal of International Economics* 14 (1983).

4. The previously cited issue of the *Journal of International Economics* provides a useful guide to the current state of the theory. Other useful recent sources are Bhagwati and Srinavasan (1982) and Bhagwati (1983).

5. Bhadwati (1983), Vol 2, p. 231.

6. Ibid.

7. See Bhadwati (1983), Chs. 53 and 54.

8. Ibid.

9. Ibid.

10. See, for example, Krueger (1978) and Little (1982).

11. Early and influential books were those by Kindleberger (1969) and Vernon (1971 and 1977). For a recent survey with an extensive bibliography, see Kindleberger and Audretsch (1983).

12. See Vernon (1971).

13. For an explicit theoretical treatment of direct foreign investment as a phenomenon of firm integration, see Krugman (1983).

14. Hennart (1982) analyzes foreign direct investment as the expressed preference of a firm for internal control of its operations as distinct from reliance on markets.

15. See, for example, Levy and Sarnat (1970), Prachowny (1982), and Ragazzi (1973).

16. See, for example, Kindleberger and Audretsch (1983) and Stobaugh and Wells (1984).

17. This has been suggested in many places in the preceding discussion. As another example, Aliber (1970) makes the argument that direct foreign investment springs from capital market imperfections.

18. See Caves (1971) and Hennart (1982).

19. See Helpman and Razin (1983).

20. See Hymer, S. H. (1976).

21. See Kierans, E. W. (1983).

22. See Krugman, P. R. (1983).

BIBLIOGRAPHY

Aliber, R. "A Theory of Foreign Direct Investment." In C. P. Kindleberger (ed.), *The International Corporation*. Cambridge, Mass.: MIT Press, 1970.

Bhagwati, J. *Essays in International Economic Theory* Vol. 2, *The Theory of International Factor Mobility*. Cambridge, Mass.: MIT Press, 1983.

Bhagwati, J. and T.N. Srinavasan. *Lectures on International Trade*. Cambridge, Mass.: MIT Press, 1983.

Caves, R. "International Corporations: The Industrial Economics of Foreign Investment." *Economica* 38 (1971), 1–27.

Helpman, E. and A. Razin. "Increasing Returns, Monopolistic Competition, and Factor Movements." *Journal of International Economics* 14 (1983), 263–276.

Hennart, J.-F. *A Theory of Multinational Enterprise*. Ann Arbor: University of Michigan Press, 1982.

Hymer, S. H. *The International Operations of National Firms: A Study of Direct Foreign Investment*. Cambridge, Mass.: MIT Press, 1976.

Kierans, E. W. "Money, Multinationals and Sovereigns." In C. P. Kindleberger and D. B. Audretsch (eds)., *The Multinational Corporation in the 1980s*. Cambridge, Mass.: MIT Press, 1983.

Kindleberger, C. P. *American Investment Abroad: Six Lectures on Direct Investment*. New Haven, Conn.: Yale University Press, 1969.

Kindleberger, C. P. and Audretsch, D. B. *The Multinational Corporation in the 1980s*. Cambridge, Mass.: MIT Press, 1983.

Krueger, Anne, O. *Liberalization Attempts and Consequences*. Cambridge, Mass.: Bollinger 1978.

Krugman, P. R. "The 'New Theories' of International Trade and the Multinational Enterprise." in C. P. Kindleberger and D. B. Audretsch (eds), *The Multinational Corporation in the 1980s*. Cambridge, Mass.: MIT Press, 1983.

Levy, H. and M. Sarnat. "International Diversification of Investment Portfolios," *American Economic Review* 60 (1970), 668–675.

Little, I. M. D. *Economic Development: Theory, Policy, and International Relations*. New York: Basic Books, 1982.

Prachowny, M. J. "Direct Investment and the Balance of Payments of the U.S.: A Portfolio Approach." In F. Machlup, W. Salant, and L. Tarshis (eds.), *International Mobility and Movements of Capital*. New York: National Bureau of Economic Research, 1982.

Ragazzi, G. "Theories of the Determinants of Direct Foreign Investment." *International Monetary Fund Staff Papers* 20 (1973), 471–498.

Stobaugh, R. and Wells, L.T., Jr. (eds.), *Technology Crossing Borders: The Choice, Transfer, and Management of International Technology Flows*. Boston: Harvard Business School Press, 1984.

Vernon, R. *Sovereignty at Bay: The Multinational Spread of US Enterprises*. New York: Basic Books, 1971.

———. *Storm Over the Multinationals: The Real Issues*. Cambridge, Mass.: Harvard University Press, 1977.

Chapter Seven

The Financial Component of Foreign Direct Investment: Implications for Developing Countries

Donald R. Lessard

Foreign direct investment (FDI) involves the transfer across national boundaries of resources, including such intangibles as know-how and access to a global production and marketing system as well as funds, in return for claims on all or part of the future profits of the foreign venture. Thus, it is both an industrial and a financial phenomenon, in contrast to much of the literature that insists it is one or the other. FDI is similar to licensing or contracting in terms of the resources transferred, but it also displays the characteristics of portfolio equity investment in terms of the character of the claims acquired in return for the transferred resources.

This chapter focuses on the nature of the financial claims created through FDI and their effect on the welfare of the host country. These claims are viewed as "sharing rules," which allocate the financial rewards and risks of microlevel activities, typically specific enterprises or projects, between the foreign investor and the host country. Since these rules divide the expected financial returns of the investment between the investor and the host country, it is natural to view the negotiation of investment terms as a zero-sum activity. However, this is not always the case. Efficient sharing rules can provide gains to one party without reducing the benefits to the other in several ways. They can do so by

1. creating incentives for the appropriate design and efficient management of the activities undertaken:
2. allocating the rewards and risks of the project between the investor and the host country in line with their respective comparative advantage in bearing the risks involved; and
3. reducing the "deadweight" contracting costs that result from conflicts of interest between the various parties coupled with the impossibility of creating completely enforceable contracts across national boundaries.

Of course, these microlevel sharing rules also can lead to economic inefficiency if they result in incentives for negative-sum behavior.

Various implications at the micro- and macroeconomic level are drawn from the "sharing rule" perspective of FDI. First, *the financial contribution*

131

of FDI includes three elements: (1) *the capital provided by the foreign firm,* (2) *the risks assumed by the foreign firm, and* (3) *the improved economic performance of the project or enterprise due to the incentives provided by the ownership/contractual structure.* Appearances are often deceiving. A firm's participation in a project may not be what it appears at first glance. A firm that borrows locally in the amount of its full investment and, hence, "brings no capital" may in fact bear a substantial share of the project's risks. Further, a firm that finances the entire project, but receives a host government guarantee for its borrowing, may have little or nothing at risk.

Second, *FDI is only one possible form of foreign involvement that provides for a sharing of risks and returns and, hence, creates incentives for particular behavior.* It is open-ended, exposing the firm to a broad range of risks, in contrast to various forms of incentive contracts that expose the investing firm to a narrower range of risks. The most efficient form of involvement is the one that aligns risk exposures with the comparative advantage of each party in bearing particular risks and is enforceable at a reasonable cost.

Third, *host government interventions alter the sharing of risk and reward in ways that are not always obvious.* Tax systems imply one set of sharing rules. Financial interventions, including concessional credit and loan guarantees, modify these basic rules, as do regulations regarding local financial participation. Further, host taxes interact with firms' home country taxes to determine the overall sharing of returns.

Fourth, *conflicts arise when there is asymmetry in mechanisms for realizing financial returns between the foreign investor and local firms or the host government.* The foreign firm can realize its returns through dividends, interest, fees, and the over- or underpricing of its real transfers. In the case of a joint venture, the local firm has a similar set of mechanisms, but its real interactions can be either more or less extensive than those of the foreign firm, while the host government has tax and regulatory mechanisms for capturing a share of the benefits of a given activity in addition to its direct participation. This possibly asymmetry can lead to conflicts of interest that may seriously distort investment and operating incentives and, perhaps, even block what otherwise would be desirable projects. These conflicts are likely to be most serious when there are controls on profit remittances and other forms of direct financial participation.

This chapter is organized in five parts. "Financial Dimensions of FDI" illustrates the sharing rules implicit in various types of financing and fiscal arrangements, while "Alternative Sharing Rules . . . " discusses their implications for efficiency in the dimensions of management incentives, risk allocation, and contracting costs. "Identifying Appropriate Contracts. . . . ," examines special issues that are likely to be of particular importance in three different contexts: (1) extractive undertakings with large "up-front" expenditures, (2) manufacturing FDI where most of the resources transferred are intangibles, and (3) manufacturing investments oriented toward production for a local market. "The Role of FDI . . . " extends the sharing rule perspective to the national level and contrasts the characteristics of FDI and other forms of contingent finance with general obligation borrowing, the dominant form of external financing employed by developing countries in recent years. The last part concludes the study.

FINANCIAL DIMENSIONS OF FOREIGN DIRECT INVESTMENT

Foreign Direct Investment: Financial or Industrial Phenomenon

At an abstract level, the pattern of international investment, in terms of both the location and ownership of specific undertakings, is the result of the interaction of the supply of investment opportunities and the demand by investors for these opportunities. At an aggregate level, countries with large opportunities relative to available resources tend to draw resources from those countries with fewer opportunities relative to current available resources. Thus it is analogous to the savings/investment interactions among individuals in a simple, closed economy.

Since investment decisions involve trade-offs between *current outlays* and *future, uncertain returns*, the supply/demand equation involves the determination of a price for time (real interest rate) and a price for risk (risk premium). While the determination of the interest rate has been a standard element in economic analysis for some time, the determination of the price of risk and its implication for the valuation of individual undertakings has been developed in the last 20 years. While models of this process differ greatly in their assumptions and degree of complexity, a basic conclusion is that, in equilibrium, the only risks commanding a premium are those that contribute to the variance of aggregate consumption. In other words, risk elements that are idiosyncratic to particular projects, and can be eliminated through diversification, do not represent risk from the viewpoint of society as a whole and, hence, affect the desirability of a specific investment only through their impact on expected future cash flows.[1]

From a financial perspective, firms act as agents on behalf of shareholders. Thus, in theory, their investment decisions reflect a "shadow calculation" of the value that shareholders place on the cash flows resulting from the new undertaking. This is the basis for the net present value rule advocated by academics and increasingly adopted in practice.[2]

FDI is an interesting special case of international investment for several reasons. First and foremost, as noted throughout the literature reviewed in by Eckaus in chapter 6, the time and risk profile of the operating cash flows associated with a particular investment are specific to a particular investing firm. The reason for this is that FDI usually involves the transfer of intangible assets and the incorporation of the venture into an international sourcing, marketing, and technological support system. For example, when General Motors considers an investment in auto production for a specific market, it is shifting countless man-years of experience of auto production and marketing to that country, as well as supplying specific capital goods and components from its existing system. When it invests in a plant to produce components in a particular country for world markets, it not only transfers its know-how, but also integrates this narrow band of activity into its worldwide production of autos. Therefore, the cash flows anticipated by GM are different than those facing, say, Toyota or Hyundai, and certainly different than those facing an indigenous firm. Thus, GM may encounter attractive opportunities in countries that are net international lenders and may not face comparable opportunities in countries that are net borrowers on world markets.

Differences in the profitability (net present value) of a project from different perspectives can be traced to differences in four factors: (1) the initial capital outlay, including investments in intangible assets such as know-how; (2) the pre- (local) tax operating cash flows of the project; (3) the taxes paid out of these operating cash flows, as well as amounts appropriated in other forms by nonshareholder stakeholders, including but not limited to the host or home governments; and (4) the risk-adjusted discount rates that each party applies to the net of tax cash flows that it *expects to appropriate* either directly or indirectly from the project.

The value of the project to a local joint-venture partner differs from its value to a foreign firm because of differences in appropriate cash flows resulting from transfer risks, cross-border taxes, and different externalities within the respective firms arising from differences in the discount rates the two parties may apply because of the different opportunities they face. Similarly, the differences between the value of the project to either firm and the host society differ by the inclusion of taxes and other externalities, the adjustment of prices of inputs and outputs to reflect their social opportunity cost, and any differences in the discount rate due to the society's time and risk preferences as well as its scope for diversification. These differences between private (financial) and social (economic) perspectives are summarized in Figure 7.1

In general, the multinational firm faces higher expected operating cash flows in cases where its experience and joint economies more than compensate for its lack of knowledge of local circumstances and the inevitable costs of operating at great geographical, political, and cultural distance. It faces less-risky operating cash flows in cases where its worldwide scope allows it more flexibility in responding to shifts in world or local conditions.[3]

Figure 7.1   Three Perspectives on Project Profitability

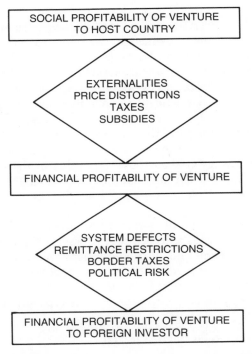

Second, since FDI involves investment across national boundaries, the time and risk profile of the cash flows that the investing firm expects to obtain differ from the underlying operating cash flows of the project, not only by the proportion captured by the host country's fiscal system, but also by the proportion captured by the host country through exchange controls and other mechanisms as well as through potential unilateral modification of the firms' terms of participation, including the extreme of expropriation. While there is a similar wedge between total operating cash flows and the cash flows appropriable by a firm within a single country, the cross-border case typically is more complex because of the existence of macroeconomic transfer risks and the absence of effective mechanisms for the enforcement of contracts.

In some cases, this typically negative relative impact on the multinational firm is offset by its ability to circumvent taxes or transfer controls facing the indigenous firm through the former's multiplicity of channels for cross-border transfers, including dividends, fees, interest on direct or fronting loans, transfer pricing,[4] or by a favorable interaction between home and host taxation.[5] In general, though, these mechanisms at best place it on par with indigenous firms that do not face the same transfer risks or double layer of taxation.

Third, since the foreign firm makes the "shadow calculation" of value on behalf of its shareholders, the time and risk parameters that it incorporates in the discount rate for a particular project are likely to differ from those of the host society if the local capital markets are not fully integrated into world markets, as is typical of developing countries. Thus, the foreign firm is likely to place a different value than an indigenous firm on a project with a given time and risk profile of remittable cash flows.

In general, the multinational firm employs a lower discount rate to a particular project than an indigenous firm when the time and risk parameters of its shareholders are lower than those applicable in the host country, or where the risk of a particular undertaking can be diversified to a greater extent in the context of the home capital market than in the indigenous financial economy.[6]

The advantage of foreign firms relative to indigenous firms in undertaking particular projects thus reflects three factors: (1) differences in operating cash flows due to tangible and intangible economies of scope, (2) differences in the proportion of the operating cash flows appropriable by the firm, and (3) differences in the time and risk parameters they employ. Of these three, (1) and (3) are likely to be positive while (2) is typically negative.

Financial Sharing Rules Implicit in FDI

FDI is defined generally as ownership by a firm of ten percent or more of the equity of a foreign firm. This balance sheet definition, though, sheds little light on the nature of the claim of the foreign firm to the cash flows anticipated from the undertaking, or of the real linkages between the foreign firm and the local undertaking. In some cases, a 100 percent equity position will entitle a firm to only a small fraction of the operating cash flows of the project (before local taxes, royalties, and other forms of government participation). In others, an arrangement with no explicit ownership take may entitle a firm to a substantial share of the underlying financial gains. Thus, in analyzing the likelihood of FDI, as well as its attractiveness to the investing firm and the host society, it is worth examining the true financial claims embodied in FDI. We do this by focusing on so-called sharing rules, rules for splitting the operating cash flows that will be generated under various circumstances between the various parties. This form of analysis is applicable to all forms of financial contracts, whether they involve full foreign ownership, ownership-based joint ventures, contractual joint ventures such as coproduction agreements, or simpler sourcing, marketing, or technology transfer contracts.

Three stylized sharing rules for a project involving a normal distribution of one-time financial returns are illustrated in Figure 7.2, together with the probability distribution of implied investor returns. The first (Panel A) is a *linear* rule, where the investor's return is proportional to the total project return. The second (Panel B) is *linear with an upside limit* where the investor shares in the project return up to a specified limit, S, and receives P_{max} thereafter. The third (Panel C) is *linear with a lower limit* where the investor receives a specified payoff, P_{min} (perhaps zero) when project returns fall below the critical level, S, and participates proportionally in returns above that point.

Actual investments, of course, are much more complex than our simplified example, with financial payoffs occurring over many years, often with some form of statistical dependency from one period to the next. The sharing rules implied by different investment arrangements typically are more complex as well, with various nonlinearities that may apply to current or to cumulative payoffs. Nevertheless, as is shown in the following section, these simple characterizations of sharing rules provide useful insights regarding the sharing of risks, the incentives created, and the stability of any particular investment.[7] First, though, we provide some examples of the types of sharing rules implied by different contract/ownership arrangements.

In its simplest form, FDI involves a 100 percent equity investment in a project. In the absence of taxes, such an investment implies a linear sharing rule such as the one illustrated in Figure 7.2 (Panel A). If the venture is structured as a local corporation with limited liability, though, the investing firm need not "accept" a negative financial return. It can walk away from the venture and allow it to declare bankruptcy. It will do so if the present value of future returns is negative as well, otherwise it will absorb the current loss as an investment in order to obtain the future returns. Thus, the payoff function to the firm is linear with a lower limit (Figure 7.2, Panel C).

If the firm borrows 50 percent of its investment, its payoffs become either lines A or B in Figure 7.3, depending on whether or not the parent firm guarantees the debt payments.[8] When projected into a cumulative distribution, as illustrated in Figure 7.2 (Panel B), limited liability results in a truncation of returns at zero. Note that the dispersion per unit of investment is increased, as is the expected dollar payoff divided by the equity investment. However, if borrowing is at a "fair" rate, the value of the project to the investor is unchanged. This fact can be seen in Figure 7.3, which shows that the combination of the cumulative distribution of returns to debt and equity equal the cumulative distribution of the all-equity-financed project.[9]

If the firm's local borrowing is guaranteed by the host government, the firm then faces returns that are linear with a lower bound.

Figure 7.2.   Alternative Sharing Rules

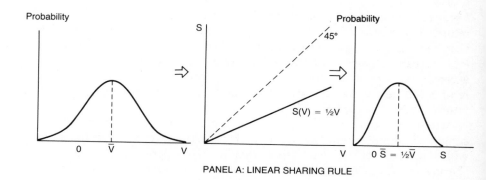

PANEL A: LINEAR SHARING RULE

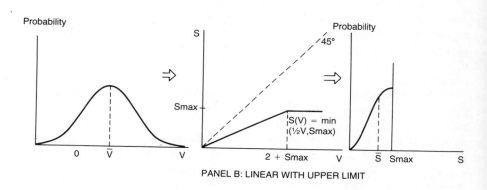

PANEL B: LINEAR WITH UPPER LIMIT

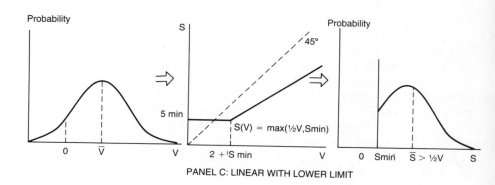

PANEL C: LINEAR WITH LOWER LIMIT

Figure 7.3   Effect of Borrowing on Investor Returns

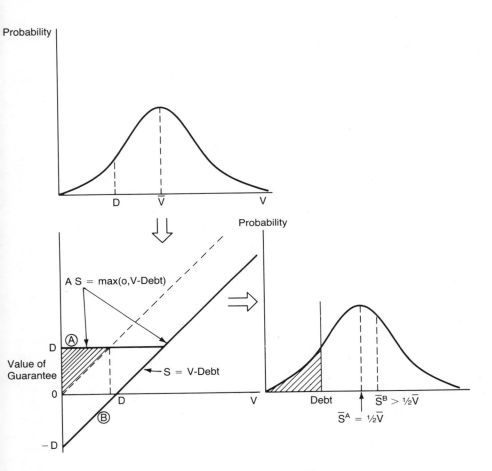

When an income tax is introduced, the payoff structure is further altered. The government becomes a "shareholder," but one that does not accept a negative return. Hence, even with all equity finance, the payoff relationship becomes nonlinear, and the cumulative distribution of returns is truncated. With taxes and borrowing, interest is deductible and, hence, borrowing reduces taxes, correspondingly increasing the value of the undertaking to the firm.[10]

While there exist many more financial structures, implying different sharing rules, these simple illustrations provide a basis for understanding the major issues associated with the alternative financial structures.

Contrast of Sharing Rule and Balance Sheet Perspectives

A common complaint voiced against multinational firms is that they do not bring capital, but instead borrow locally to finance their activities. Therefore, it is argued, they do not contribute to aggregate capital formation, but simply shift it to their operations. The sharing rule perspective on FDI introduced above typically results in quite a different picture. Even if a firm borrows the full amount of its local expenditures, it is generally able to do so because of the parent firms' backing, and hence its "share" moves in line with project outcomes, even negative ones.

A more interesting question in such cases is why firms choose to borrow so much locally. In some cases, such borrowing propensity reflects underpriced credit and involves an implicit subsidy. In others, it represents an attempt to bypass existing remittance limitations or to offset transfer risks, an effort that can be successful only if the payment restriction or transfer risks are less severe for banks and other lenders than for direct investors. Finally, it may be a way to reduce the local tax take. These considerations should be of concern, but for the reason that they represent departures from efficiency rather than the surface reason that the firm appears not to be providing capital.

The opposite situation also occurs at times. A firm may appear to be taking large equity risks, but in fact may be sheltered on the downside by explicit or implicit government guarantees of its borrowing. We return to this point in the third section of the chapter, "Identifying Appropriate Contracts . . . ," when we discuss financial interventions.

ALTERNATIVE SHARING RULES AND THE EFFICIENCY OF FDI

The attractiveness of foreign investment depends on the perspective taken. The investing firm is seeking the maximum present value of remittable cash flows (financial returns), where the present value calculation employs the time and risk parameters of the firm's home capital market value of the project's cash flows, given their time and risk profile. The host country, in contrast, wishes to maximize the economic or social value of the project, including not only the local financial returns but also relevant spillover and distributional effects.

It is tempting to view the entry negotiation as a zero-sum process whereby the benefits of a given undertaking are split between the two parties, and perhaps a local joint-venture partner as well. However, this perspective overlooks the fact that, in many cases, the process is not zero-sum in that some arrangements allow greater benefits than others to one party without decreasing the benefits to the other party. Clearly, to obtain the maximum benefit, the government must negotiate well or, alternatively, create a strong competitive climate for local opportunities. However, it should also concern itself with the efficiency of the arrangements, which will ultimately determine the net gain to be divided between the two.

As noted in the introduction, the efficiency of the sharing rules embodied in FDI can be analyzed in terms of three dimensions:

1. the incentives they create for the design and management of the activities undertaken,

2. the way they allocate the rewards and risks of the project between the investor and the host country in terms of their comparative advantage in bearing the risks involved, and

3. the "contracting" costs that evolve as the result of conflicts of interest between the various parties, coupled with the impossibility of creating completely enforceable contracts across national boundaries.[11]

Each of these is examined below.

Managerial Incentives

The managerial incentives provided by a given contract are eloquently summarized in the following statement by eighteenth-century traveler Arthur Young, quoted by Kindleberger [1979]: "Give a man the secure possession of a bleak rock, and he will turn it into a garden; give him a nine-year lease of a garden, and he will convert it into a desert." In this case, the lessee's interest is limited in time, and he has no incentive to preserve or improve the project's profitability beyond that point. Similarly, a contract that limits an investor's return to a fixed maximum will have a similar effect on the investor's incentives to further improve or expand the project.[12]

In general, FDI implies the involvement of a foreign firm that brings special knowledge of particular activities. Hence, there is no way that the host government can completely specify or regulate its behavior. This fact implies that in order to insure corporate behavior appropriate from the host country's perspective, the foreign investor should have a claim that is roughly proportional to the net benefits of the project to the national economy. In the absence of distortions in the host economy or of other externalities of the firm's activites, an equity position (a linear share) serves this purpose. This is one of the key theoretical benefits of FDI relative to various "unbundled" purchases of foreign technology or capital.

In practice, however, the benefits to the foreign firm often do not correspond closely to the host country's benefit. Reasons for this imbalance include prices that do not reflect society's opportunity cost because of tariffs, subsidies, or other distortions; tax regimes that result in nonlinear private profit shares; and/or risk of unilateral alterations of the investment claim such as windfall profits taxes or renegotiation of natural resource contracts.

Allocation of Exogenous Risks

Most investments involve gambles on outcomes beyond the control of the parties involved, as well as on outcomes partially under their control. Examples of risks outside the control of the foreign investor or the host country, in the case of natural resource projects, include geologic and (world market) price uncertainties. With manufacturing projects, there are uncertainties over market demand, technology, consumer tastes, and competitor behavior, among others.

To the extent that home and host country capital markets are not perfectly integrated, it is likely that the contribution of these gambles to the risk of aggregate consumption in the two economies will differ. Hence, investors in one country or the other will have a comparative advantage in bearing these risks and will place a higher value on cash flows with a given time and risk profile.

Large divergences in the systematic nature of particular risks are most likely in the case of commodity-exporting countries that rely very heavily on one or two products. Clear examples are the oil exporters, as well as several of the mineral producers. Such countries should be able to benefit by entering into contracts that shift a substantial proportion of these risks to foreign investors.[13]

Contract Stability and Self-Enforceability

A major obstacle to any form of cross-border investment is the limited enforceability of contracts with sovereigns, coupled with the discretionary powers of sovereigns. Any contract that bridges two jurisdictions requires that both agree, explicitly or tacitly, to enforce the contract within their systems.

Contracts with sovereigns are difficult to enforce since, clearly, a sovereign can reject a claim within its own territory. Further, courts typically do not recognize a claim against a foreign sovereign and, even when they do, the remedies that can be applied are limited. In the absence of an invasion to seize a country's assets, claims are limited to those assets present in a court's jurisdiction. Even when the contract is with a private agent within the foreign country, many of the same obstacles to enforcement are present. Further, even when the private party complies with the contract, the sovereign may be unable or unwilling to allow the necessary transfer of resources.

Problems arising from this limited enforceability are further complicated by the fact that governments have a great deal of discretion over policy choices that influence their ability to meet foreign claims, as well as those of domestic firms or banks. Many of these policies are matters that need not constitute a breach of contract, such as shifts in monetary policy, limits on exchange remittances, changes in competition and trade policies, and so on.

The ability of the host government to influence outcomes, coupled with limits on the legal sanctions that can be imposed on it in case of nonperformance, imply that contracts with developing countries have little financial value unless they are self-enforcing. That is, the contract will not be honored unless it is in the self-interest of the contracting parties and the respective sovereigns to honor the contracts under virtually all circumstances.

FDI often includes elements that increase self-enforceability.[14] Such elements include patterns of integration into upstream and downstream networks that limit the value of the stand-alone project, continuing flows of new technology, and continuing access to foreign markets. However, these forces typically are most useful to protect against such extreme actions as expropriation, but place few effective limits on a country's policy discretion. In this regard, FDI suffers relative to bank lending, since lenders have a fairly strong common interest that allows them to act collectively, in concert with multilateral institutions, to place limits on a borrowing country's discretion.

IDENTIFYING APPROPRIATE CONTRACTS FOR SPECIFIC SITUATIONS

This section illustrates the general principles discussed above by examining the *efficiency or appropriateness* of particular forms of participation in three different contexts: extractive projects, manufacturing projects, and projects that are attractive by reason of financial incentives, especially those entailing some form of guarantee.

The appropriateness of a contract depends upon the extent to which it matches the risk exposure of the various parties with their comparative advantage in bearing particular risks, subject to the enforceability of the resulting contract.

Extractive Projects

Extractive ventures stand out for three reasons. First, the host country provides the resource to be exploited and, typically, takes some type of financial claim in addition to taxes as its payment. Thus, sharing rules are often quite complex.[15] Second, because of the magnitude of the projects involved and the frequent dependence of developing countries on one or a few key exports, the host country and the foreign investor are likely to differ substantially in their ability to diversify the exogenous risks of the project. Third, given the one-shot nature of most such projects, coupled with the possibility of extreme outcomes, the sharing rules tend to be subject to renegotiation, a form of uncertainty that typically results in deadweight losses.

Any analysis that focuses on the present value (or rate of return) going to each party under the "most likely" outcome is likely to miss most of these considerations. A case in point is the contract that was negotiated between the government of Panama and the Texas-Gulf Corporation for exploiting the Cerro Colorado copper project, which, fortunately for the country, was never undertaken.[16]

At the time the contract was negotiated, it was hailed by many as a victory for Panama, since it gave the government an 80 percent equity share in return for an investment limited to the ore body and the necessary infrastructure. However, to do so the government also had to undertake to guarantee the project's entire borrowing, borrowing that was much greater than such a project could support on a stand-alone basis. Further, the government promised to pay Texas-Gulf a management fee, a significant fraction of which was tied to gross rather than net revenues.

A summary of a Monte Carlo analysis for a Texas-Gulf project clearly shows that Texas-Gulf's share is relatively flat across outcomes while that of the host government starts very low and rises sharply with overall project returns. Using somewhat arbitrary assumptions, the expected net present values are split roughly equally between Texas-Gulf and the Panamanian government, but the latter bears over 80 percent of the risk. In other words, even assuming that it applies the same risk and time parameters as Texas-Gulf, its share of project value is substantially less than 50 percent. Further, the different risk exposures create some very inappropriate incentives for design and management of the project by Texas-Gulf, requiring an unreasonably large degree of regulation by the Panamanian government.

Another interesting example is the resource rent tax (RRT) currently being applied in Australia.[17] In its extreme form, the RRT limits the investor's take to a fixed rate of return on its costs regardless of the profits of the venture. While this undoubtedly increases self-enforceability in the case of good outcomes, it entails a number of problems. First, it provides operators with incentives for different choices than the host country would make if it had the same information and expertise. Second, since it provides the investor with no participation in windfalls, it does little to shift exogenous risks. Finally, if properly priced, a project requires relatively high rates of return over costs in cases of marginally commercial discoveries, thereby creating a contracting risk on the downside, in that it does not provide participation in windfalls.[18]

Manufacturing Ventures

Typically the motivation for FDI in manufacturing, either for the domestic market or for foreign markets, is the possession by the investing firm of certain intangibles, such as process or product know-how, which can be employed at little incremental cost to the firm or from which it is able to achieve joint economies because of the positioning of the local undertaking in the firm's worldwide production and marketing system. Thus the investment opportunities facing a firm, to a large extent, reflect the firm's own circumstances and not the aggregate savings/investment balance of the host country. Further, many of the risks inherent in such projects are at least partially under the control of the investing firm. Thus, the major dimension of efficiency is in the incentives the sharing rules imply for management choices. In cases where local joint ventures are desired, the sharing rules may either exacerbate or ameliorate potential conflicts between the foreign and local parties that arise because of the asymmetry of channels the two possess for realizing their financial returns.

Many Latin American countries, probably unwittingly, have put in place FDI controls and incentive mechanisms that are pervaded with conflicts and, hence, quite inefficient. A classic example is a country that imposes tight restrictions and high taxes on profit remittances and yet contends that it wants to encourage joint ventures. The clear incentive of the restrictions is to develop alternative channels for profit remittances such as transfer pricing and parallel loans, but this is in conflict with the interests of potential local partners. Thus, in order to comply with the ownership goals, the firm has to give up the value of these alternative channels and do so in a credible way. Another example of conflict is a country perceived as politically risky by investors that seeks to attract foreign investment with tax holidays. Typically, these holidays are most beneficial when profits are retained, but the political risks weigh against such retention. Hence, the government gives up tax revenues, but does not necessarily gain corresponding benefits.

A similar problem arises when firms can remit profits only out of their own export revenues. In such cases, the value of a given opportunity is greatest for conglomerate firms with many linked ventures, even though these firms may supply less-appropriate technology or be less efficient along other dimensions than other firms. Further, in such cases, firms are unlikely to maximize local value added, and they will benefit from manipulating inward or outward transfer prices. Thus, in order to insure socially desirable behavior, some form of regulation must be imposed in such cases to overcome the distortions created by the blocked currency. Such analysis lies behind much of the advice that in order to benefit from FDI a country must align its prices with world prices. Otherwise, it has no assurance that what firms do in their own self-interest will be in the interest of the host country.

The Efficiency of Financial Interventions

In competing for foreign direct investment, both industrialized and developing countries increasingly resort to financial incentives in the form of concessional credits, loan guarantees, and tax holidays of various sorts.[19] A general question that should be asked in such cases is whether the economic and social externalities of the undertaking justify the transfer being made. Whether such interventions are an efficient way to make a grant of a given financial value, however, is a question that should be raised more often, as it appears that financial interventions often lead to less efficient sharing of project benefits.

The various financial interventions employed by host governments can be modeled in terms of how they modify the time and risk profile of remittable, appropriable cash flows anticipated by the foreign investor. These altered time and risk profiles, in turn, can be examined in terms of the three dimensions of efficiency discussed above.

Loan guarantees, for example, eliminate or reduce negative outcomes, hence providing an incentive for firms to select more risky projects even if the overall risk-reward trade-off is not attractive. Further, if a project goes poorly, the existence of a guarantee with its implied overhanging claim creates incentives for the firm to abandon the project more quickly than it would if it were all equity financed.

Cheap credit, if it is tied to investment in capital goods, as is often the case, provides incentives for more capital-intensive investment. Further, if it is tied to imported goods, it leads to a bias against local inputs and so on.

While it is difficult to derive general conclusions, the sharing rule perspective provides new insights regarding not only the financial value or cash grant equivalent of various incentives, but also their likely consequences for efficiency.

THE ROLE OF FDI IN A COUNTRY'S OVERALL EXTERNAL FINANCING[20]

Floating rate bank credit has become the predominant form of external finance for developing countries in recent years, rising to more than 70 percent of new financing in the late 1970s and early 1980s. Some of the costs to borrowers of this heavy reliance on bank financing are now painfully apparent, with many borrowers suffering large cuts in their standard of living because of their debt service requirements. In retrospect, using the sharing rule perspective developed above, it is clear that bank financing and other forms of general obligation credit have important limitations and that a larger share of developing countries' external obligations should be in the form of foreign direct investment and other forms of finance that are contingent on the success of particular projects, enterprises, or export sectors.

There are three major reasons why heavy reliance on bank finance is undesirable. Bank finance (or other forms of general obligation borrowing):

1. entails variations in debt service requirements that only accidentally correspond to changes in the borrower country's ability to service debt;

2. requires repayment regardless of the performance of the borrowers' macroeconomies or specific projects or programs, and hence shifts risk only through default; and

3. provides lenders with no stake in the outcome of the borrowers' macroeconomies or specific projects or programs, and, hence, does not give any responsibility for the selection or execution of programs or projects to the suppliers of capital.[21]

These points are taken up in the remainder of this section.

Debt Service Mismatch

Most developing countries experience fluctuations in revenue owing to world economic cycles, shifts in terms of trade, and domestic political and economic events. International finance should provide a basis for smoothing national consumption over time in periods of low income and replenishing reserves or repaying debt in periods of high income. However, if a country already has substantial external obligations, it may have difficulty in borrowing more, and indeed the obligation to service its existing debt may rise and intensify the fluctuation in its underlying income.

In a world with perfect information and complete enforceability of claims, the part of the perverse variation in debt service due to fluctuations in inflation would not be a problem. Claims would be rolled over unless the present value of a borrowing country's future net exports fell short of outstanding claims. In other words, illiquidity would never be an issue in such a world, and the only risk would be that of insolvency. However, given limited information and enforceability, rolling over is not a sure thing, and the arbitrary shortening of maturities via increases in LIBOR (London Inter-Bank Offer Rate), as well as the shortening of available maturities, can create problems for borrowers as well as for the system as a whole.

Limited Risk Sharing

Most commercial bank loans to LDCs (and all World Bank loans) involve implicit or explicit government guarantees. Thus, while the funds may be earmarked for a specific project or program, their repayment is not contingent on that project's outcome; the risk of success or failure of the specific project or program is borne by the guarantor.

This nonspecific nature of bank credit has two effects. First, it trivializes the role of private banks and public institutions in project evaluation or oversight of national economic strategies. Since all claims are general obligations of the sovereign, a loan to a good project is no better than one used to maintain consumption in the face of a reversal in the terms of trade. Second, and probably much more important, it means that risks inherent in specific projects or strategies are shifted only through nonperformance at the country level. Such nonperformance is a calamitous event, with high costs to borrowers and lenders alike.

Limited Shifting of Responsibility

In addition to not shifting specific risk from borrowing countries to lenders, the general obligation and noncontingent character of loans to developing countries imply that specific lenders have little or no stake in the success or failure of specific undertakings. Instead, their recovery of the amount loaned depends on the borrower's overall ability to pay and the penalties it faces if it does not.

This situation is in sharp contrast to contingent finance—direct foreign investment or quasi-equity investment such as production shares of incentive contracts—where success of the project is a critical determinant of the investor's financial return. Clearly, in such cases the financier has a strong interest in assuring that the project or program being financed is well conceived and executed. Further, to the extent that industrial country interests control outcomes critical to a program or project's success, inducing those countries to accept a stake causes them to influence outcomes in ways that are favorable to the project. This consideration is important at the national level when a country faces a large exposure to policy decisions of foreign governments or firms, such as changes in the terms of access to particular markets for products or strategic inputs for domestic industries.

CONCLUSIONS

Foreign direct investment involves the exchange of intangible factors of production for financial claims whose value is at least partially dependent on the success of the undertaking. The specific form of the foreign firm's share in project benefits, though, is the result of many factors in addition to the balance sheet definitions of participation. These include local taxes, financial incentives, and threats to appropriability of profits.

The resulting sharing rules are important determinants of the efficiency of FDI along three dimensions: managerial incentives, risk spreading, and contract stability. All deserve careful attention in the design and operation of control systems and incentives for FDI. Every investment should be examined in terms of the sharing of risk and reward and not just the stated ownership percentages and financing structures.

The risk spreading and incentive implications of foreign share financing are important at an aggregate, national level, as well as at a project or enterprise level. Our conceptual framework suggests that most developing countries should include some form of share financing in their external financing, even though they recently have relied more heavily on general obligation finance. The extent to which share financing is important depends on the country's overall obligations relative to its likely foreign exchange earnings, its comparative advantage in bearing particular risks, and on the extent to which it wants to shift some of the responsibility of its selection and execution of projects or programs to foreign interests.

Even if these aggregate-level considerations are not strong in a specific case, a country may want to employ substantial foreign share financing in order to make up for incomplete internal mechanisms for spreading risk and creating appropriate managerial incentives. In such cases, though, an important further consideration is whether the form of the foreign share financing employed will stimulate or retard the development of appropriate domestic markets.[22]

NOTES

1. A critical assumption underlying this conclusion is that there exist complete, perfect markets for spreading and pooling risk within an economy. If this is not the case, risks that are diversifiable at the level of the economy will be borne by some individuals and, hence, will have negative welfare impact.

2. In simple terms, the net present value rule states that a firm should accept a project when the value of future cash flows, discounted at rates that reflect the time and risk parameters determined in the market, is greater than zero. For a clear discussion of its rationale, see Brealey and Myers (1984).

3. This point has long been recognized in practice, but only recently has been incorporated in the academic literature on FDI. See in particular Kogut (1984).

4. For a fuller discussion of this point, see Lessard (1979). For an empirical examination of MNCs' transfer pricing practices in Asian countries, see LeCraw (1984).

5. An example is the case where a foreign firm operating as a branch is able to offset start-up expenses of a local venture against its foreign tax liabilities while an indigenous firm must carry these losses forward until the project becomes profitable.

6. If financial markets were perfectly integrated, of course, the same financial parameters would apply in all countries and the diversifiability of the risk of any project would be the same regardless of the perspective taken. However, taxes, transfer risks, and the absence of the necessary institutions (including mechanisms for cross-border enforcement of contracts) result in the partial or total segmentation of national markets. In this sense, the multinational firm is acting as an alternative mechanism for spanning these hitherto segmented markets, albeit probably as by-product of its industrial advantages rather than as a prime motivation.

7. The analysis of claims that can be represented as nonlinear functions of the value of some underlying asset is known as *contingent claims analysis*. For a review of applications to investment analysis, see Mason and Merton (1985).

8. If the investor does not guarantee the debt, it will make the payments on the debt only if it deems the present value of the future cash flows from the venture to be positive.

9. This is a clear implication of the Modigiani-Miller Theorem, which states that the value of a firm (project) is unchanged by the division of claims into two or more classes. See Brealey and Myers (1984) for discussion of this basic principle.

10. There is considerable debate in the corporate finance literature over the extent to which firms gain from issuing tax-deductible debt given the differential treatment at the level of the individual investor of interest and capital gain income. However, in the case of a small country, interest tax deductibility for foreign investors will result in a unambigous decrease in tax revenues and an increase in the value of the undertaking to the investor.

11. A fourth dimension of efficiency from the viewpoint of the host country is the minimization of third country taxes, for example, the minimization of the investor's home country taxes associated with the investment in question.

12. This point has been made by several analysts with regard to the resource-rent tax imposed by Australia, which places an upper limit on investor returns. See, for example, Dowell (1978) and Ball and Bowers (1982).

13. See Lessard and Williamson (1985) for further discussion.

14. See Vernon (1983) for examples.

15. The exception is the case where a bonus option is paid at the outset and all other returns to the government are in the form of taxes.

16. This example is based on primary documents for the Cerro Colorado project as well as commentaries on the project by CEASPA (1980). The calculations are the author's and are based on some highly simplifying assumptions.

17. The RRT was first advocated by Garnaut and Clunies-Ross (1975). See the references in note 12 for recent, critical discussion.

18. For a more extensive discussion of the efficiency dimensions of contracts for oil and gas exploitation, see Blitzer, Lessard, and Paddock (1984).

19. For a general discussion of investment incentives and their effects, see Guisinger and Associates (1985).

20. This section draws substantially on Lessard (1986).

21. A fourth drawback of bank financing is that it concentrates the impact of default losses on a narrow segment of the world financial market, creating the potential for systemwide impact far out of proportion to the magnitude of any default.

22. For further discussion of this point see Lessard and Williamson (1985) and Van Agtmael (1984).

REFERENCES

Ball, Ray and John Bowers. "Distortions Created By Taxes Which are Options on Value Creation." *Australian Journal of Management* 2, no. 8 (December 1982).

Blitzer, Charles, Donald Lessard, and James Paddock. "Risk Bearing and the Choice of Contract Forms for Oil Exploration and Development." *The Energy Journal* 5, no. 1 (1984).

Brealey, Richard and Stewart Myers. *Principles of Corporate Finance.* New York: McGraw-Hill, 1984.

CEASPA (Centro de Estudios Anthropologicos y Sociologicos Panamenos). *El Proyecto Cerro Colorado,* 1980.

Dowell, Richard. "Resources Rent Taxation." *Australian Management Journal* 3, no. 4 (October 1978).

Garnaut, Ross and A. Clunies-Ross. "Uncertainty, Risk Aversion, and the Taxation of Natural Resource Projects." *Economic Journal,* June 1975.

Guisinger, Stephen, and Associates. *Investment Incentives and Performance Requirements: Patterns of International Trade, Production, and Investment.* New York: Praeger, 1985.

Kindleberger, Charles. "Contract and Ownership in International Business." Reprinted in Charles Kindleberger (ed.), *Multinational Excursions.* Cambridge, Mass.: MIT Press, 1984.

Kogut, Bruce. "Foreign Direct Investment as a Sequential Process." In Charles Kindleberger and D. B. Audretsch (eds.), *The Multinational Corporation in the 1980s.* Cambridge, Mass.: MIT Press, 1984.

LeCraw, Donald. "Some Evidence on Transfer Pricing by Multinationals." In Alan Rugman and Lorraine Eden (eds.), *Multinationals and Transfer Pricing.* London: Croom Helm, 1984.

Lessard, Donald. "Transfer Prices, Taxes, and Financial Markets: Implications of Internal Financial Transfers within the Multinational Firm." In Robert Hawkins (ed.), *Economic Issues of Multinational Firms.* Greenwich, Conn.: JAI Press, 1979.

————. "International Finance for Developing Countries: The Unfulfilled Promise." *World Bank Staff Working Papers No. 783,* Series on International Capital and Economic Development, No. 2. (January 1986).

———— and John Williamson. *Financial Intermediation Beyond the Debt Crisis.* Washington, D.C.: Institute for International Economics, 1985.

Mason, Scott and Robert Merton. "The Role of Contingent Claims Analysis in Corporate Finance." In Edward Altman and Marti Subrahmanyan (eds.), *Advances in Corporate Finance.* New York: Dow Jones-Irwin, 1985.

Van Agtmael, Antoine. *Emerging Securities Markets.* London: Euromoney Publications, 1984.

Vernon, Raymond. "Organizational and Institutional Responses to International Risk." In Richard Herring (ed.), *Managing International Risk*. New York: Cambridge University Press, 1983.

Chapter Eight

Trade Policy and the Impact of Foreign Technology

William A. Fischer

The ability to develop new industrial products and processes is associated with the process of economic development. In fact, it is often not the products or processes themselves that are desired, but the industrial capabilities embodied in them.

The less developed countries' preference for industry does not arise from the sheer pleasure of producing industrial goods. Industrialization is simply a proxy for concomitant changes in labor productivity, technological diffusion, "learning by doing" and the resulting economic environment which appears to be relatively more conducive to development.[1]

The acquisition of foreign technology often serves as a means of rapidly achieving access to "improved" industrial products and processes. Hence, international technology transfer represents a central issue in the policies of industrialization. Technology transfer is not, however, a culturally neutral phenomenon. Technology reflects characteristics of the society and situation in which it was developed. As a result, the acquisition of foreign technology involves a series of trade-offs between a variety of often conflicting societal goals. The technology transfer decision is one with multiple policy dimensions revolving around the costs and benefits of allowing the penetration of foreign influence via the national markets.

Technology Transfer and Influence Transmission

Despite the fact that the "communications" nature of the technology transfer process has been demonstrated in a variety of studies,[2] it is not an entirely evident proposition. Consequently, this aspect often tends to be ignored in more hardware-oriented discussions of foreign technology acquisition. In order to be able to appraise the impact of foreign access to a particular market competently, it is important to emphasize that any technology, no matter what its level of sophistication, embodies within it the norms and values of the society in which it was developed. Products produced in the more industrialized countries contain resource, usage, and fashion biases that tend to reflect the preferences of the societies in which they evolved. Modern manufacturing technologies developed in the industrialized world carry within them assumptions as to levels of adequacy in operating environments, preventive maintenance, worker capabilities, work-force organization, and others. These assumptions suggest that the adoption of such technologies by users in developing countries requires either acceptance of these assumptions or heightened risk of technological failure. Perhaps most significantly, the actual presence of foreign manufacturers in a market brings with it a variety of social and managerial expectations that can create a direct confrontation between differing cultures. In each case, however, the essential equation remains the same: Foreign technology is accompanied by foreign influence. A fundamental cost of employing technology transfer as a means of short-cutting an indigenous technology development process is the willingness to accept a degree of foreign influence over product design, process development, product utilization, and organizational design and management that would otherwise not be present. It is the purpose of this chapter to consider what the scope of such influence might be and to assess what is known to date about its actual impact.

Arguments for Protecting Indigenous Industry

While the nature of the influence of the transmission might not be immediately evident from the literature on technology transfer, the arguments of market protectionists have long recognized the possible consequences inherent in such activities. The mercantilists, for example, regarded the importation of foreign products into the home market as an undesirable economic event because of the loss of monetary wealth involved. Jean Baptiste Colbert, 1619-83, finance minister under Louis XIV of France, wrote: "The whole business of commerce consists in facilitating the import of those goods which serve the countries' manufacture, and placing embargoes on those which enter in a manufactured state."[3] The author goes on to point out that

the export of improved tools and machinery was almost universally prohibited, because of the fear of helping competing industries in foreign countries. England did not abandon this prohibition until well into the nineteenth century. This was evidenced by the fact that the plans for the first cotton mill in the United States at Pawtucket, Rhode Island, had to be smuggled into this country by Samuel Slater.[4]

Among the earliest arguments for protectionism came from America's first secretary of the Treasury, Alexander Hamilton (1757-1804). In his 1791 *Report on Manufactures*, he argued for the employment of tariffs to protect "infant" industries that were just beginning to appear in the newly independent United States of America and that, he felt, were ill-prepared to compete against more established European firms. By 1815, as a result of the success of manufactured imports from British factories, the infant industry argument had gained considerable attention in the United States. Since that time, the infant industry issue has become an important part of the protectionist debate in both the more-developed and less-developed countries.

In brief, the infant industry argument has been that it is useful to allow newly developing domestic firms to grow within a protected environment before they are subjected to direct foreign competition. In such cases, protectionism works to limit foreign technological influence to that which can be gained either indirectly through the mimicry of product design or through the acquisition of foreign process technology. Foreign direct participation in the organization and management of local industry, are typically limited to subsidiaries or affiliates that include some local involvement.

Arguments against Transnational Corporate Involvement in Markets of Developing Countries

The arguments relating to technological influence that have been raised in opposition to the entry of transnational corporations (TNCs) into the markets of developing countries have been advanced for a variety of reasons. The whole issue of "appropriate" product and process technology, which addresses the sensitivity of the TNCs to local cultural preferences and factor endowments, is a key issue in discussing the attractiveness of TNC entry. Similarly, the suitability of advertising and distribution methods have also been questioned as to their appropriateness. Other issues that must be considered in appraising the desirability of allowing foreign access to developing-country markets include the impact on local manufacturers and merchants of TNC competition and the upgrading of local technical and managerial skills resulting from the TNC presence.

Any subsequent attempt to appraise the desirability of opening up local markets to foreign competition and influence must, of necessity, recognize the multiple economic, social, and political dimensions involved. Dunning has suggested four goals as being mentioned frequently in the literature: (1) economic—type and quality of products available; (2) equity—distribution of income and assets; (3) sovereignty—right to control one's own destiny; (4) participation—need of people to be involved in the decision-making process.[5] These four can serve as criteria in respect to issues of interest to this chapter.

DIMENSIONS OF TECHNOLOGICAL INFLUENCE

Technology transfer can occur in a variety of different ways resulting in a variety of different outcomes. The "appropriateness" of the transfer mechanism depends upon the outcome desired. Ruttan and Hayami have categorized technology transfer into three major types: (1) hardware transfer, when only access to the technology itself is desired; (2) information transfer, when the hardware alone is not enough and "know-how" is desired; and (3) capacity transfer, when the ability to translate the technology into indigenously produced new generations of technology is desired.[6] The relative degree of appropriateness of each transfer is a function of both the technology and the recipient of the transfer. When industrialization is the ultimate objective, mastery of the technology is most likely to be the nature of the technological capability desired. Such mastery implies, in the long run, an ability to perform the entire ongoing innovation process locally.

The innovation process, which ultimately results in a marketable product, involves a spectrum of activities ranging from idea formulation to the manufacture and distribution of the product.[7] The Charpie committee's report to the U.S. Commerce Department in 1967[8] indicated, in fact, that the research and development portion of the innovation process amounted to only a small part of the cost and time involved, a finding confirmed in several more recent studies. This conclusion suggests the dangers of focusing merely on product or process development in understanding technology transfer. Accordingly, we borrow from Ruttan and Hayami and describe technological transfer policies designed to achieve mastery over a technology in order to support national industrialization policies. This mastery requires attention to: (1) access to the product; (2) an ability to produce the product(s) indigenously; and (3) a command of the knowledge-skills necessary to design, develop, and manage the technology.

The remainder of this chapter discusses what is known from previous studies about the role of foreign influence in facilitating mastery in developing countries over each of these three capabilities. It should be kept in mind that the following discussion is exploratory in the arguments it asserts and represents a distillation of available evidence rather than the gathering of new data.

One other qualification should be raised before turning to the body of the chapter. A great deal about TNC behavior can be determined by reference to its primary market orientation,[9] in that some are oriented toward serving their home market. Even their overseas activities are designed to serve primarily the home market. These are called "home" market firms. Others engage in activities overseas in order to establish a presence in foreign markets and to sell in these markets. These are called "host" market firms.

Finally, the most sophisticated TNCs go offshore to create globally integrated production/marketing systems. These are called "worldwide" market firms. Most of the studies reviewed for this chapter seem to ignore the effects of market orientation and, as such, provide only a portion of the information needed to appraise accurately the desirability of allowing foreign access to developing-country markets. Available data are so scarce, however, that despite such limitations, we must rely on data from such studies.

ACCESS TO PRODUCT

The Effects of Import Substitution and Neoprotectionism

Given the lengthy experience that the world economy has had with a variety of restrictive trade practices, it is somewhat remarkable that there are so few unambiguous conclusions regarding the outcomes of import substitution and neoprotectionism measures designed to protect local industry from foreign competition. Most likely, this paucity of information stems from the rather complex and confusing interrelationships, between competitive success and a variety of other, difficult-to-control, variables. Nonetheless, given the initial motivation for this chapter, which is to understand the infant industry protection issue, it remains important to address the basic question: "What have been the outcomes of import substitution policies enacted to protect infant industries from foreign technological influence?"

The essential argument that underlies infant industry protection is that such industries need protection from older, better endowed, and better established foreign competitors during some sort of formative period so that the "infants" can eventually develop into mature enterprises that can stand up to foreign competition without support. Relying on a variety of tariffs and nontarriff-barriers, import substitution to protect both infant and not-so-youthful industries became a fashionable development strategy during the 1950s and 1960s. Resources were directed to that end.

The proponents of the strategy believed that the accumulation of capital, skills and technology initially spearheaded in import-competing sectors would in due course spill over into other sectors. In almost all cases, import substitution was viewed as a catalytic agent rather than merely as a source of industrial goods.[10]

By far the most successful employment of infant industry protection was that of Japan in the postwar period. Aided by the erection of a number of policy and nonpolicy barriers that effectively blocked foreign access to the Japanese market, Japanese industry was able to rebuild from the devastation of World War II and to engage in extremely demanding domestic competition before venturing out to tackle the established industrial giants of Western Europe and the United States. It seems clear, however, that infant industry protection worked in the Japanese case primarily because of an already well-developed industrial infrastructure that had existed long before World War II and as result of aggressive government policies that stimulated and supported export-oriented activites.[11] In fact, Ahmad, in a review of import substitution policies, concluded that

. . . the growth of import substitution in manufacturing sectors is positively correlated with the growth of exports. . . . In this supply-oriented view of the matter, therefore, import substitution and export expansion, far from being antagonistic as commonly assumed, are compatible and symbiotic.[12]

This view is partially supported by Schmitz, who wrote:

The problem is that it is inherently difficult to produce evidence which shows that protection under import substituting industrialization generated externalties and learning which would have been lost without it. But it may not be accidental that some of the successful exporters were countries in which import substitution was relatively successful in building up an industrial structure which was not merely limited to local production of consumer goods.[13]

The close relationship between import substitution and export expansion dramatizes the timing involved in such activities. Import substitution and infant industry protection, in and of themselves, do not necessarily improve a developing nation's mastery of technology. Instead, protectionism leads to a diminution of access to foreign products (and technologies) and to a misallocation of resources devoted to the locally produced products that are available. An example of the former can be found in the reluctance of subsidiaries of protected foreign pharmaceutical firms in Brazil to engage in new product development when their existing products were already shielded from competition by the grant of monopoly privileges.[14] In Portugal, on the other hand, a reliance on import substitution strategies for the infant Portuguese automobile industry led to the proliferation of inefficient, small-sized assembly plants, rather than to a strong, growing, internationally competitive industry.[15] Both of these examples are illustrative of the negative consequences that Bela Belassa has associated with import substitution:

Countries applying inward-oriented industrial development strategies were . . . characterized by the prevalence of sellers' markets. . . .[And] The existence of sellers' markets provides little inducement to cater to users' needs. In the case of industrial users, it [leads] to backward integration as producers [undertake] the manufacture of parts, components, and accessories themselves in order to minimize supply difficulties. This outcome, observed in capitalist as well as socialist countries, [leads] to higher costs, since economies of scale [are] forgone.[16]

Ignoring economies of scale, to which Belassa refers, can lead to the illusion of product diversity, while in reality resulting in high-cost items not competitive on the world market and to lack of access to world-class products. One graphic example of such a situation was the Chilean automobile industry in the early 1960s, when

22 assembly firms were processing less than 8000 vehicles, which meant a production run of roughly 400 cars per plant per year. In addition, the industry offered an incredible choice of 27 different makes of cars, with the result that local suppliers were unable to mass produce components of a standard specification.[17]

Given the foregoing discussion, it is not unreasonable to suggest that import substitution can lead to increased vulnerability for a closed economy. The radical opening up of the Chilean economy associated with the Chicago-school experiment there in the post-Allende period, combined with a serious recession, led to a three percent reduction in the manufacturing sector's importance to gross domestic product and an eight percent decline in employment in the period between 1970 and 1978.[18] While it is difficult to ascertain exactly what the role of increased foreign competition was in the determination of these outcomes, it is clear that the previously protected electronic equipment, transportation materials, textiles, clothing, and footwear industries and a variety of industrial intermediates were seriously affected by the increased competition. Furthermore, even the numbers associated with this experience understate the extent of Chilean vulnerability in that they fail to show the dramatic decline in industrial wages that allowed many firms to survive the shock of external competition. Industrial wages dropped from an index of 100 to 1970 to 47.9 in 1975 and then rose to 74.9 by 1979.[19] Nor do the numbers reflect the shift from the manufacturing of local products to the distribution of imports, which also characterized the survival strategies of many Chilean firms.

In Kenya, where import substitution and growing pressures for Africanization of industry led to the establishment of local manufacturing subsidiaries by foreign transnational corporations, case studies of Kenyan soap and footwear manufacturers indicate that local firms experienced reduced sales and reduced income as a result of the opening-up of the domestic market to foreign competition. Other pertinent effects of foreign competition were: (1) an increased move among domestic manufacturers toward the mechanization of production processes, despite the functional superiority of hand-made soap; (2) significant product-mix diversification;

(3) increased import intensiveness (i.e., raw materials and packaging to suit the mechanized production processes); and (4) increased subcontracting for foreign firms that wished to enter the Kenyan market without manufacturing there themselves. Such subcontracting represented one way in which the Kenyan firms could increase the turnover necessary to run the mechanized production processes at an economic level. There was a general retreat of domestic firms out of manufacturing and back into repairing in the face of the superior price competitiveness and product diversity of the foreign competitors.[20]

Nigerian industries, including several that were previously protected by import substitution policies (tobacco products, brewing, cotton textiles, cement, and sugar refining) also experienced displacement in the face of foreign competition once their markets were opened up. The situation of small artisan and semiskilled (handicraft) producers appears to have been both helped and hindered by foreign competition. While it seems that significant displacement occurred as a result of imports and by direct investment by transnational producers, there is also evidence that indigenous manufacturers were encouraged to produce goods to serve local tastes, using imported raw materials. In respect to the effect of foreign competition on Nigeria's indigenous manufacturers, there is no evidence to suggest "the existence of firm displacement, the outright elimination or closing of indigenous firms engaged in the production of a roughly comparable product." As Biersteker points out, however, this situation might have reflected the fact that the existing Nigerian manufacturers in the markets into which foreign competition was drawn were not sufficiently comparable to the foreign competitors to be displaced: "Thus the prospect for any direct takeover or elimination of established domestic firms was virtually impossible, at least until a substantial indigenous industrial sector emerged." In markets where indigenous firms had made the initial investment, foreign competition captured an increasing portion of market share and, then, in some cases, gave up a limited amount of market share to emerging Nigerian competitors. In the cigarette and beer industries, domestic production virtually replaced foreign imports, but transnational firms controlled all of the domestic production. In industries in which foreign firms initiated investment, on the other hand, indigenous firms have experienced far less success in winning market share, and to the extent that they have won any it has apparently been as a result of government pressure for indigenization.[21]

In general, over the wide range of industries and national experiences cited here, the lesson seems fairly clear that protected industries, sheltered from competition, enjoy dubious advantage in potential competition against foreign competitors once the national market is opened up. In case after case, local manufacturers have been unable to compete with world-class competition on the bases of price, real product variety, or quality.

This conclusion agrees with a summary of import substitution experiences in the 1950s and 1960s by Little, Scitcovsky, and Scott,[22] who argue that import substituting industrialization resulted in too much protection and led to an inefficient allocation of resources. Some of their specific criticisms can be summarized thus:

1. Excessive administrative regulation gave rise to bureaucratization, corruption, uncertainty and delay, thus inhibiting productive private initiative.

2. Import restrictions led to an exchange rate that was higher than would have emerged under a free trade regime, thereby reducing possible gains from exporting.

3. Protection of local industry raised the prices of manufactured goods relative to agricultural products, and together with the overvalued exchange rate, reduced the proceeds from agricultural exports.

4. Since import controls for capital goods were somewhat more liberal than for consumer goods, and credit for factory expansion was relatively cheap, factories tended to be overequipped, thereby leading to underutilization. Even so, profits were possible because the domestic market was protected from import competition.

5. For very similar reasons, industry tended to be overly capital-intensive and biased against the employment of labor.

6. The reduction of imported consumer goods was achieved at the expense of increased imports of equipment and industrial inputs, which led to even more dependence on foreign supplies and heightened pressure on foreign exchange reserves.

7. Industry can grow only as fast as the domestic market unless its products are exported. Protection and import substitution, however, created an inefficient industry which was not able to compete in international markets. The result was an inevitable slowing down in the expansion of export-substituting industrialization.[23]

With specific reference to the use of import substitution to protect infant industries, Schmitz cites an unpublished paper by Bell,[24] which reports the following, within the original author's caveat to recognize the danger of extrapolating from a very limited set of case studies:

[L]earning in infant enterprises and industries has been highly variable; common characteristics of the maturation path of industries do not emerge, neither on the duration of infancy nor on the magnitude of its costs. The weight of the evidence suggests, however, that relatively protracted maturation periods and correspondingly high infancy costs are more common. When the firms or industries are set in their differing contexts some pattern seems to emerge. The more successful learners tend to come from LDCs with a relatively long industrialization experience stretching back at least to the 1950s (e.g., Argentina, Brazil or India). Much of the evidence of low rates of progress is drawn from economies in which significant industrialization only began in the 1950s (e.g., Bangladesh, Thailand or Tanzania).[25]

In fact, from the literature reviewed for this study, it appears reasonable to conclude that only in those cases where import substitution was enacted in concert with policies designed to encourage eventual international export competition (e.g., Japan) do there appear to be the sort of results desired in terms of gaining mastery of acquired technology. Ahmad explains,

Successful industrial exporting requires that domestic production problems must be satisfactorily resolved not only with respect to cost but also to quality, standardization, knowledge of foreign markets, advertising and sales effort. . . Trade in manufactures tends to be most intensive in products which, though identical, are highly differentiated. Unless the less developing countries attain that level of product differentiation, the growth of their manufactured exports will remain a slow and painful process.[26]

Import substitution policies that fail to encourage the development of such a "protected/competitive" domestic market do not appear suitable for the emergence of internationally competitive industries.

The Effects of Direct Foreign Investment by TNCs

The direct entry of transnational corporations into a developing economy introduces a variety of influences on product design and availability that will likely affect the ability of local industry to master the skills noted above, associated with successful industrial exporting and, by implication, successful mastery of technology. From the studies reviewed for this chapter, it appears that much (if not most) direct foreign investment by transnational corporations in developing countries came about either (1) after export experience in the relevant market had been gained, or (2) in an effort to protect or gain access to a market so as to preempt entry by an oligopolistic competitor, or (3) in response to some form of locally inspired import substitution. It appears evident that when direct foreign investment does take place, the products offered by the investing enterprise typically represent the product line already offered by the parent corporation rather than an attempt to develop unique products for the local market. In this regard, Langdon quotes managers of two transnational subsidiaries operating in Kenya:

Internationally, we have 4000-5000 products—mention it and we make it. Now, of course, the whole idea is to capitalize on the corporate signature—not only in the product formulation but also in the marketing know-how. The brand-name emphasis and so on. . . .

[The parent] has some 5000 products I can choose from to promote here. So I don't really need to look for anything new—they've usually a possible one for any area I'd have in mind.[27]

Thus, the entry of TNCs into a foreign market does not necessarily mean that local tastes or needs influence the design of the products offered. Nonetheless, despite this reluctance to develop "local" products in developing countries, the presence of direct foreign investment by transnational corporations in a market typically results in an increase in product variety in that market. This increase is simply the result of the greater number of products available from the parent, as well as some limited willingness, which develops over time, to adapt available products to local wants. On this latter point, we rely on Dunning's conclusions:

Empirical studies, in general support the contention that the presence of MNEs (multinational enterprises) tends to increase product differentiation and promotional behavior in host countries. Almost certainly the range of products produced by MNEs, as a whole, is greater than it would have been had their foreign markets been served by exports.[28]

With respect to product quality, there appears to be general agreement that the products produced by TNCs are of higher quality (measured by international standards of reliability, standardization, and aesthetics) than those produced by local firms.[29] According to Stewart, this superiority is attributable to the greater export orientation of the TNCs' subsidiaries in that they are obligated to compete in sophisticated world markets requiring high quality.[30] Higher quality, however, does not necessarily mean technological state-of-the-art in the products made available in the local market. This fact is illustrated strikingly by the decline in the sophistication of computer technology in India during the 1960s when India relied on foreign computer manufacturers for access to new product technology. On the other hand, the presence of IBM in India during that period was credited with setting standards for price and product service that were lost after IBM's withdrawal from the Indian market.[31]

The creation of demand through advertising and the shaping of market desires represents a very important influence over product technology of particular relevance in situations where foreign (especially TNC) competition is allowed into a market either through exports or through direct foreign investment. In almost every study examined, aggregate market demand for products grew following the entry of foreign product offerings. While some of this growth was undoubtedly due to population increase and general economic development, it would appear that a significant share of that enhanced demand was attributable to the presence of foreign products and advertising undertaken to support those products. Critics view this influence with considerable alarm, taking it to be a factor in bringing about erosion of local cultural heritage.

The importing of norms and values and the structuring of modes of representation [through advertising] strike at the innermost self of individuals, at their cultural identity and at the way in which they envisage the potentialities of life.
    The structuring of social consumption patterns by TNCs is a particularly revealing example of their socio-cultural influence. The fact is that TNCs are conducive to the introduction into the developing countries of a "consumer logic" such as already prevails in Western societies. . . . a process which tends to accentuate the cultural destructuring of the Third World nations and seriously jeopardizes any chances of a national, endogenous transformation of economic, social and cultural structures.[32]

Advertising is, in fact, a major competitive weapon used by foreign competitors who enter developing-country markets. The advertising budgets spent by TNCs in such markets are impressive. Undoubtedly, a portion of this advertising does indeed result in cultural dislocation as consumers in developing markets are encouraged to desire products that represent alien social, economic, and cultural situations. The case of Nestle's powdered baby formula is often cited as a prime example of strong advertising pressures leading to widespread demand for a product that was "inappropriate" for a variety of reasons. Similar examples include the displacement of a wide variety of locally produced traditional products, such as porridges and chewing sticks by heavily advertised breakfast cereals and toothpastes.[33] On the other hand, the advertising of foreign competitors in the Kenyan market led indigenous firms to improve their advertising and marketing skills and product offerings. Presumably, such skills are essential if local firms are ever to become successful exporters. Advertising might, it could be argued, be the least essential of those skills required for the prospective exporter. A study of Korean exporters, for example, revealed that foreign buyers were relied on to do most of the advertising abroad. But even so, great emphasis was placed on mastering marketing and product design skills through observation of foreign practices.[34]

Assessment on Access to Products

While the data reviewed here regarding access to product technology are fragmentary and often contradictory, it does appear that some overall conclusions can, nonetheless, be drawn from this diverse set of observations. In the first place, import substitution, in general, and as a protective device for infant industries in particular, does not appear to be a particularly effective instrument in improving local access to product technology. Local firms "protected" by such mechanisms tend to become increasingly uncompetitive, and the net result is that the local consumers suffer without any noticeable gain in national capabilities. Furthermore, the design and enactment of such protective barriers are not necessarily straightforward. The late Paul Douglas pointed out several difficulties with infant industry protection:

1. It is almost impossible to predict which industries will become self-supporting and which will fall by the wayside. Since the claims of promising infancy will be advanced for a wide range of industries, uncritical acceptance of the argument could and would lead to encouraging a multitude of new industries which ultimately would not be able to hold their own. In the meantime, we would have wasted some of the resources of the nation on industries which could never grow up and reduced our national and individual prosperity in the process.

2. Those who benefit from the tariff [or other protective mechanism] will refuse to admit that they ever grow up, and even in hoary age will continue to demand protection. The textile and metal industries first raised their infant cries after the War of 1812. These pleas have continued for a century and a half. They were successfully made during and after the Civil War, and again at the turn of the century, and they reappeared with full vigor in the 1920s. Today, the very same groups are still beating the drums for further protection. The textile and steel manufacturers argue as though they were indeed in a perpetual state of infancy. Instead of welcoming the chance to grow up and fend for themselves, they refuse to be weaned and insist rather on drawing sustenance from the breast on an indulgent mother, although they wear the whiskers of old age.[35]

Referring to Dunning's criteria for appraising the entry of foreign competition into a developing market, it would appear from the literature surveyed here that the *economic* criterion appears to be met in the sense that the entry of foreign competitors into developing-country markets almost always results in a larger number of higher quality products than was the case in the previously sheltered markets. Performance against the *equity* criterion, however, is not nearly as unambiguous. While there are instances in which consumers at lower income levels have benefited from price competition fostered by the entry of foreign products,[36] there is also evidence that many foreign products have been luxury items targeted at elites within developing markets.[37]

Measures of *equity* revolving around industry structures are also ambiguous. Dunning, for example, notes that TNCs tend to be concentrated in those industrial sectors where hierarchical (i.e., internally controlled by the firm) rather than market-type transactions predominate. In any case, within these industries, the entry of TNCs leads to a greater concentration of sellers.[38] A case in point is the experience of a number of Latin American nations, where transnational corporations control staggering shares of important markets. In Brazil, for example, the percentage of assets owned by foreign firms in 1977 was: 99.6 percent in motor vehicles, 94.1 percent in electric and communication, 88.5 percent in pharmaceuticals, and 62.1 percent in food.[39] Such concentration supports Dunning's hypotheses. On the other hand, studies of industries in Hong Kong[40] and India[41] report either no change in seller concentration or reduced concentration following the entry of TNCs into the market. In terms of locational effects on equity, the more sophisticated products of TNCs offered in Kenya required more sophisticated markets, more reliance on advertising, more capital-intensive production processes, a well-developed repair and replacement infrastructure, reliable international communications and transportation modes for headquarters personnel. Also, such firms emphasized close political contact with the local government.[42] All of these factors led to a propensity for such firms to locate in the largest cities, Nairobi in particular.

Any discussion of performance against the *sovereignty* and *participation* criteria must, in a sense, treat them both together when considering access to product. It would appear that developing countries suffer as a result of the entry of foreign products and producers in the sense that most of these firms are not actively producing products unique to their local markets but are, instead, attempting to adapt already existing product designs. As a result, local interests are not well represented in the development of product technology and must, instead, accept someone else's values embodied in the technology, or else do without. In the case of India, it appeared that IBM had a plan for the development of the Indian computer industry that was contrary to that of the host government.[43] This posture can clearly be construed as an encroachment on national sovereignty, no matter what the merits of the corporate plan. On the other hand, it must be remembered that such loss of sovereignty is found everywhere that technology is the property of private corporations, and that without such private interests much of the technology that characterizes modern industrial life would not be available.

INFLUENCE IN PROCESS TECHNOLOGY

Discussions about the influence of foreign corporations and production process technology in developing countries are almost exclusively concerned with the issue of what has come to be called "appropriate technology." The central argument is that the process technology employed by the TNCs is developed for resource availabilities that are considerably different from those present in many developing countries. As a result, the technologies are often "inappropriate" with respect to national resource endowments. One recent review of this literature reported on studies of capital intensiveness in Pakistan, India, Brazil, Ghana, and Indonesia.[44] It found TNC subsidiaries to be employing more capital-intensive technology than their local counterparts. Studies of industries in Korea, Mexico, the Philippines,

Taiwan, Thailand, and Kenya, on the other hand, have reported less or equal degrees of capital-intensiveness on the part of foreign firms. Obviously, there is no clear-cut answer to the question of "appropriateness" in manufacturing technology. Nor is the employment of labor intensiveness necessarily the best choice for a surrogate for "appropriate" process technology. Likewise, the studies reviewed for this chapter yielded somewhat contradictory findings regarding the preference of TNCs for more capital-intensive process technology.

In general, the studies reviewed for this chapter suggests that Dunning was correct when he observed that the activities of TNCs in a developing country market "improve the technical competitiveness of firms in the recipient country. . . ." Furthermore, the activities of TNCs appear to be most likely found in industries where their process technology provides them with competitive advantages, either within the developing country market or at home.

MNEs [multinational enterprises] play their most important role in those sectors characterized either by above average technological intensity or product differentiation, for example, the chemical, engineering, motor vehicles and food, drink and tobacco industries. By contrast, indigenous firms . . . dominate in labor intensive producing goods which require fairly standardized technology, for example, textiles, wearing apparel and leather products.

The importance of foreign affiliates of MNEs in high and medium technology industries suggests that the transfer of technology of MNEs . . . has helped to build up these sectors in these countries.[45]

Examples of process technology modernization as a result of competition from foreign producers are to be found, for example, in the increased mechanization of production processes of indigenous Kenyan soap manufacturers when faced with foreign competition.[46] Other examples are those Hong Kong manufacturing industries marked by significant foreign competition and where the presence of the more highly capital-intensive foreign firms makes similar investments more acceptable (or, perhaps, less avoidable) for local firms. It also appears likely that the presence of foreign competition in such industries tends to drive out inefficient local competition, thereby resulting in industries in which the remaining firms are those that were most efficient before the competition ensued.[47] In the opinion of Chen, this process leads to the TNCs being "much more important agents of technology transfer than [are] local firms."[48] A similar finding comes out of a study of direct foreign investment in Portugal, which concludes that

[A] it is undeniable that labor productivity of foreign affiliates is higher than that of their domestic [i.e., Portuguese] counterparts [and] [B] in the absence of foreign direct investment inflow—and even bearing in mind the possibility of utilization of alternative ways for obtaining technology—the Portuguese industrial structure would certainly be more biased towards traditional sectors.[49]

There are a number of important factors inherent in capital-intensive production processes that both explain the preference of the TNCs for such processes and establish differences in competitive behavior between TNCs and local firms. Perhaps the most significant of these is the relationship between product quality and mechanized manufacturing operations.[50] Perceptions of product quality in sophisticated consumer markets tend to be heavily influenced by the reliability of the products. Product reliability, in turn, is dependent upon standardization in the manufacturing process. Such standardization requires capital-intensive manufacturing because labor-intensiveness introduces too much human variation. It is not surprising then that the TNCs, which tend to be much more oriented toward export markets,[51] and which often have internationally recognized brand names to protect, tend to be more capital-intensive. In fact, Keddie's study of 57 investment decisions by 31 TNCs in Indonesia found that product quality was, by far, the most important reason for adopting high-investment-cost technology for production processes.[52] Lecraw, however, in studying a small sample of exporting firms in several light manufacturing industries in Thailand, found that firms producing intermediate products as part of a TNC international sourcing network tended to be even more capital-intensive than were those firms exporting finished products. He reasoned that the export-oriented firms relied on more labor-intensive production processes since they were competing in the world market on the basis of price, while the producers of the intermediate products chose more capital-intensive processes "since they perceived a high risk of variation in quality and disruptions due to labor problems, and were willing to increase costs to reduce these risks."[53]

Product-mix strategies also appear to affect the suitability of various manufacturing processes and, in repetitive manufacturing situations, result in significant variations in the efficiency of capacity utilization in the production process. Yeoman's comparison of the degree of adjustment of production processes employed by foreign subsidiaries of TNC producers in the pharmaceuticals, machinery and equipment, and household appliances industries[54] led to the conclusion that in the latter industry, where cross-elasticity of demand for products was especially high, and where the cost of labor and depreciation as a percentage of the producer's selling price was moderate, there was a far greater willingness to adopt more labor-intensive process technologies than was the case in the other two industries. These relationships were particularly evident at one small-appliance manufacturer where "major [product] design changes were infrequent. [And where] the firms in this segment of the industry competed with relatively standard items, and a number of Japanese companies had successfully entered the market." Similarly, the one machinery and equipment manufacturer to have adjusted its production process to local conditions was an elevator manufacturer whose "marketing skills [through product differentiation] had kept the cross-elasticity of its product line from being the highest of any in the sample."[55] Lecraw also found among several light manufacturing firms in Thailand that firms specializing in brand-name products, and investing heavily in advertising and selling, invested far more in manufacturing equipment than did their counterparts with a more commodity-type product. Presumably, the former could better afford the investment in capital equipment as "the production costs for these firms were a less important component of total costs. [And] the managers of these firms also tended to perceive a higher risk in loss of variability of quality than did the managers of production-oriented firms." On the other hand, he pointed out,

firms that followed a strategy of competing on a price basis with low marketing costs and an undifferentiated product chose a more efficient technology than did marketing-oriented firms. These production-oriented firms needed low production costs in order to compete, because of the higher level of price competition as well as the fact that their production costs were a high proportion of total costs.[56]

According to Ansalem, the findings on the relationship between product differentiation and production process technology can be summarized as follows: "Firms that do not differentiate their products face greater price competition and, hence, greater pressure to minimize costs, thereby leading them to pay more attention to the possibility of adapting technology to factor costs."[57] His own study of TNC firms in the textile and paper industries in four developing countries (Colombia, Brazil, Indonesia, and the Philippines) tended to support this proposition.

While the exploitation of the lower labor costs in developing countries is one way to appraise the relative efficiency of different production processes, the set-up costs involved in broad product lines in repetitive manufacturing situations introduces still another basis for efficiency comparison. In most instances of automated production processes (except for those in which "smart" manufacturing technologies, such as numerically controlled machine tools or flexible manufacturing systems, are employed—which is rarely the case in developing countries), the offering of broad product lines results in production control difficulties. Examples of such difficulties are large inventory accumulations and/or delivery delays, for allowances have to be made for the relative long product-batch runs associated with optimizing the costs of manufacturing changeovers. According to Langdon, a familiar pattern occurs whenever TNCs extend their international oligopolistic competition to the markets of developing countries.

[TNC] subsidiaries enter into oligopolistic competition with each other by product-differentiation rather than price rivalry and, in doing so, attempt to draw on and reproduce as wide a range of parent products as possible. Parent efforts to defend as wide a range of former exports as possible, when persuaded to invest for defensive reasons, lead to similar wide subsidiary product ranges—and changeover inefficiencies.[58]

The manufacturing cost consequences of such product mix policies can be significant. Kenyan textile manufacturers provided Langdon with some striking examples:

One firm, for instance, described how its production of ten different types of cloth, each in five different colors, added 10 percent extra to weaving costs and 20-30 percent extra to printing costs (compared to the costs of producing one type in one color). Another textile factory reported that the production of its wide range of clothtypes (15-16) resulted in capital-output ratios 20 percent higher than if a single standardized product were manufactured. Other consumer goods subsidiaries reported similar inefficiencies—including a food manufacturer making 20 variations of one basic product. . . .[59]

A further manufacturing-related inefficiency was described:

[S]light differences among brand-name variations of the same basic product reduce [the potential for increased indigenous supply] linkages, because they reduce potential output runs for local production, and thereby made such production uneconomic. Toothpaste tubes, for instance, could all have been purchased in Kenya; but because of brand (and size) differentiation, only one brand (out of four or five) had large enough levels of output to justify local manufacture—the rest had to be imported. The same effect was evident in firms using cans and bottles in differentiated markets; often these containers had to be imported because size and design variations took potential production runs below an economic level. Similar points were made by subsidiaries in textile and blanket manufacturing, the electrical products industry, and tent manufacturing.[60]

TNCs subsidiaries integrated with the parent corporation also tend to reduce the sourcing and use of local manufacturing equipment. In Kenya, to expand the previous examples, "very little equipment was produced locally for the TNC sector; and even in the case of material inputs, the great bulk of subsidiaries reported importing more than 70 percent of their supply."[61] Similarly, in Thailand, Lecraw reported that TNCs typically followed limited search routines, concentrating on available "inappropriate" technology, before selecting manufacturing equipment.[62] As a result, he found that Japanese subsidiaries obtained 80 percent of their equipment from home sources, while European and American subsidiaries sourced 57 percent and 51 percent, respectively, of their manufacturing equipment from home suppliers. "Interestingly enough [however], while firms based on other LDCs obtained 25 percent of their equipment locally, Thai-owned firms obtained only 13 percent locally," thus suggesting that the TNCs were not alone in relying on foreign technology.

Assessment of Influence in Process Technology

In appraising the effects of foreign influence on process technology in developing countries, using Dunning's criteria, it seems evident that the *economic* criterion is supported by the presence of foreign competition and by direct foreign investment, in that the variety and sophistication of the process technology employed in developing markets and by locally owned firms tends to increase as a result of greater access to markets by foreign competitors. This relationship was most graphically seen, among the studies reviewed for this chapter, in the high correlation that Chen found between foreign investment in Hong Kong industries and rates of technical progress, and his conclusion that it is foreign investment that leads technological progress rather than the converse.[63] According to Chen, it is the greater propensity of foreign firms to undertake labor training and bring new technologies to Hong Kong that account for this difference.[64] In almost all cases, foreign competition sparks greater efficiency and higher quality in the manufacturing process and this should result in a net overall good.

To the extent that increased use of capital-intensive manufacturing processes is labor-displacing, serious equity considerations accompany any discussion of the economic benefits brought about by increased foreign influence in developing-country markets. Since relatively cheap labor is a comparative advantage of the developing countries, technologies that reduce the labor content of products are "technically inappropriate." Sophisticated markets, however, often require a degree of product quality only obtainable using mechanized production processes. It is therefore conceivable that the increased use of labor-intensive ("appropriate") technology could ultimately result in a larger displacement of labor than experienced at present, if local exports lose favor in international markets as a result of quality failures. Quality concerns and the inertia in engineering design have resulted in some equity losses for the developing world as TNC subsidiaries and local producers continue to rely on foreign sourcing for manufacturing equipment and materials. Such practices lead to outflows of scarce foreign exchange and the supression of local industry growth. On the other hand, brand-name producers cannot afford to take chances with local inputs that suffer from a high variance in quality and reliability and the use of which might imperil the brand-name's reputation.

The choice of process technology, like the issue of access to products, links the criteria of sovereignty and participation closely. It is quite evident that the choice of foreign technology often introduces alien concepts of time, work organization, man-machine relations, and a variety of other industrially sensitive values into developing country economies. Furthermore, as Vaitsos has pointed out, resource allocation and technology decisions of transnational corporations are based primarily on the worldwide interests of the firm and affected by "international multiplant production activities."[65] In many cases, the developing country is regarded by the TNC as a source of resources rather than as a market to be served. In such instances, there is little reason to believe that the interests and actions of the firm will necessarily be in harmony with those of the host country. It is not the purpose of this chapter to comment on the merits or demerits of such events but, rather, to point out their linkages to the issue of technology acquisition and local development and to suggest that such introduction of foreign influence results in a subtle erosion of sovereignty to the extent that the receiving organization is unable to participate in the original design of the technology. In many, if not most, cases, imported foreign technology is subject to very little adaptation, much less design change, to fit the operating and cultural contexts of the developing world. Hence, the loss of sovereignty is not a trivial concern.

ACQUIRING MASTERY OVER TECHNOLOGY

The ultimate objective of the technology transfer experience on the part of the recipient country is eventually to gain mastery over the technology so that in the future it will be able to develop its own indigenous technology to suit its particular needs, or at least to be able to identify and select the foreign technology best suited to its situation and, if necessary, to modify that technology. Such mastery requires that relevant research and development be supported within the developing country so that indigenous technical resources are established and local needs considered in the design, implementation, and use of new technologies. However, the great majority of all the world's R&D, and scientific and technical manpower, are presently located in industrialized countries. Given the small scientific and technical communities in most developing countries and the expense involved in establishing an active R&D program in any industrially relevant field, it is not surprising that the developing world should look to TNCs as one possible vehicle for building local industrial R&D capabilities.[66]

The propensity of TNCs to establish R&D activities in the developing world and the nature of the work undertaken in such facilities is largely dependent upon the market orientation of the firm.[67] Overall, the amount of transnational corporate R&D undertaken in the developing countries is relatively small, and that which is done tends to be largely development or field-station type of work.[68] Those companies most likely to locate applied research and development activities in developing countries are firms whose primary orientation is serving the "host" market. Such firms typically exhibit a relatively low scientific content in the R&D performed and, consequently, do not represent means of gaining access to the sorts of advanced science and technology that many national planners associate with industrial R&D in developed countries.

In process industries, where major technological efforts on products and processes are not crucially linked to each other or to the main production centers and markets, it appears that such factors as international experience and cost advantages tend to promote greater reliance on foreign R&D. In engineering industries, on the other hand, where innovation centers around product development and testing, it seems much more difficult to separate any part of major R&D activity from the main market and the centers of decision making. . . . In these industries, greater technological intensity seems to create a greater centralization of research activity. In terms of absolute value of R&D expenditures, it is these engineering industries which predominate in overseas research; however, most of this research seems to be concentrated on relatively minor technological activity and on techniques which are relatively mature.[69]

A further consideration, in this regard, is that the foreign subsidiaries of "host-market" firms tend to exhibit a considerably greater degree of autonomy within the transnational corporation and, as a result, do not necessarily enjoy guaranteed access to scientific and technical advances made elsewhere within the corporate family.[70]

Although those firms primarily oriented toward serving their "home" markets do not typically consider the placement of R&D offshore as being of interest to them, they may, nonetheless, wind up having oversees R&D activities in developing countries as a result of a need to support their overseas operations. Such cases generally relate to operations located in developing countries to obtain raw materials or low-wage labor. As a result, when they locate an R&D activity abroad it is almost always a testing, developing, or engineering group dedicated to maintaining the production process and the quality of product. Although the activities of such groups can evolve into more sophisticated work, such is not normally the case. Firms pursuing the most technically sophisticated products, on the other hand, tend to serve "worldwide" markets and concentrate their R&D resources in central laboratories that offer economies of scale. These laboratories are almost always in developed countries where there are communities of scientists and engineers to which the firm desires access. In many science-based industries the "critical mass" of R&D professionals deemed necessary to justify investment in an R&D laboratory is often so large that it either strains the available population of trained nationals in a particular field,[71] or else is so expensive that it is unlikely that such a laboratory represents a viable economic investment.[72]

When TNCs choose to locate R&D activities in developing countries, however, they appear to perform more R&D than do their host country competitors. A recent study of R&D performance by TNCs and local companies in Portugal,[73] for example, supports this conclusion. Although in most industries the ratio of R&D expenditures to technology payments were significantly greater in domestic Portuguese firms than in the foreign affiliates, with the exception of those in chemicals and metallurgy, the foreign affiliates reported significantly higher ratios of R&D expenditures to output. In the Hong Kong textiles, apparel, plastics, toys, and electronics industries, foreign-owned subsidiaries tended to spend more on R&D than did the local firms. However, a higher percentage of local firms carried on R&D than did affiliates of TNCs.[74]

Related to R&D work and the effect of such on developing countries is the issue of patents and the ability of TNCs to dominate the granting of national patents. In so doing, they influence the rate and direction of local scientific and technical advances. Undoubtedly, the role of patent protection in advanced industrialized nations has been in many ways a very positive one. Kingston relates that "patents certainly underwrote the growth of the German chemical industry on the basis of scientific research. Those who invested in Edison's earlier inventions (all protected by patents) obtained returns which were well up to the dreams of avarice."[75] In developing countries, however, with small communities of local inventors, too often the national patent system has the appearance of protecting the interests of the better-endowed inventors of the developed world and shutting off inventive opportunities for local nationals. This is particularly apparent in those cases where patent protection is granted for a product that will never be produced locally, thus placing the nation in the ironic position of effectively blocking the developing of its own indigenous innovative resources.

Manpower and Management Training

One of the important benefits associated with TNC activities in a developing country is its presumed ability to train local workers and management in advanced techniques. Earlier in this chapter, it was argued that TNC affiliates operating in developing economies are often considerably more efficient than their local counterparts. Although technology is clearly one reason for such differences, it is not the only reason. One very large contributor is that the management of TNC affiliates tend to be more sophisticated and their workers better trained. In Zaire, for example, comparisons of labor productivity of local textile firms against similar factories in Britain and Canada led to the conclusion that the often significantly lower productivity in Zaire was not due to lower motivational attitudes but, rather, to the lower qualification of workers.[76] Part of this deficiency was attributable to "insufficient training, lack of incentives, poor management-worker relations, and possibly low efficiency of management." Indeed, in 1983, the World Bank emphasized the need for managerial improvement in one of the major sections of its annual *World Development Report*.[77]

In the 1979 report of the Industrial Sector Advisory Group to the Secretary General of the United Nations Conference on Science and Technology for Development, the role of the TNCs as agents of technical skills acquisition and professional development was highlighted.[78] Similarly, a recent study for UNESCO observed that

TNCs are also one of the vehicles for the transmission of a new educational model, either directly by means of their action in respect of vocational training through the intermediary of their subsidiaries, or indirectly by the changes they bring about in social, economic and cultural spheres. As the propagators of a specialized education whose content is directly related to its being turned to full account under modern industrial conditions, as the holders of knowledge in branches of technology which Third World countries lack and lastly, as the users of adaptable, decentralized educational management models, TNCs bring their full weight to bear against the cumbrousness, unsuitability and lack of any genuine cultural foundation of the education systems which often prevail in the Third World.[79]

Review of the direct educational activities of TNCs in training their developing country work forces suggests strongly that the TNCs are, in fact, training a significant number of workers in modern industrial skills and that they are increasingly doing it on a multinational basis in corporate training centers.[80] The payoff from such activities is clearly illustrated in the case of Hong Kong, where

the evidence clearly points out that the local firms pay very little attention to the training of workers. A much smaller proportion of local firms takes up the training of workers and if they do, they tend to spend a very small percentage of their value added on training. Thus, the major contribution of foreign firms in Hong Kong manufacturing is not so much the production of new techniques and products, but the training of workers at various levels. The provision of training at the practical level is of extreme importance for industrial development in Hong Kong.[81]

The presence of TNCs in developing country markets can also have a significant indirect effect on local education by creating a demand for technical and managerial education among citizens who hope to enter the modernizing industrial sector. As a result, more students may apply to postmiddle school educational institutions, and more of these institutions strive to improve the quality of the education offered and to modernize the curricula. While it is impossible to quantify such effects, there is substantial qualitative evidence to support the existence of such a phenomenon.[82]

Assessment of Influence in Mastery of Technology

The presence of a growing amount of R&D activity by TNCs in developing countries attests to the benefits, relevant to a nation's attempts to gain mastery over available technology, flowing from a policy of allowing foreign competitors access to the national market. Such benefits would accrue under Dunning's *economic* criteria. To be realistic, however, the overseas R&D role of the TNCs within the developing countries is, as yet, not very large,[83] and that R&D which is being undertaken tends not to be very sophisticated. Nonetheless, for many countries, such R&D represents the only practical means presently of promoting industrial innovation. Furthermore, to the extent that TNCs engage in the upgrading of national technical and managerial skills, whether directly or indirectly, such talent presumably represents a contribution to a nation's talent pool and should, therefore, constitute a net plus in terms of economic capability.

One of the keys unlocking the ability of a developing counry to achieve the *economic* benefits described above depends upon the ability of such talent to flow out of the TNC sector and into the locally owned sector. At present, there is little indication that this is, in fact, what typically happens. More usually, it would seem, local workers and managers trained within a TNC, and given increased responsibility there, are likely to remain with that firm. If they move at all, it will be to another TNC. In the case of Hong Kong, such reticence to move has been explained in terms of the financial advantages accruing to employees of TNCs: "In the foreign firms, the fringe benefits are usually more and the employer-employee relationship usually better and the labor turnover rate is therefore usually lower. This perhaps explains to some extent why foreign firms are more willing to provide training for workers."[84] As a result of the infrequency of personnel shifts out of the TNC sector within a developing country's economy into the local sector, there is a possible *equity* loss. Many of the mastery benefits attributed to the presence of the TNCs are not well captured, at least in the short run, by local interests.

In terms of Dunning's *sovereignty* criterion, it would appear that the promise of technical skill and managerial development associated with the presence of TNCs within a developing country represent potential gains in a nation's ability to protect its sovereignty with respect to future technology transfer. In too many cases, developing countries enter into technology acquisition or development programs without complete knowledge of the field, or wind up mismanaging projects that would otherwise be beneficial. There are even cases of products banned domestically in the United States, being accepted as imports into nations where adequate scientific and technical skills are not available to prevent such occurences.[85] Presumably, the improved training and experience in R&D, which is likely only through employment in a TNC laboratory (if present), would protect against such abuse.

R&D and the training provided by TNCs possibly constitute the most efficient vehicles for increasing the degree of participation by developing countries. They do so by increasing LDC capacity to influence the rate and direction of technical activities in their economies. The evidence from a wide variety of studies suggests that the TNCs have moved away from dependence on expatriates in most roles. The exceptions tend to be the top management positions in their foreign affiliates. In fact, even at the top management level there is some evidence of movement toward establishing more participation by local nationals. However, the movement of such managers to levels of responsibility above that of the affiliate is still uncommon.[86] It does seem clear, nonetheless, that progress toward greater participation in technological development within many developing countries in the foreseeable future depends upon active participation between local nationals and TNC managements. To some extent, *long-run* gains in technological sovereignty are best achieved through local national participation in schemes that reduce national sovereignty over technological change in the *short run*.

CONCLUSIONS

An examination of the major components of the technological innovation process reveals a multitude of ways in which foreign technical influence can enter a developing country market and alter the rate and direction of technological achievement in that society. Such situations involve trade-offs between benefits and costs; but still it is possible to draw several general conclusions from the material discussed in this chapter.

For all intents and purposes, it appears that import substitution, as a strategy to protect infant industry, is not likely to succeed. Given such protection, the level of competition necessary to stimulate industrial development is not such as to facilitate the healthy growth of the protected industry. For import substitution to work, careful attention must be given to the ongoing technical development of the protected industry and to the deliberate and gradual growth of competition.

Transnational corporations, allowed to operate within a developing economy, either through exports, licensing, contracting, or direct investment, represent a "fast" method of bringing modernizing technical influence into an economy. There are, however, significant equity, sovereignty, and participation costs that must be borne by the developing country in return for the technology. The presence of TNCs within developing economies has been found by the studies reviewed above to result generally in greater product variety, better quality, more efficient utilization of process technology, better training of local workers in modern technical skills, and a greater commitment to R&D than is typical of local enterprises.

NOTES

The terms "transnational corporation" (TNC), "multinational enterprise" (MNE), and "multinational corporation" (MNC) are used interchangeably in this chapter to refer to any large corporation based in an industrialized country with production, service, and/or processing facilities located in several foreign countries. These foreign facilities may be owned wholly or in part by the "parent" corporation, leased by it, or operated under license or contract with little or no cross-border ownership involved.

1. Jaleel Ahmad, *Import Substitution, Trade and Development* (Greenwich, Conn.: JAI Press, 1978), p. 4.

2. William A. Fischer, "Empirical Approaches to Understanding Technlogy Transfer," *R&D Management* 6 (1976), 7–13; and David J. Teece, *The Multinational Corporation and the Resource Cost of International Technology Transfer* (Cambridge, Mass.: Ballinger, 1977).

3. Paul H. Douglas, *America in the Market Place* (New York: Holt, Rinehart and Winston, 1966). p. 52.

4. Ibid., pp. 52–53.

5. John H. Dunning, *International Production and the Multinational Enterprise* (London: George Allen & Unwin, 1981), p. 359.

6. V. W. Ruttan and Y. Hayami, "Technology Transfer and Agricultural Development," *Technology and Culture, Part I* 14:2 (1973), 24–31.

7. Erik A. Haeffner, "The Innovation Process," *Technology Review*, March-April 1973, 19–26.

8. Daniel V. De Simone (for the Panel on Invention and Innovation), U.S. Department of Commerce, *Technological Innovation: Its Environment and Management* (Washington, D.C.: U.S. Government Printing Office, 1967).

9. Jack N. Behrman and William A. Fischer, "Transnational Corporations: Market Orientations and R&D Abroad," *Columbia Journal of World Business* 15 (Fall 1980), 55–60.

10. Ahmad, p. 22.

11. William A. Fischer, *Postwar Japanese Technological Growth and Innovation: A Comparative Review of the Literature* (Washington, D.C.: The Program of Policy Studies in Science and Technology, The George Washington University, 1974).

12. Ahmad, p. 56.

13. Hubert Schmitz, "Industrialization Strategies in Less Developed Countries: Some Lessons of Historical Experience," *The Journal of Developing Studies* 21 (October 1984), 13.

14. Jack N. Behrman and William A. Fischer, *Overseas R&D Activities of Transnational Corporations* (Cambridge, Mass.: Delgeschlager, Gunn & Hain, 1980), p. 107.

15. Vitor Corado Simoes, "Portugal," in John H. Dunning, ed., *Multinational Enterprises, Economic Structure and International Competitiveness* (London: John Wiley/IRM, 1986, p. 28.

16. Bela Belassa, *The Process of Industrial Development and Alternative Development Strategies, Essays in International Finance* No. 141, International Finance Section, Department of Economics, Princeton University, December 1980.

17. L. L. Johnson, "Problems of Import Substitution: The Chilean Automobile Industry," *Economic Development and Cultural Change* 15 (January 1967), 202–216, as cited in Ahmad, p. 34.

18. Alejandro Foxley, *Latin American Experiments in Neoconservative Economics* (Berkeley: University of California Press, 1983), pp. 76, 78.

19. Ibid., p. 70.

20. Steven W. Langdon, *Multinational Corporations in the Political Economy of Kenya* (New York: St. Martin's Press, 1981), pp. 74, 87.

21. Thomas J. Biersteker, *Distortion or Development? Contending Perspectives on the Multinational Corporation* (Cambridge, Mass.: MIT Press, 1978), pp. 103–118.

22. Ian Little, Tibor Scitovsky, and Maurice Scott, *Industry and Trade in Some Developing Countries: A Comparative Study* (New York: Oxford University Press, 1970).

23. List compiled by author.

24. R. M. Bell, *"Technical Change in Infant Industries: A Review of the Empirical Evidence"* (Sussex, Science Policy Research Unit, University of Sussex, 1982), mimeo.

25. Schmitz, p. 6.

26. Ahmad, p. 56.

27. Langdon, p. 56.

28. Dunning, pp. 192–193.

29. Francis Stewart, *Technology and Underdevelopment* (Boulder, Colo.: Westview Press, 1977); Louis T. Wells, Jr., "Economic Man and Engineering Man: Choice of Technology in a Low-Wage Country," *Public Policy* 21 (Summer 1973), pp. 319–342.

30. Ibid.

31. Joseph M. Grieco, *Between Dependency and Autonomy* (Berkeley: University of California Press, 1983), pp. 27–30, 48.

32. Jean-Louis Reiffers, Andre Cartapanis, William Experton, and Jean-Luc Fuguet, *Transnational Corporations and Endogenous Development* (Paris: United Nations Educational, Scientific and Cultural Organization, 1982), pp. 154–155.

33. Langdon, p. 132.

34. Yung Whee Rhee, Bruce Ross-Larson, and Garry Pursell, *Korea's Competitive Edge* (Baltimore: The Johns Hopkins University Press for the World Bank, 1984), pp. 61–65.

35. Douglas, pp. 34–35.

36. Langdon, p. 89.

37. Robert H. Ballance, Javed A. Ansari, and Hans W. Singer, *The International*

Economy and Industrial Development: The Impact of Trade and Investment on the Third World (Totowa, N.J.: Alanheld, Osmun, 1982), p. 235.

38. Dunning, pp. 188.

39. Jean-Max Baumer, Albrecht von Gleich, Renate Heierli, and Karsten Jaspersen, *Transnational Corporations in Latin America* (Amsterdam: Verlag Reugger, 1982), p. 119.

40. Edward K. Y. Chen, *Multinational Corporations, Technology and Employment* (New York: St. Martin's Press, 1983), p. 62.

41. Ballance et al., p. 247.

42. Langdon, p. 73.

43. Grieco.

44. Chen, pp. 102–104.

45. Dunning, pp. 323, 332.

46. Langdon, p. 74.

47. Chen, p. 89.

48. Ibid., p. 64.

49. Simoes, pp. 13, 26.

50. Louis T. Wells, Jr., "Economic Man and Engineering Man," in Robert Stobaugh and Louis T. Wells, Jr., eds., *Technology Crossing Borders* (Boston: Harvard Business School Press, 1984), pp. 50–54.

51. Stewart, p. 51.

52. James Keddie, "More on Production Techniques in Indonesia," in Stobaugh and Wells, pp. 72–77.

53. Donald J. Lecraw, "Choice of Technology in Thailand," in Stobaugh and Wells, p. 99.

54. Wayne A. Yeoman, "Selection of Production Processes by U.S.-Based Multinational Enterprises," in Stobaugh and Wells, pp. 21–44.

55. Ibid., pp. 42–43.

56. Lecraw, p. 99.

57. Michel Ansalem, "Technology Choice for Textiles and Paper Manufacture," in Stobaugh and Wells, p. 124.

58. Langdon, 121.

59. Ibid., p. 122.

60. Ibid., pp. 113–114.

61. Ibid., p. 107.

62. Lecraw, p. 96.

63. Chen, pp. 43–51.

64. Ibid., p. 66.

65. Constantine Vaitsos, "Foreign Investment and Productive Knowledge," in Guy F. Erb and Valeriana Kallab, eds., *Beyond Dependency* (Washington, D.C.: Overseas Development Council, 1975), p. 76.

66. Jack N. Behrman and William A. Fischer, *Science and Technology for Development* (Cambridge, Mass.: Oelgeschlager, Gunn & Hain, 1980).

67. Behrman and Fischer, "Transnational Corporations."

68. Behrman and Fischer, *Overseas R&D Activities*.

69. Sanjaya Lall, "The International Allocation of Research Activity by U.S. Multinationals," *Oxford Bulletin of Economics and Statistics* 41 (November 1979), 313–331.

70. William A. Fischer and Jack N. Behrman, "The Coordination of Foreign R&D Activities by Transnational Corporations," *Journal of International Business Studies*, Winter 1979, pp. 28–35.

71. Ibid., pp. 73–76.

72. Edwin Mansfield, David Teece, and Anthony Romeo, "Overseas Research & Development by U.S.-Based Firms," *Economica* 46 (May 1979), 187–196.

73. Fernando Goncalves, paper prepared for the Portuguese Workshop on Innovation-Based Technology, Povoa de Varzim, Portugal, October 17, 1984.

74. Chen, pp. 55–58.

75. William Kingston, *The Political Economy of Innovation* (The Hague: Martinus Nijhoff, 1984), p. 82.

76. Eckhard Siggel, "On the Nature of Technology Shelves Facing Less Developed Countries: Some Hypotheses and Case Studies," *The Journal of Developing Areas* 18 (January 1984), 227–246.

77. *World Development Report 1983* (Washington, D.C.: The World Bank, 1983).

78. The Industrial Sector Advisory Group to the Secretary General of the United Nations Conference on Science and Technology for Development, *The Contribution of Transnational Enterprises to Future World Development* (Vienna: United Nations Conference on Science and Technology for Development, August 20–31, 1979), pp. 14–15.

79. Reiffers et al., p. 183.

80. Ibid, pp. 194–208.

81. Chen, p. 61.

82. Reiffers et al., pp. 208–225.

83. Behrman and Fischer, (see note 66) p. 91.

84. Chen, p. 61.

85. Jack G. Kaikati, "Domestically Banned Products: For Export Only," *Journal of Public Policy and Marketing* 3 (1984).

86. Joseph D. Peno, Jr., "Multinational Corporate Behavior in Host-Country High-Level Manpower Markets: The Implications for Technology Transfer and Foreign Investment Control in the Less Developed Host Countries," in Dimitri Germidis, ed., *Transfer of Technology by Multinational Corporations* (Paris: Organization for Economic Cooperation and Development, 1977).

Part Four

RESPONSES OF
FOREIGN INVESTORS

Chapter Nine

The Multinational Corporation and the Host Country Environment

John S. Schwendiman

It is interesting to me that the Chinese are concerned with understanding the futures of foreign business through the end of this century, but from a different vantage point in a different culture and country from my own. I am in a real sense a "futurist," trying to understand what the key factors or driving forces are in the unfolding of economic, social, political, and technological events and trends into the future.

The essence of long-range planning is not in making decisions in the future; it is making decisions *today* with a basis of the best possible facts and assumptions about the future. The question that I attempt to answer is: "As multinational corporations look at China or any country, how do they analyze the future of the country as a location for business activities, particularly in terms of direct investment, but also in terms of the many ways in which international business is conducted?"

At the outset I repeat and enlarge upon a point made by others. Foreign private companies exist to make a return for investors—a profit derived from the utilization of capital and human resources. Profits in this world are by no means guaranteed in free or open market societies or in commerce that crosses borders. In a real sense, profits must not only reflect a reasonable return to capital, but also a return to compensate for the risk that many times there will be no profit at all, only losses.

Companies do not exist to be charitable institutions. They do not "give away" that which is of greatest value to them—whether capital, technology, management know-how, or "competitive advantage." There is always a calculation of cost and benefit, with the emphasis being heavy on the benefit or profit side. As someone put it: "There is no such thing as a free lunch." Companies do not have to make a specific investment in a specific country. They can and do say "no."

Negotiations between a multinational corporation and its host country are always complicated. There are interests, "sticking points," on both sides. I believe that a clear understanding on the part of both host country officials and foreign business representatives of the concerns, criteria, and priorities of potential private foreign investors can greatly help the negotiation process. It can positively influence the role that foreign investment can play in the national development of a country.

The first two sections of this chapter include specific examples of why foreign investors are often wary of their host countries, why they are often difficult to negotiate with, and why they so carefully negotiate their investment arrangements. Whether it was Mexico in the 1930s; Peru in the 1960s; Argentina, Chile, Angola, Iran, or Libya in the 1970s; or Yugoslavia, Brazil, Canada, or Korea in the 1980s, events have occurred that have caused substantial losses for foreign investors and have caused them to be wary. In fact, the level of foreign investment for many companies, including my own, in the mid-1980s, is down substantially from a few years ago.

POLITICAL RISK

The role of the multinational corporation in the economic development of a country can take many forms. Involvement can range from direct investment in wholly owned manufacturing facilities to joint ventures or licensing arrangements for technology. For an involvement to make a long-term positive contribution it must be of long-term benefit to both parties, the multinational corporation and the host country.

Although U.S.-based natural resources companies (in mining and petroleum, for example) were heavily involved in resource-rich developing countries for many decades, the broad internationalization of U.S. business interests has come since the 1950s. Many large U.S. companies have gone from virtually no involvement in international markets to half or more of their business now being outside their home (or base) country. This is somewhat in contrast to many European companies that, because of relatively much smaller home country markets, have been much more internationally oriented for a longer period of time.

Companies investing in other countries have always been concerned about relations in the host countries. For many years the potential problem of expropriation was a significant concern to investors. In recent years expropriation (in the traditional sense) has probably become less of a concern. However, other concerns have arisen to replace those of outright expropriation. The term "creeping expropriation" has sometimes been used to describe a process perceived by the investor as one in which the policies of the host country in effect strangle an enterprise, and accomplish over time, in a de facto sense, an expropriation. A company is seen to have reached this point when it has virtually no control of its capital resources or its profitability because of rules, regulations, or discriminatory policies.

Companies have tried and are trying to be cognizant of the potential problems (or risks) they face in a given host country environment. Business strategies are developed to deal with potential risks. Louis Wells of Harvard has written much about building on a company's strengths in developing a strategy for dealing with a host country.[1]

The events that occurred in Iran late in 1978 and into 1979 with the overthrow of the shah and subsequent negative experiences for many investing companies (especially those based in the United States) spawned the further emergence of a field that had begun years earlier. "Political risk analysis" became a new term about which many managers talked. Companies hired "experts," often people retired from the U.S. Foreign Service or the Central Intelligence Agency, to make political assessments of countries as a part of the strategic planning and management process.

The high-growth period of the use of political risk analysis by U.S. companies is over, and the emphasis has subsided. There remains, however, a basic caution and sensitivity that was lacking previously for many companies. The wide range of relevant consultant services has become somewhat institutionalized and professionalized with the establishment in 1980 of the Association of Political Risk Analysts, currently with over 400 members in the United States and Europe.

There is a difference between "normal business risks" and "environmental (economic, social, and political) risks." The business environment and the rules and practices governing business are generally fairly stable, but with time they may change due to the interaction of economic, social, and political forces. Political risk assessment is broadened here to include economic, social, political, and business environment factors. To aid in an understanding of this subject, I will use many examples from the experiences and programs of The Dow Chemical Company, many of which, however, can be generalized to a large number of U.S. companies.

INTERNATIONALIZATION AND EXPERIENCE OF THE DOW CHEMICAL COMPANY

Rapid expansion in international markets, through direct investments, licensing, joint ventures, and export sales was the great engine of growth for the Dow Chemical Company in the 1960s and 1970s. From an international base in 1960 of less than 10 percent of sales, by 1980 the company reached the point of having over 50 percent of its sales and profits come from outside the United States. In 1984 total worldwide sales were in excess of $11 billion. The company fully expects that in the future non-U.S. business will provide over one-half, and perhaps even more, of corporate sales and profits.

The Dow Chemical Company operates manufacturing plants in approximately 30 countries and sales offices in 70. There is hardly a country in the world that is not the specific responsibility of some Dow manager. Being involved in Dow's international business has been a proving ground for many of the company's top corporate officers. Of the top 20 who are members of the company's management committee, 14 have had significant international management experience.

Dow's experience with international growth is not atypical of the experiences of many companies. Investment followed export sales. Dow's first investment outside the United States was in Mexico in the early 1950s. At the time, the firm's rapidly growing Texas manufacturing division considered the Mexican market and the small investment there as a logical extension of its business. In 1952 Dow and Asahi Chemical Company in Japan established a joint venture, Asahi-Dow, which was to grow and develop for 30 years. When Asahi-Dow split up by mutual agreement of the partners in 1982, it had become an $800 million sales company.

These early investments were not followed by additional ones until the 1960s. In the meantime a global sales organization, based on exports from the United States, and an international division (Dow International) came into being. The first European plants, at Terneuzen in The Netherlands, were begun in 1962. At Terneuzen, Dow set out to do for the European market, under the beneficial trade arrangements of the European Economic Community, what it was best at doing in the United States, building a very large, world-scale, highly integrated and efficient chemical production complex for the manufacture of large-volume commodity chemicals and plastics. With that idea for a base, Dow became the largest U.S. participant in the European chemical market. Dow's 1984 European sales approximated $4 billion.

The mid-1960s brought a change in the way the international business was managed. A regional management concept was introduced, and geographic "areas" were established: Dow U.S.A., Dow Canada, Dow Latin America, Dow Europe, and Dow Pacific. Today, additionally, there are subareas for Brazil, Middle East/Africa, and Japan. Regional headquarters were established, with the headquarters for Dow Chemical Pacific being in Hong Kong.

The area organization was overlaid in a matrix fashion with centralized product management groups called "corporate product departments" (now "global product management units"), with responsibility for global product strategies. In practice, the power base in the company shifted from centralized to decentralized management, with the area managers becoming very powerful in the company. At one point (in 1979), all area presidents were also members of the company's largely internal board of directors.

The evolution is now in the direction of individual globally managed businesses, the first of which are pharmaceuticals, agricultural products, and consumer products. Centralized management and control over these major sectors of the company is now emerging. Admittedly, no two multinational companies have evolved in exactly the same way. However, patterns do emerge and can be studied. Basic issues such as organization, control, preferred ways of doing business, and personnel management have to be resolved, no matter what product or technology is involved.

With the establishment of the area concept came the first attempts to develop investment projects in the so-called developing countries. It was at this point that Dow first confronted directly the challenge of evaluating country environment risk. Some early experiences pointed up the necessity of a more formal approach to risk assessment and management in Latin America and subsequently in the Pacific area. But for Canada, Europe, and the United States itself, there were no formal procedures for assessment. Managers who had spent many years on the international side of the company continued, until the end of the 1970s, to make basically intuitive judgments as far as managing enterprises and risks was concerned.

In 1966 and 1967 Dow had been invited by the government of Chile to build a petrochemical complex. The project was to be a joint venture, but majority ownership would be in Dow's hands. The plants would produce basic plastics. The business outlook was good, recommendations were made, and the company's board of directors authorized a $30 million investment (which would be over $100 million in today's dollars), of which a major portion would be financed by borrowing external to Chile.

As is the case with any large capital-intensive petrochemical project, the design and actual construction of the Chilean plants took more than three years. In 1970, with six months remaining before the plants were to be started up, Salvador Allende was elected president of Chile. His campaign promises had been to change completely the basis of the economy, expropriate foreign investors, and throw off foreign influences. The Dow project, although a joint venture with a Chilean government company, was large and visible. It was a time of decision, but Dow decided to finish the plants, run them, live up to the contracts, and be "a good corporate citizen."

Nonetheless, some two years thereafter, Dow was expropriated. The legal term in Chile was "intervened." Dow was one of the last foreign companies to be taken over, but that was still six months before the coup that ousted Allende. In the meantime, business conditions deteriorated rapidly. Inflation was runaway—over 900 percent in Allende's last year. The balance of payments was a disaster. No foreign exchange was available. Dow costs went up faster than prices because there was an attempt to control chemical product prices, but not raw materials. Profits disappeared. The situation was dismal. Later, several months after the coup that ousted Allende, the new military regime approached Dow and asked the company to return. That meant going back into a very shaky environment, but Dow went back and is still there.

It was during the same period that an even larger project was being developed for Bahia Blanca in Argentina. That project had already cost over $2 million of development money and moving expenses for the project team when a new government came into power, a government that changed the rules for that kind of investment almost 180 degrees. Dow decided not to do anything further, dropped the project, and moved its people home.

During this period, both corporate and area management asked a lot of tough questions. Was there any way in which these problems could have been foreseen? Could Dow's strategies have been developed or adjusted to deal more explicitly with foreseen or unforeseen risks? What could be done differently for the future?

It was out of these difficult experiences that in 1971 an effort was begun in Dow Chemical Latin America that resulted in Dow's Economic, Social, and Political Assessment Program (ESP Program, for short). ESP is a systematic framework for analyzing the many factors in a country and business environment that may impact on a foreign investment by Dow.

Other companies have had varied experiences. The oil companies had to cope at much earlier dates with expropriation. Exxon Corporation, for example, had by the late 1960s a well-developed program for environmental assessment both at its New York headquarters and in its regional operating companies. Others, previously noted, did not formalize any assessment activities until they had been badly hurt in the aftermath of the ouster of the shah of Iran.

BASES AND CONTENT OF COMPANY ENVIRONMENTAL ASSESSMENT PROGRAMS

Companies approach the assessment of country environments with different methodologies, but the same kinds of issues appear for consideration, no matter what the methodology. Before considering the specifics of what is assessed, however, it is appropriate to define the concept of "risk." What does it mean to speak of "risk" in a host country environment?

There are at least two broad categories of risk to be distinguished. First is "normal business risk," what might also be called "commercial risk" or "competitive risk." These risks are the natural consequences of being in business: the risk that one's competitors may offer a better product, or a lower price, or better technology, or more attractive terms, or better delivery, or a completely new product that eliminates the need for that presently being produced. These risks all operate against a background of a basically stable business environment.

There are also "environmental risks," those that arise out of economic, social, and political events, trends, or shocks, that can cause the business environment itself to change. These changes in business environment frequently mean changes in the "rules" or ways of doing business. They may be favorable, unfavorable, or possibly neutral. But change brings uncertainty, and it is uncertainty that people look at as being an important environmental risk.

Many analysts and students of business have used the term "investment climate" to refer to countries and their business environments. I do not believe that there is a single "investment climate" for a country. Rather, there is a whole range of investment climates, depending on the nature of the product, the project, the importance of the sector, and other factors. (This view is why Dow finds the reports of generalized country risk assessment services and consultants of little relevance or use in decison making.)

Two authors have addressed this subject:

For most companies, in fact, *countries don't have risks; projects have risks.* And the degree to which an individual project is at risk in a particular country will vary with such factors as the size of the fixed investment, the degree to which investment is bunched at one moment in time or strung out over a longer period, the stability of the project's basic technology, the extent to which the sector is divided among many smaller or a few larger firms, the extent of vertical integration and its importance to the project's economics.[2]

Dow's experience in Brazil illustrates the point. Dow has major chloralkali production in Brazil, what is called a basic chemical. On the other hand, the company has a major pharmaceutical business, which faces a completely different set of rules and regulations. Then there are commodity plastics such as polystyrene, and such specialty products as epoxy resins and styrene-butadiene latexes, not to mention agricultural chemicals. Each of these businesses faces different challenges and risks.

For an industrial company, it is the economic, social, and political risks associated with a specific project, in the context of the total country economic, social, and political environment, which are important. For example, in Dow the economic evaluation (capital project analysis) for a major new manufacturing plant proposal generally projects ahead 12 to 14 years. From the time a decision is made to build a plant it can take three to five years for engineering, construction, and start-up. If the plant has been linked to a growing market demand, it may well be two to three years more before full-capacity utilization is reached. Peak profitability (with efficient full-capacity production) thus comes at around seven years into the project.

The time horizon for Dow's economic, social, and political assessment studies, therefore, becomes five to seven years. If it cannot be seen quite clearly that the host country political and economic situation, and the rules under which the investment is to be made, are going to remain stable seven years into the future, then it is very questionable whether the investment should be made. Alternatively, the company must find some way, or strategy, to hedge against perceived risks. The problem of time horizon varies with the type of industry and company. The problem for a capital-intensive chemical company is quite different from that for a consumer products company. The focus of analysis is also different from that of a banking institution, which may look primarily at the ability of a country to repay its debts.

Few companies conduct risk analysis to reach "on" or "off" decisions regarding investments, although such analysis is an important part of the decision process. Once a worthwhile commercial opportunity has been found and proposed, risk analysis can be used to assess the noncommercial risks so that they can be understood and dealt with. That is, strategies can be developed to minimize the risks and maximize the opportunities. Ideally, only after a project has been developed, its risks analyzed, and ways to minimize them devised, can it be compared with other projects in the corporate system, similarly developed, which compete for limited capital and managerial resources.

In Dow's ESP Program there are four basic structural elements, similar to those found in many multinational companies: (1) a business condition checklist or index, (2) a checklist or index of basic pressures for change, (3) a summary of key factors and assumptions, and (4) a range of scenarios or "alternative futures."

The business conditions checklist is made up of approximately 40 key descriptors of business conditions in the prospective host country. These include: real economic growth rate, availability of local capital, price controls, infrastructure, profit repatriation rules, freedom to reinvest, skill levels of work force, labor stability, investment incentives, and attitudes toward foreigners. When each factor is evaluated against a scale of "goodness" or "badness" (in terms of impact on a company or project), an index can be created. The checklist can be used in a retrospective, present conditions, or prospective mode.

The concept of a checklist of "pressure" factors (those factors that could result in pressures building either for positive or negative change in the business environment) goes back to a book by Peter Drucker entitled *The Age of Discontinuity*.[3] Discontinuities in trends give business planners the most headaches. Typically, in business forecasting one looks for trends and postulates continuation of such, perhaps with cyclical components added. Drucker pointed out that when discontinuities occur, the seeds of that discontinuity generally were there well before the event. The task of risk assessment analysts is to find those seeds that are germinating, sprouting, growing, and perhaps even being fertilized, but that are not obvious in trend lines. The Dow checklist of over 40 types of potential pressures to watch includes: balance-of-payments structure and trends, vulnerabilities to external shock, economic growth versus expectations, where opinion leaders are headed, stability of leadership changes, relations with neighboring countries, terrorism or unrest, balance of economic and social progress, population composition and demographic trends, and attitudes toward foreigners and foreign investments.

For example, take the question of vulnerability to external shock. Back in the late 1960s and early 1970s Brazil was growing very rapidly. GNP growth per year in real terms was 8-10 percent. Things were really booming in Brazil. One of the questions people asked then was, "What could possibly cause Brazilian growth to slow down?" As it turned out, a major cause of eventual slowdown in Brazil was external to the country. The two oil crises/shocks of 1973/74 and 1978/79 were enough to slow down growth and push Brazil, which had borrowed heavily on international markets to finance its growth, into a financial crisis.

Relating this concept to China, I believe the analyst today must ask: "What, if anything, in the form of an external shock on China, could have a significant impact?" I will not attempt to answer that; I only raise the question.

Another factor I would comment on here is economic growth versus expectations. This subject is commonly referred to in the literature of economic development as possibly leading to a "crisis of rising expectations." That is, the capacity of an economy to deliver an ever increasing volume of consumer goods and services to the population and still maintain adequate levels of investment. This problem has been severe in Mexico and other Latin American nations.

With reference to China, an analyst could ask this question: "Has the opening or loosening up of the economy to a much wider variety of consumer goods created a momentum that could be difficult to slow should that become necessary?" Again, I do not presume to know the answer, but I believe the question is one that should be asked.

However, to return to the two checklists: By considering all of the factors and potential pressures listed, one can identify the eight or ten factors critical to the success of a specific project or country involvement. These key factors, and the basic assumptions that must underlie them, become key indicators to be monitored on an ongoing basis. As such, they become the basis for continuing country assessment and review.

A fourth element of structure in Dow's program, which is widely used among other companies as well, is the "scenario" approach. Key factors and assumptions must be generated before scenarios can become useful, because the scenarios must be built upon them. Different types of scenarios can be created. In Dow's case, four country/project scenarios are normally developed. The first is a "most likely" scenario for the key economic, social, political, and business factors for seven years into the future. A second scenario postulates, "If things go better than expected, how much better might they be?" This second is the basis for an "optimistic scenario. A third question is asked, "If things go worse, what might characterize the situation?" A "pessimistic" scenario is thus formulated. To focus on things of greatest importance to the company, a "disaster" scenario is drawn up. This last does not necessarily mean a country disaster scenario, but what would constitute a "disaster" for the company. When the scenarios have been developed, subjective probabilities can be assigned and compared by various people, if desired, to portray the results to the company's management.

RESOURCES FOR COUNTRY INFORMATION, INSIGHT, AND INTERPRETATION

In conduction business environment analyses, companies use many different sources of information. Among those external to the country, sources used by analysts include the following:

1. *"Think-tank"* specialists, such as those at Georgetown University's Center for Strategic and International Studies, the Hoover Institution, and the Council on Foreign Relations in New York City.

2. *U.S. Department of State* country desk officers and political and economic analysts, who are often well-informed.

3. *U.S. Department of Commerce* country desks, although these people focus primarily on the commercial and business environment. (Analysts generally find the Commerce Department an excellent source of trade and market data.)

4. *World Bank (IBRD)* personnel involved in "missions" to various countries. (These people are often willing to talk about their views, though their written reports are generally confidential.)

5. The *International Monetary Fund* publications such as *International Financial Statistics*, which are a key and consistent source of data.

6. The *U.S. Export-Import Bank* officers can be very helpful with their insight.

7. *International banks* maintain extensive files of country data. (Their officers and economic-political analysts are generally willing to share their views.)

8. *Managers in other companies*, both in the same and in different industries, can relate their experiences and give first-hand impressions if they are operating in the country under consideration.

9. *University centers of international studies* have many scholars and faculty who have spent lifetimes studying various countries and cultures. Examples are the Institute of Latin American Studies at the University of Texas at Austin, the Middle East Research Institute at the University of Pennsylvania, the Center for Chinese Studies at the University of Michigan, the School of International Studies at the University of Washington, and the Center for African Studies at the University of California at Los Angeles.

10. *Regional organizations*, such as the Organization of American States for Latin America, likewise have many resources.

11. *"Rating" organizations*, such as Business International, Frost and Sullivan, Business Environment Risk Index (BERI), and the Economist Intelligence Unit have built up large date bases on countries.

12. There are a large number of *consultants* who specialize in economic, social, political environment studies for clients. Examples are Probe International Inc., Multinational Strategies, Inc., International Business-Government Counsellors, Inc., and firms such as Keller-Dorsey Associates and Oxford Analytica in the United Kingdom, and a host of individual consultants, frequently former government people.

13. *Journalists* can also be helpful with observations, although often they look only for a current "story" rather than for the historical context and meaning of events.

Analyses of countries should also include visits to the countries by key decision makers and analysts. In order to get broad view of the local business environment and the pressures for change (discontinuities), the visitors should be involved with a wide cross-section of people. Such local resources to be investigated can include:

1. *Bankers*, both local and international, resident in the country.

2. *Local businessmen*, who can give a feeling for how the foreign investor has been or will be received.

3. *Foreign businessmen* operating in the country who can provide another viewpoint on essentially the same issues. (It is always good to compare the perspectives of local and foreign businessmen and note the congruence or divergence of views on key issues.)

4. The *U.S. Embassy*, which has economic, political, and commercial people who can give an immediate "on-the-spot" review, which can be compared with the viewpoints reported in Washington.

5. Conversations with university *students and professors* can give an important perspective on emerging issues and conditions.

6. *Customers* and potential customers are a good source of information on the key business conditions in the target market.

7. *Political or government leaders* may be visited, but one generally does not learn anything more than what these people are saying publicly. (In countries where an organized political opposition exists, members of the opposition may also be contacted.)

8. Local *publications and journalists* can give a good feel of who the "opinion leaders" are and what viewpoints they are espousing.

9. To the extent possible, *labor leaders* may be consulted. (If the project in question has a high labor content, it is very important for the investor to know excactly what kind of labor needs it will be facing.)

Neither of these lists is meant to be complete, but they do cover a range of resources that can be investigated. Probably no two analysts will approach an assignment in the same way, so the weighting given to each kind of resource is variable.

Environmental assessment ideally should not be merely a one-time process, done only when a major project is being developed, but rather be a continuing part of a program for sustaining good relations with the host country. Also, evaluation needs to be ongoing in order to cope with changes and contingencies. Over time, good relationships with local sources can be developed. But assessment specialists should always probe beyond the easy and obvious to get an early feeling for changes that may be coming.

CONCLUSIONS

In contrast to years past, multinational corporations today, particularly those that are U.S.-based, are much more sensitive to political, economic, and business conditions in their host country environments. The experiences of Dow Chemical cited in this chapter are not untypical of those of many other companies.

More sensitivity to such issues has probably resulted in better business strategies being developed and in more productive and definitive negotiations between multinational corporations and host countries. On the one hand, host country negotiators are better prepared than ever before. They have more experience, expertise, and understand better how multinational corporations operate. On the other hand, the companies understand better the needs, concerns, and priorities of their host countries. In particular, they are more sensitive to going where they are wanted or desired.

The most important factors that companies consider in evaluating a host country environment vary because of planning horizon, nature of the business, capital and/or intensity, and other things. The specific checklists may differ in particulars but not in breadth. The use of internal evaluation systems or hired consultants results in the investigation of the same kinds of issues. Preeminent among concerns, however, is the necessity for the rules for foreign investments and the conduct of business to be stable—not necessarily unchanging, or unevolving, but nevertheless stable. It is the uncertainty of random change that causes companies to decline otherwise attractive opportunities.

This consideration leads to the concept of time horizon. Companies that are heavily capital-intensive have much longer time horizons than companies using capital equipment that can be set up in six months rather than five or six years. The Pepsi-Cola joint venture in Shenzhen is an example of a company that went into production within a six-month period. Companies that must make large capital investments over several years are very reluctant to enter into ventures with fixed termination or "renewal" dates of 10, 15, or 20 years.

Also deserving of emphasis is the distinction I have made between business conditions as they now exist and may exist in the future *and* the underlying political, social, and economic driving forces or pressures that may cause those business conditions to change, sometimes in an evolutionary way, but sometimes very abruptly.

Knowledge by host country officials of how their country's environment is viewed by potential investors can be very useful to the host country in developing its policies for foreign investors and in its negotiating stance. Perhaps it may be useful to suggest some of the views held by people outside China today. In so doing, I make no value judgment as to the correctness or incorrectness of these views. I would point out, however, that often it is perceptions rather than objective facts that influence decision makers.

A recent *Fortune* magazine article on China had this to offer:

For companies willing to pay the price, put up with the bureaucratic guff, and gamble that China will stay on course for a while, the payoff could be worthwhile. Since the 19th century, when merchants dreamed of selling "oil for the lamps of China," as the catch phrase went at that time, Westerners have been dazzled by the potentially huge Chinese market. It's still largely out of reach for most consumer products from the West, since the average annual income of China's more than one billion consumers is about $300. But that's bound to change fast since the economic reforms are designed, among other things, to put cash in the pockets of ordinary Chinese.[4]

A key phrase in this quotation is "stay on course." There seems to be a widespread feeling among observer groups that China is headed in a correct direction—on a course that, with time and experience, will make China increasingly attractive to foreign investors. At the present time, however, there are some nagging doubts expressed by people as they look at China over the last 50 years and observe that it has a history of sudden ideological swings. Companies are looking for assurance that when the present administration passes from the scene there will not be a reversal of the policy of opening to foreign investment.

Another perception is that China is one of the most expensive places in the world in which to do business.

Still another perception is a desire that joint ventures not be set up with a termination date in the contract. This is likened to planning a wedding and specifying a divorce date in advance. Such a policy tends to make both partners hold back a bit in giving their best effort to assure the success of the enterprise. Many companies want to come to China to conduct mutually profitable business, but they do not want to give away their technology by putting their "crown jewels" or most valuable technology and know-how into a joint venture, particularly if a forced separation is planned.

Another perception is perhaps portrayed best in a recent article from *The Economist* magazine:

The most intractable difficulty, though, is remitting foreign exchange. Earnings are all in local currency, the yuan. What do you spend it on? In Shenzhen, even the electricity has to be bought in foreign currency. Most businessmen reckon that the single most important change China could make to attract more investment would be to provide guarantees that local earnings can be converted into foreign exchange and remitted home.[5]

One final quotation: "China's modernization plans require some joint ventures to talk in billions, but few projects so far have exceeded $20 million."[6]

I have heard managers of major multinational corporations say, "China will be the world's greatest business frontier for the next twenty years."

There is a great desire on the part of many U.S. and other multinational companies to enter the China market. For some companies it seems as though they might do almost anything to get their "foot in the door," even agreeing to stipulations that they would find unpalatable elsewhere in the world. However, getting one's foot in the door is different from going all the way in. In other words, a company might be willing to put $5-10 million at risk, but not $100 million *before* seeing how the smaller investment works out over time.

It seems to me that changing these perceptions takes time. It is impossible to hurry the process. It takes foreign investors time to gain experience and confidence. I believe that $10 million in investments cannot be hurried or rushed into commitments of $100 million or more, in spite of the assurances given or incentives offered. Skeptics remain.

NOTES

1. See, for example, L. T. Wells, "Negotiating with Third World Governments," *Harvard Business Review*, January-February 1977, 72–80.

2. Paul M. Sacks and Stephen Blank, "Forecasting Political Risk," *The Corporate Director*, September/October 1981, 10 (emphasis added).

3. Peter Drucker, *The Age of Discontinuity*, New York: Harper & Row, 1969.

4. *Fortune*, February 18, 1985, p. 29.

5. *The Economist*, February 16, 1985, p. 66.

6. Ibid.

BIBLIOGRAPHY OF USEFUL WORKS

Alsop, Ronald. "More Firms are Hiring Own Political Analysis to Limit Risks Abroad." *Wall Street Journal*, March 30, 1981, p. 1.

Baily, Kathleen C. "Profiling an Effective Political Risk Assessment Team." *Risk Management*, February 1983, 23–46.

Blank, Stephen et al. *Assessing the Political Environment: An Emerging Function in International Companies*. New York: The Conference Board, 1980.

Brown, Alan, S. "Handicapping the Foreign Investment Gamble." *Chemical Marketing Reporter*, September 21, 1981, pp. 30–35.

Bryon, Christopher. "In Search of Stable Markets." *Time*, May 25, 1981, p. 69.

Ensor, Richard (ed.). *Assessing Country Risk*. London: Euromoney Publications, 1981.

Ghadar, F., Stephen J. Kobrin, and Theodore H. Moran (eds.). *Managing International Political Risk: Strategies and Techniques*. Washington, D.C.: Ghadar and Associates, 1983.

Ghadar, F., and Theodore H. Moran (eds.). *International Political Risk Management: New Dimensions*. Washington, D.C.: Ghadar and Associates, 1984.

Haendel, Dan. *Corporate Strategic Planning: The Political Dimension*. Beverly Hills, Calif.: Sage, 1981.

Haner, F. T. "Rating Investment Risks Abroad." *Business Horizons*, April 1979, 18–23.

Kobrin, Stephen J. "When Does Political Instability Result in Increased Investment Risk?" *Columbia Journal of World Business*, Fall 1978, 113–122.

_____. "Assessing Political Risk Overseas." *The Wharton Magazine*, Winter 1981-82, 25–31.

_____. *Managing Political Risk Assessment*. Berkeley: University of California Press, 1982.

Kraar, Louis. "The Multinationals Get Smarter About Political Risks." *Fortune*, March 24, 1980, pp. 86–100.

Lacquer, Walter. "The Press, the Devil, and World Coverage." *The Washington Quarterly* 5 (Summer 1982), 99–102.

Moran, Theordore H. (ed.). *International Political Risk Assessment: The State of the Art*. Washington, D.C.: Georgetown University, 1980.

Rogers, Jerry (ed.). *Global Risk Assessments: Issues, Concepts and Applications*. Riverside, Calif.: Global Risk Assessments, Inc., 1983.

Rummel, R. J., and David A. Heenan. "How Multinationals Analyze Political Risk." *Harvard Business Review*, January-February 1978, 67–76.

Sacks, Paul M. and Stephen Blank. "Forecasting Political Risk." *The Corporate Director*, September/October 1981, 9–14.

Schwendiman, John S. *Strategic and Long-Range Planning for the Multinational Corporation*. New York: Praeger, 1973.

Shreeve, Thomas W. "Be Prepared for Political Changes Abroad." *Harvard Business Review*, July-August 1984, 111–118.

Vernon, Raymond. "Storm Over the Multinationals: Problems and Prospects." *Foreign Affairs*, January 1977, 243–262.

Wells, Louis T. "Negotiating With Third World Governments." *Harvard Business Review*, January-February 1977, 72–80.

Chapter Ten

Overview of Corporate Reactions

Richard D. Robinson

Two years ago, my associates and I conducted research in the United States to ascertain management response to the opportunities and problems created by government intervention in the international marketplace through the introduction of incentives and disincentives.[1] The focus was primarily on developing countries, but not exclusively. It was felt that one had to view management reaction in the context of the *world* economy, for many industrialized countries compete vigorously to attract foreign capital, management, and technology.

The central question asked was: Did executives believe that what governments were doing influenced their decisions as to the direction and nature of corporate involvement in foreign markets?

In the process of the research, we interviewed at some length executives in 51 corporations in 12 industries (plus 5 conglomerates that were unclassifiable), ranging in size from $50 million to over $10 billion in annual sales and in employment from 4,300 to over 600,000. The degree to which these firms were active overseas varied enormously, from 5.6 percent of total sales to 60.5 percent, and from 6.1 to 70.6 percent of total assets. Five claimed that over half of their total assets were located outside the United States; 15, over 35 percent. Twenty-three firms report 20 or more foreign affiliates, and 20 reported affiliates in more than 15 countries. Others had no or very few offshore affiliates. Organizational form varied from the mere exporters to the true multinationals. Of the 51 corporations, only 10 alleged a preference for 100 percent ownership of any overseas venture, while 13 indicated a preference for joint ventures, 1 opted for technology transfer contracts only, and 25 reported a flexible policy in this regard. Experience in international business ranged from a century or more to five years or less.

I cite this detail simply to convey the notion that it was unlikely that the responses we received were heavily biased by industry, firm size, degree of overseas commitment, control and ownership strategy, and length of experience in overseas markets.

PERFORMANCE REQUIREMENTS

In our survey of corporate experience and executive opinion, we were able to separate out 12 areas in which host governments had either explicitly or implicitly imposed performance requirements on foreign business firms. In some cases, of course, these requirements had been placed on both foreign and domestic enterprises, although it was not the purpose of our study to address that issue directly. The areas in which requirements had been imposed were: exports, ownership, employment of foreign nationals, local content, employment, investment, production level, local research and development, training, product, level of technology, and location.

It was noted that the requirements did not always run in the same direction. In some cases, a host government tried to depress foreign ownership; in others, to increase it. In some instances, the use of foreign technicians and managers might be discouraged; in others, the reverse. In some situations, a host government might require the transfer of "modern" or "advanced" technology; in others, "appropriate" or labor-intensive. In some cases, the commitments imposed might not be entirely consistent, such as the requirements that "high" technology be used (assuming that meant capital-intensive technology) and a high level of employment be maintained at the same time, or the imposition of production limits (if that meant that economy of scale could not be achieved) and simultaneous pressure for more exports.

It was not always easy for a corporation to respond to these host government requirements. For a firm organized into regional profit centers—for example, North America, Latin America, Middle East, Africa, Europe, and the Pacific—an export requirement could mean that some other region would have to import. Unless that import were fully competitive in terms of price, quality, and delivery, the other regional headquarters might well resist. Even so, those other corporate divisions undoubtedly had already developed a network of suppliers with whom they were accustomed to work and with whom they were linked by contract. An example was the automotive firm that had been obliged to export from Mexico to keep its Mexican affiliate operating. The logical buyer was the North American company, the management of which resisted vigorously. The Mexican product was not competitive with other sources, and the North American division of the corporation was a profit center. How was the firm with approximately 60 plants scattered around the world expected to export from all of the countries in which it was producing? Nor was it only the developing countries that felt compelled to press for exports because of persistent balance-of-payments problems.

It may be true that corporations organized by product group, in which each global product group was a profit center, had a somewhat easier time in satisfying export requirements—that is, as long as the products did not move from one product division to another. The logistical decision could be made by a single decision-making body. However, it cannot be claimed that our study demonstrated this to be true. All one can say is that it would be surprising if it were not.

We came across no instance in which a firm had been obliged to post a bond or deposit funds in a blocked account as tangible guarantee that it would fulfill a specific performance requirement.

Executives in several firms expressed uneasiness about possible nonfulfillment of commitments made. An interviewee in one firm reported that his management was quite worried about promising what it could not deliver in terms of specific requirements for exporting, external financing, ownership, and employment. In another firm, an executive admitted that management was very much concerned about living up to commitments in Mexico with respect to exports. But in another, management felt that the Norwegian government had not lived up to its side of the bargain and, hence, the firm was absolved from fulfilling the employment commitment it had made.

Export Requirements

We noted at least 17 countries that had requested that firms enter into export commitments, most frequently from Brazil (11 cases) and Mexico (6 cases). In some instances, a commitment to export had led to the relaxation of ownership requirements (Mexico and India) or to a reduction of the local content requirement (Australia and Mexico). In others, such a commitment had been a precondition for the right to import At least one country had treated all of the local affiliates of a given U.S. firm as a single unit for the purpose of calculating export credits for import rights (Brazil). The trade-off between exports and import rights varied somewhat from country to country and, apparently, even from company to company within a single country. The standard seemed to have a one-to-one trade-off; that is, a dollar's worth of exports would give the right to purchase a dollar's worth of foreign exchange for imports, but it might go as high as three to one (as it had in Brazil in at least one case). In Yugoslavia, a local affiliate had been required to earn all of its foreign exchange requirements, whether used for imports or remittances of earnings, fees, and depreciation allowance. In some cases, a firm had been required simply to export a given percentage of its production. Five firms had refused to enter into such commitments but no pattern emerged. The question had arisen in one country (Mexico) about whether a U.S. affiliate could capture the export credits (that is, credits arising out of exports that could be used to secure license to import) earned by a local subcontractor. The rule of thumb seemed to be that such was possible if the foreign customer of the subcontractor's export were the parent or an associated firm of the U.S. affiliate, or if it could be demonstrated that the exports had been made possible by the subcontractor's association with the affiliate. One way to be certain of capturing export credits, of course, was for the affiliate to invest significantly in its subcontractors. The Mexican affiliate of one U.S. firm had acquired minority interest in a number of its Mexican suppliers to lay claim to the latter's export credits, which had then made possible imports and greater production in Mexico—and more business for the suppliers as a result. The problem of interdivisional or interregional sales within an international corporation has already been discussed.

Despite much negative comment and general misgiving, most firms, when faced with an export requirement, had nonetheless gone on with their investments. At least 29 cases were recorded during the course of this inquiry. It is impossible to estimate, of course, how much investment had not taken place because of the imposition of export requirements, but one judged not much. We heard of only the five instances, one each in Brazil, Colombia, Ireland, South Korea, and Venezuela. Whether firms were living up to the commitments was another matter; although, when linked to import rights, such commitments were relatively easy to monitor and enforce, assuming that the administration was honest.

Ownership Requirements

Both the experience and attitudes that surfaced during our inquiry varied substantially from firm to firm and from country to country. Executives in virtually all firms in which interviews were conducted addressed this issue in one way or another. Several referred to the difficulty of maintaining adequate control in the absence of a majority interest. Executives in others were not concerned; their firms had entered into management contracts with minority equity participation and seemed perfectly content. There was concern about the division of earnings with partners who had not contributed to an enterprise in a way that was commensurate to their equity and, hence, claim on earnings.

One firm in Mexico was permitted 100 percent ownership on the basis of a commitment to export 100 percent. Another firm had been protected by "grandfathering" in Mexico. (The same had been true of a firm in the Philippines.) Yet many managements reported considerable pressure from the Mexican government to limit the foreign participation to 49 percent. One executive felt that his firm would be in a position to do a lot more for both Mexico and itself it if were to become more active in Mexico. It was the ownership restraint that was binding. Another firm had a wholly owned operation in Mexico and had been under no pressure to relinquish any equity. An executive felt that the operation was probably too small to merit attention. Another felt that his company could maintain its 100 percent position if it increased production. In any event, he doubted that there were any local buyers. Another corporation had been permitted to retain 100 percent ownership in its Mexican venture for five years. Still another had heard nothing about any Mexican ownership being demanded by the government.

One executive reported that this firm had been under no pressure in Brazil to relinquish any ownership. Yet another reported that his company had not been permitted to enter the country without a local partner. In this case, the industry was perhaps the important variable. The former had been in the electronics sector; the latter, in heavy industrial machinery. Another, a chemical producer, had been encouraged to buy out its local partner in Brazil, and there had been no government interference when still another, a machinery producer, had converted its Brazilian joint venture into a wholly owned subsidiary.

An engine manufacturer had been under pressure by the Indian government to reduce its equity in a local venture below 50 percent, a pressure the firm had resisted. As yet, it had not been forced to yield. Another, a supplier to the automotive industry, had been under pressure in Canada to reduce ownership from 100 to 75 percent, but it had resisted, and nothing further had been heard. Also, a farm machinery manufacturer had been discouraged from majority ownership by the French government.

The South Korean government had used the promise of 100 percent ownership in one case, if the U.S. company, a chemical producer, would become involved on a minority-contractual basis in a much larger project. The same company had insisted on 100 percent ownership in Brazil but had readily accepted a 49 percent involvement in a large Yugoslav project. The country and the reward made a difference.

In total, some 33 instances of host government requirements relative to ownership were reported from 12 countries:[2] 11 from Mexico, 4 from Brazil, 3 from Indonesia, and the rest scattered, with no more than two cases per country. There were only seven specific instances reported in which ownership requirements were cited as a principal reason for noninvestment: two each in Mexico and Brazil, one each in Morocco, Nigeria, and France. The reverse may also happen. That is, a corporation may be pressed to take on a greater share of ownership than it really prefers.

An executive reported that the Tunisian government had put pressure on his corporation to assume *at least* a 20 percent equity position in its distribution-assembly operation there, which had been operating strictly on a license basis. The idea was to force the commitment of the corporation in order to identify it more closely with the success of the local operation. The executive observed that there were, in fact, some advantages for the corporations in these independent assembler-distribution contractual relationships, inasmuch as it was possible for the firm to extract itself from situations where the economics of the market so indicated, whereas it was very much more difficult if it had committed itself heavily via major capital expenditures. Hence, the logic of the Tunisian government pressure was revealed.

Requirements to Limit Employment of Foreign Nationals

Very few executives expressed any concern over entering into commitments to reduce expatriate personnel. As one put it, "We normally hire local people in any event." Another observed that it was company practice to turn over local management to local nationals. An executive in a third firm felt that there should not be "arbitrary limits" on the number of foreign employees, and he cited Nigeria as a bad example. He opined that the country was trying to localize its work force too rapidly and in too arbitrary a manner. An executive in a second firm likewise felt that it was important that the number of expatriates given entry into a country should not be too restrictive. But yet another observed that his company could understand the desire of host governments to have as many local nationals employed as possible, including management. It was, in fact, in the interest of his firm to move in that direction as well. An executive in one firm explained that the training of local people was always a problem. The company had an international staff of approximately two dozen people who moved into a country as a start-up team. When a new plant was running successfully, they were moved on to another development. He went on to comment that the right to bring these people in was an important consideration. For example, in negotiating with the Egyptian government, the firm had insisted on the free access of its personnel.

Local Content Requirements

Firms in our sample had faced local content requirements at least in Argentina, Australia, Brazil, Malaysia, Mexico, Nigeria, Spain, Thailand, and Turkey. The only countries cited more than once in this regard were Mexico (six instances) and Brazil (four instances). In one case, a U.S. firm in Australia had been able to trade off exports or a reduced local content requirement. The same firm had enjoyed a reduced local content commitment for increased exports in Mexico on a dollar-for-dollar basis. Still another had been able to negotiate a downward reduction of a local content rule because it had taken over an ailing Spanish enterprise and had agreed to maintain employment. Another had gone into Thailand in anticipation that soon the government would require final processing locally.

Local content rules became particularly serious when the U.S. firm was not a highly integrated manufacturer in the United States and there were not available to it competent subcontractors in the country in which it was investing. For example, a firm in Brazil reported that it had been forced to manufacture in-house a higher percentage of a given machine than it did in the United States, by reason of the local content rule. It could not find adequate external suppliers. The result was higher cost, thereby rendering exports even more difficult, because maximum economy of scale could not be reached for certain parts that were manufactured customarily in large volume by U.S. suppliers.

Two firms, one in Mexico and one in Turkey, cited the local content rules as contributing reasons for their nonentry. Another had rejected a Nigerian project for the same reason, at least in part. (However, this firm had, in fact, faced local content requirements in another situation, Mexico, where it had nonetheless gone into a minority-owned venture.) There were no other cases of blocked investment. One other general observation: local content rules appeared particularly onerous with respect to the automotive industry, but apparently such controls had not caused any firms to desist from investing and expanding when the economics of the situation promised financial reward. We concluded that such requirements had not been generally significant in diverting or blocking investment.

Employment Level Requirements

One corporation had been required by the Canadian government to give an employment guarantee when it had acquired a local firm, but the company had not been able to live up to this commitment. However, it was a small operation, an executive observed, and it would probably be overlooked. Similar requirements had been imposed by the Panamanian and Nicaraguan governments, but there the company had been able to fulfill its commitments. Another had made an employment commitment in Brazil, but still another had encountered no such pressure. An executive noted that no further expansions of investment would be authorized in Colombia and Venezuela without company guarantees of exports and employment. As part of a general agreement, one company had agreed to maintain the employment level in a Spanish enterprise that it had taken over. All together, we found exactly nine investment projects in relation to which employment commitments had been given, one each in Brazil, Canada, Egypt, Nicaragua, Nigeria, Norway, Panama, Spain, and Venezuela. In two others, Indonesia and Malaysia, companies had undertaken to employ given percentages of certain ethnic groups (*prigumi*, or indigenous Indonesians, in Indonesia, and *bumiputra*, or indigenous Malays, in

Malaysia). In no case did it appear that an investment had not taken place because of the requirement that an employment commitment be given.

Investment Level Requirements

One firm reported that it had made a commitment to a certain level of investment in Brazil, which seemed to be quite common practice. This appeared to be more of a statement of intent, however, than an actual commitment. Another had been required, when seeking a license to expand production in Indonesia, to make a commitment that it would invest a specific amount over a given number of years. These were the only two instances specifically mentioned, but one can assume that in all cases where an entry screening process, investment incentives, or negotiated entry agreements were in place, the foreign business firm would have made some sort of investment commitment. Problems of evaluation were mentioned by several executives. Such problems arose when intangibles were to be capitalized as part or all of the foreign investment in the event that used machinery would be contributed as capital.

Production Level Requirements

Here again, many of the commitments were more in the nature of statements of intent, on which basis various permits and incentives had been given. But this was not always the case. A requirement for a certain level of production had been forced on one firm in Mexico—along with export and local content requirements—in order to get an open-ended management contract with respect to a local venture in which the U.S. firm had a 40 percent equity interest, the balance being held by the government. This was the only explicit quid pro quo in which a specific production commitment had been part of the price of a government commitment of some sort. In any event, this commitment is possibly the most difficult to monitor from the point of view of the host government, and it would appear to be a little real value. The economics of the market, plus the impact of government incentives, will determine the level of production.

Local Research and Development Requirements

Fifteen firms reported foreign research and/or development activities in 18 countries: Belgium (1), Brazil (4), Canada (2), Costa Rica (1), France (3), West Germany (3), Honduras (1), Ireland (2), Japan (4), Luxembourg (1), Mexico (1), New Zealand (1), Nicaragua (1), Peru (1), the Philippines (2), South Africa (1), Switzerland (1), and the United Kingdom (4). In addition, one firm reported 19 foreign laboratories; another, 1 marine-related research station in Latin America. One other claimed to have R&D activities but did not specify where.

Only one incident was reported in which a host government had virtually required a U.S. firm to undertake local R&D, and that had been in France. An executive in a pharmaceutical company observed that the French government, in issuing product licenses, had insisted on a commitment to develop local technology. The company had been told, in one recent instance, that it might get a better price review if it were to engage in local R&D. (Pharmaceutical prices were under control.) Another firm reported that the Indonesian government had declared that it would give preference in granting licenses for expanded capacity in one industry to those firms with R&D and "a technology of international standard." However, an executive said that the firm had not been under any pressure to do R&D *locally*. Nonetheless, other companies, not included in this present survey, had reported Indonesian pressure for local R&D activity at the time of application for capacity extension.

Training Requirements

Although training was obviously a very common activity by virtually all direct foreign investors and many technology transfer contractors, only two firms mentioned the imposition of specific requirements in this regard. One had undertaken the obligation to train a local Indonesian to replace an incoming foreign technician. The granting of the latter's work permit was contingent upon the commitment. Another company had agreed to a specific training program in Kenya as a condition for entry. In this case, an executive observed that the firm had been glad to enter such a commitment because it wanted to do the training anyway. A third had enountered rigid controls in France with respect to the training required for new insurance agencies. In this instance, the French subsidiary had failed because of the company's inability to hire good salespeople. In no case was such a commitment referred to as a disincentive to investment. On the contrary, it was often cited as an indication of realism on the part of the host government.

Requirements for Products, Level of Technology, and Plant Location

Commitments to satisfy requirements imposed as conditions for entry and/or the granting of incentives were frequent, but only those having to do with product had given any trouble. In some situations, executives reported, it had been impossible to secure permission to produce locally because an indigenously owned firm was already manufacturing the same or comparable good. An executive in one firm, a food processor, opined that possibly 15 or 20 national markets were closed to his firm for this reason, and he gave Brazil, South Korea, and Mexico as specific examples. This view was corroborated in another food processing firm. All together, we encountered 19 specific instances in which firms had encountered difficulties by reason of the product with which they were involved: Brazil—computers, food processing, industrial instrumentation, steel; Canada—restaurants, timber; Egypt—canning; France—computers, insurance; West Germany—employment services, insurance; Japan—insurance; South Korea—food processing, vehicles; Mexico—food processing; Nigeria—vehicles; the Philippines—land ownership; Taiwan—vehicles; and Venezuela—steel. Withdrawal or blocked investment had resulted in virtually all cases. We did not become aware, however, of any situation in which requirements imposed relative to technology or plant site had been a significant factor in an investment decision.

Summary of Export Requirements

All together, executives in the 51 firms reported 126 instances in which host governments had imposed performance requirements of some variety, or over two per company. There is no claim that this constitutes anything like a complete listing of those actually encountered by the 51 corporations, but they were the ones that surfaced in conversation with knowledgeable managers. It should also be borne in mind that one of the prime purposes of each interview was to ascertain the significance of performance requirements in the recent allocation of corporate resources overseas. The general finding was that performance requirements were not very significant. As can be seen, only 33 cases of nonentry due to these requirements were indicated, or 26 percent. If one were to eliminate those cases of investment blocked by reason of sectoral restrictions, which is more realistic, then the percentage drops to 13.

INCENTIVES

It was very difficult, we found, to discuss performance requirements divorced from incentives. A country might, on the one hand, enforce an export requirement or, on the other hand, reward a firm for exporting. The reward, however, might be such that the firm could not really remain competitive within the market without the reward. Export credits might be required for an import license, or they might be used as credits against taxes that would be otherwise levied against local profits.

During the course of the inquiry, we identified essentially six types of incentives:

1. Subsidies (for land and plant, debt, research and development, imports, exports, energy, raw material inputs, and infrastructure)
2. Tax reduction (on imports and on revenues)
3. Market protection
4. Import rights
5. Guarantees (on availability of foreign exchange for remittance of earnings, on right to import of essential materials, and against expropriation)
6. Government procurement

Not all firms in the survey paid attention to the variety of incentives offered by host governments.

It was clear that most firms did include "up-front" incentives—that is, those committed by a host government prior to the actual execution of an investment project—in their financial analysis. Other incentives, which were essentially promises to be delivered later, were heavily discounted, if counted at all. Tax holidays came in this category. Most executives echoed the notion that incentives did not turn a bad project into a good project. The economic justification of an investment had to stand on its own. One observation bears repeating. In estimating the viability of a particular incentive, management was well advised to evaluate its rationale. If the incentive did not make economic sense in terms of host government interests, then it was unlikely to last long.

Corporate experience with specific types of host government incentives—subsidies, tax reduction, market protection, import quotas, guarantees, and government procurement—sheds some light on both their frequency and effectiveness.

Subsidies

Fifteen firms reported 29 cases in which government subsidies had been received. We counted as a subsidy any input priced below the market. Both the United Kingdom and Ireland had been particularly generous, as well as Spain in certain cases. Subsidies in one form or another were reported from Australia, Bahrein, Belgium, Brazil, France, Ireland, Malaysia, Mexico, Saudi Arabia, Singapore, Spain, the United Kingdom, and West Germany. These had taken the form of:

- Training allowances in Belgium, Ireland, Spain, and the United Kingdom
- Grants for capital equipment in the United Kingdom
- Subsidized energy in Australia, Mexico, and the United Kingdom
- Commitment to cover early-year losses in Spain

- Land grants in Spain
- Grants for local research and development in France and the United Kingdom
- Subsidized raw materials in Bahrein, Saudi Arabia, and Mexico
- Grants for buildings in Ireland, Malaysia, Singapore, and the United Kingdom
- Subsidized capital (either below market price or at fixed rate) in Brazil, West Germany, Ireland, Saudia Arabia, and Singapore
- Subsidized export financing in Belgium, Brazil, France, Mexico, and the United Kingdom

Altogether, there seemed to have been seven projects that had materialized when and where they did by reason of government subsidies, five in the United Kingdom and two in Ireland. It will be noted that subsidies were not a common form of incentive among Third World countries. The reason, we suggest, is that a direct subsidy to a foreign-owned firm is a politically vulnerable use of public funds. It is very visible and may be given prior to any actual performance by the firm. If so, such a subsidy should be accompanied by some sort of performance bond, but we encountered no such cases.

Export incentives, in the form of extended long-term export financing at a low-market rate, were somewhat an exception to the general management attitude regarding incentives. These were reported from a number of countries and in some instances had contributed to decisions to produce locally to be able to qualify for the export finance. There were two instances in which this factor appeared to have been critical, both in the United Kingdom, although the availability of such finance facilities had been contributory to several other investment decisions. One firm reported that Brazilian export financing—8 percent for ten years—had been a factor in its decision to produce in Brazil. For another, the availability of favorable export credit facilities would determine whether it got further involved in South Korea and Japan.

Tax Reduction

Executives in virtually all of the firms mentioned one or more experiences with various forms of tax incentives, either in the form of reduction or total exemption from import taxes (tariffs and/or revenue taxes). In some countries, tax incentives had been contingent upon achieving specified export levels, as in Brazil. In others, Mexico for example, firms had received tax credit for exports. In a number of cases, tax incentives were clearly not critical, as for one company looking at the Ivory Coast. The corporation's tax department had not even been consulted. Another firm had generally not been able to take advantage of tax concessions, with one exception. It had taken over a plant in Brazil, and with it had come some special tax benefits.

In analyzing our interview data, we came up with only two cases in which the waiving of import duties had possibly been critical. In most cases, it was not the imposition of import duties that concerned management, but rather the inability to obtain unambiguous guarantees that the firm would be able to purchase foreign exchange and import licenses for imported materials to keep a local plant running.

Many cases of tax holidays or reduced taxes on earnings were recorded. Such were reported out of Belgium, Brazil, Egypt, France, Ireland, Malaysia, Mexico, Morocco, Peru, Saudia Arabia, Singapore, Spain, Thailand, and the United Kingdom. Several firms, which had already decided on expansion of capacity within the EEC, had opted for Ireland specifically because of the tax incentives offered. When an executive in one firm (which had been exempted from Irish taxes for 15 years) was asked what the company did with its tax-exempt profits, he replied that it tried to employ them elsewhere but that, in fact, most of them were remitted directly to the United States. It was difficult to see how the firm had really benefited.

A number of executives agreed that foreign tax holidays on income were of very limited value to their respective companies by reason of the U.S. taxation of worldwide income, subject only to credit for foreign income and wealth taxes actually paid. Corporations based in countries taxing only domestic income, or with very low tax rates on foreign-source income, had a distinct advantage. As the executive of one major U.S. corporation observed, "Tax benefits are of no great help to us for the simple reason that we want to repatriate profits as soon as possible, which means that they will be taxed anyway." A benefit was derived only by firms that wanted to increase their capital base abroad by reinvesting local profits or were in a deficit tax credit position.

However, special credit to be applied against local, nonincome taxes was of universal appeal. For example, one firm reported employment credits to Spain, which could be applied against social security tax liability. In Mexico, one firm had received an employment tax credit applicable against the value-added tax. In Brazil, another firm reported having taken advantage of the special tax deal for investing in the northeast, whereby funds that would otherwise have been paid in local taxes could be invested without being subject to tax.

During the course of our study, some form of tax incentive was reported from 19 countries (number of instances are given in parentheses): Belgium (2), Brazil (3), Egypt (1), El Salvador (1), France (1), Ireland (4), Ivory Coast (1), Korea (1), Yugoslavia (1), Malaysia (4), Mexico (1), Morocco (1), Nigeria (1), Peru (1), Saudi Arabia (1), Singapore (1), Spain (1), Thailand (2), and the United Kingdom (3). Of these 31 instances, tax incentives may have been critical to investment in 8.

Market Protection

Seemingly somewhat more effective than either subsidies or tax incentives was border protection. Typical was an executive's comment about his firm's investigation of a project in Nigeria. Management realized that if Nigeria were to open its borders to competing imports, the operation would be destroyed because of its inefficiency. In Mexico, the same firm had been promised protection from competing imports.

Although the promise of protection had apparently induced much foreign production, a number of executives cited investments that had been made in anticipation of continuing tariff protection but had later suffered by reason of government failure to protect the market. There were 15 cases reported from 12 countries: Argentina (1), Australia (1), Brazil (1), Chile (1), Ivory Coast (2), Malaysia (1), Mexico (1), Yugoslavia (1), South Korea (3), Nigeria (1), the Philippines (1), and Singapore (1).

Import Rights

One form of incentive, infrequently used but effective when it was, had to do with granting an import license or quota to the investing firm. By selling a product in the market while the investment was being made and the plant being readied for operation, a corporation could both finance part of the project from the proceeds of the sales and familiarize itself with the market for the product to be manufactured locally. The Yugoslav government had permitted one firm, in anticipation of the finalization of its investment commitment, to test market the relevant product for six months. The investment was contingent upon satisfactory results. Another firm in a Yugoslav project had been permitted to sell to the joint venture, in which it was participating, during its initial years. An executive in one firm reported a corporate policy of deliberately tying a license arrangement (this firm was not interested in investing overseas) with an up-front order, and it had done so successfully in Taiwan. Finally, the Spanish government had given a machine-building company a quota to import finished machines until the company's new plant was ready to produce. It is our feeling that this form of incentive could be very important, and the cost to the host government relatively modest. Yet we unearthed only these four instances in which it had been used.

Guarantees

Specific host government guarantees with respect to such matters as the availability of exchange for the remittance of earnings, right to import essential materials, and a commitment not to expropriate surfaced infrequently during our interviews. Executives in only a handful of companies made specific mention of such guarantees, although they were implicit in much of what others said. Ideally, the first condition one firm would look at, according to one executive, was the availability of guarantees for the import of the necessary raw materials. An executive in a second company reiterated this view. He would prefer to have the host government "invite us in, and of course, give the necessary raw material guarantee." Another firm reported that both Greece and Kenya had given guarantees of foreign exchange for essential supplies on an ongoing basis. An executive in still another firm mentioned that his management would insist on a guarantee of dividend repatriation without difficulty, a requirement reiterated by spokesmen in several companies.

However, the absence of such guarantees seemed to have blocked only one investment. This had to do with a proposed investment in Turkey. The firm had turned away when it realized that a guarantee for foreign exchange with which to import essential supplies would not be forthcoming. In some instances, of course, this guarantee was implicit in the agreement that a firm could retain all or a certain percentage of its export earnings ("retention rights") for the purchase of imports and repatriation of earnings.

Government Procurement

Another effective, but apparently rarely used, incentive is the promise of host government purchase of the product of a local plant. For example, one firm had been promised preference on government contracts in South Korea were it to produce locally. Another had allegedly made a commitment to a joint venture in Mexico in order to hold its position as the preferred supplier to the government. An executive in a third firm expressed regret that the company was not producing in Canada because of a tendency by the Canadian government to direct procurement to local firms. Finally, one division of a large conglomerate had invested in Norway in a machine-manufacturing venture with no expectation of profit on the venture. The point was that another division of the parent was involved in North Sea oil exploration. The manufacturing investment was felt to be a necessary commitment in order for the parent to get an exploration block. But again, only four instances of the promise of government procurement (or largesse in another area) was reported. In three of the four cases, the maneuver had probably been a contributing factor—if not the preeminent one—in inducing foreign investment on terms acceptable to the host government.

Summary of Incentives

In aggregate, there were 85 instances mentioned by executives in discussing recent investment decisions; in 28 of these, they may have been critical (33 percent). The most effective, although the numbers are small, were the grant of import rights and the promise of government procurement. Host government guarantees simply were not reported because they were assumed in most instances. For example, where Overseas Private Investment Corporation investment guarantees had been used, there had to have been an underlying host government guarantee.

Executives in different firms reacted in a variety of ways when pressed for judgments as to host governments' performance requirements and incentives. One, in a high-technology company, said very bluntly that the firm would not accept any incentives that placed requirements on the company on the grounds that such would be "the tail wagging the dog." Management determined how to run its business, not a foreign government. Another high-technology firm had been asked to make an employment commitment in Puerto Rico and had refused. When asked why, an executive responded, "Until we are actually in the country, we do not know how it will grow." Asked whether the commitment demanded by governments had ever killed a project, an executive in an automotive firm said that he had never heard of such an incident, adding "not even Chrysler in Taiwan when there had been a lot of restrictions imposed." With respect to the requirements imposed on his own firm in Spain, the fact that all of the agreements had been approved at the ministerial level had made management somewhat more comfortable. A spokesman for a large food processor said that he knew of no instances where one country had preempted investment over another because of better incentives.

It is important to note that our interviews made it clear that host governments made no effort to differentiate between corporations that had behaved well elsewhere and those that had not. Good behavior is defined here in terms of demonstrable sensitivity to local need and fulfillment of performance requirements imposed. We became aware of only one government that had employed independent consultants to report on the global behavior of the corporations with which it was dealing. Governments were not even monitoring very carefully the fulfillment of the commitments made by corporations operating within their own territories. The point is that without rewarding those corporations with good track records elsewhere—as well as locally—by somewhat eased entry requirements and/or greater incentives, the wrong signals go out. Certainly, the executives whom we interviewed felt no relationship between the behavior of their firm in one country and how it might be treated in the next. There was no intercountry learning. Yet it would be quite simple for a government to conduct a global survey of corporate behavior. Faculty and students in graduate schools of business and management in the United States, Canada, Western Europe, and elsewhere are perfectly able to make such studies quickly and relatively cheaply, as they have done for at least one government. Corporate behavior is unlikely to be improved significantly by unenforceable rules, but corporate behavior can be influenced by rewards based on past behavior. However, if a government does not look beyond its own border, this learning process is likely to be very tedious, if indeed it takes place at all.

NOTES

1. Report in Robinson, Richard D., *Performance Requirements for Foreign Business: U.S. Management Response* (New York: Praeger, 1983).

2. Brazil, Canada, France, India, Indonesia, Yugoslavia, South Korea, Malaysia, Mexico, Morocco, Nigeria, and the Philippines.

Index

About the Contributors

RICHARD S. ECKAUS, Professor of Economics, Department of Economics, Massachusetts Institute of Technology

WILLIAM A. FISCHER, Professor of Business Administration, School of Business Administration, University of North Carolina

NORITAKE KOBAYASHI, Professor of Management, Graduate School of Business Administration, Keio University

DONALD R. LESSARD, Professor of International Management, Sloan School of Management, Massachusetts Institute of Technology

MOISES NAIM, Dean, Instituto de Estudios Superiores de Administracion

RICHARD D. ROBINSON, Professor of International Management Emeritus, Sloan School of Management, Massachusetts Institute of Technology; Jewett Professor of International Business, University of Puget Sound

JOHN S. SCHWENDIMAN, Manager, Strategic Studies, Strategic Marketing Services Department, Dow Chemical Corporation

JOHN M. STOPFORD, Professor of Management, London Business School

LOUIS T. WELLS, Jr., Professor of International Management, Harvard Graduate School of Business Administration